Prisons in Turmoil

Prisons in Turmoil

JOHN IRWIN
San Francisco State University

Foreword by
Donald R. Cressey

Little, Brown and Company
Boston   Toronto

Library of Congress Catalog Card No. 79–88490

First Printing

Published simultaneously in Canada
by Little, Brown & Company (Canada) Limited

Printed in the United States of America

ACKNOWLEDGMENTS
The author acknowledges permission to quote material from the following sources:

American Friends Service Committee, *Struggle for Justice: A Report on Crime and Punishment in America*. Copyright © 1971 by Hill and Wang (now a division of Farrar, Straus & Giroux, Inc.). Reprinted by permission of Hill and Wang.

Anchorage Times, excerpt from a letter to the editor, 26 September 1975. Reprinted by permission.

Claude Brown, *Manchild in the Promised Land*. Copyright © Claude Brown 1965. Reprinted by permission of Macmillan Publishing Co., Inc.

Malcolm Braly, *On the Yard* (Little, Brown and Company). Copyright © 1967 by Malcolm Braly. Reprinted by permission of the author and his agent, Knox Burger Associates Ltd.

For
Jenny, Katy, Annie
and
Eloise

Foreword

This is a book about the profound changes that have occurred in prisons during the last half century. It tells why today's prison officials are openly fighting inmates and each other and why prisoners are openly fighting each other as well as prison officials.

Irwin correctly notes that those of us who were studying inmate and guard organization in the 1950s actually were studying the transformation of the prison from the Big House to the correctional institution. He observes further that this trend was followed by a movement to community corrections and, at the same time, to what he calls the contemporary prison. This latest institution has some of the characteristics of the Big House and some of the characteristics of the correctional institution. It is a place where inmates are organized in radical and ethnic groups for purposes of both defense and attack, and where wardens and guards are convinced that the former emphasis on policing and rehabilitating inmates was misguided.

If I had to do time, and could choose which of the three types of prisons to do it in, I certainly would not select the contemporary prison. In all prison settings guards are supposed to function as police officers, among other things. But in contemporary institutions they have withdrawn to the walls, leaving inmates to intimidate, rape, maim, and kill each other with alarming frequency.

I would do my time in a Big House. Although the organization in these prisons was directed at keeping inmates from bunching together in ways considered threatening to security and staff safety, there was a concordant stress on protecting prisoners from each other. In this setting, I would not have to look around every corner to see if someone was waiting to stick a knife in my throat. "If we catch a guy with a shiv in his pants leg," Warden Joseph E. Ragen of the Joliet Big House told me in the 1940s, "we can be damned sure he isn't going to be using it on me or one of the guards." He went on to say that his calculated use of spies and informers, like surprise searches of persons and cells, was essential to protect prisoners from each other.

When the correctional institution came on the scene, such concerns for policing were denounced as barbarianism or, at least, as psychological rigidity that interfered with treatment. Prisons became tougher places in which to do time, even as food improved, walls were painted pale blue or light yellow, guards were called by their first names, and prisoners psychoanalyzed each other. In the contemporary prison the rhetoric of treatment that functioned to champion humanitarianism rather than rehabilitation has been abandoned. It was thrown out by a coalition of political conversatives who thought the correctional institution was too humane, and political liberals who observed that the institution was unjustly harsh on the poorest and least powerful prisoners. Now, in the contemporary prison, there is no official rhetoric to ask guards and others to be decent, let alone to serve as police officers. As Irwin says in chapter 1, the order is dangerous and tentative.

But this is more than a book about prisons. It is a discourse on democracy. It shows, in many rewarding passages, how American penal philosophy has followed changes in the economic, political, and social life of the United States. Thus it is a study of changing conceptions of freedom, liberty, and the public good. Irwin eloquently argues that the cure for the ills of democracy is more democracy. He is a leader of the prison reform movement that would resolve the tensions of the contemporary prison democratically. Thus, he is convinced, if prisoners could ban together in what he calls a union, violence would decrease, humanitarianism would increase, and peace would prevail. Most important, both captives and captors would learn democratic ways, giving them a better idea of what the outside is supposed to be all about.

Irwin also analyzes and justifiably criticizes the theoretical framework that sociologists used in the pioneering studies conducted in the early 1950s. I did some of these studies, and this book correctly reports that I—a sociologist trained in the "Chicago" style that stressed conflict, social change, and symbolic interaction—fell in with bad companions, the functionalists. But Irwin does not tell how I was "rehabilitated," thus coming to appreciate the fact that functionalist descriptions of prison life were only partly correct. The chief agent of change was Irwin himself.

John Irwin, like Arturo Biblarz, Egon Bittner, William Chambliss, Aaron Cicourel, and Sheldon Messinger, is one of my known "sociological children." These are persons who as undergraduates in the 1950s took my UCLA undergraduate course in social disorganization, were turned on to sociology, and went on to fame and glory in the profession. Because I was not a functionalist, I "proved" in the course that there is no such thing as social disorganization, thus refuting the University of Chicago proponents who had unwittingly allied themselves with those of Harvard and Columbia. Irwin became a teacher's pet. Because he was an ex-con, he was older and wiser than most undergraduates. He also was a lot more industrious—he read voraciously and was working his way through college as a tuxedo-clad waiter in a high-class restaurant. I soon found, also, that he was extraordinarily bright.

Because John was an ideal undergraduate, I invited him, a senior, to participate in a graduate research seminar devoted to the sociology of prisons. In thirty years of university teaching I have extended such an invitation only three times. Irwin was the first to receive it.

At the first or second seminar meeting, we discussed Erving Goffman's mimeographed paper on total institutions, the foundation of *Asylums* (Doubleday, 1961). Goffman claimed that persons entering total institutions such as prisons are "stripped" of their outside status. I liked that because I, like Goffman, had come under the spell of the functionalists who explained prison happenings in terms of the events within prison walls only. Irwin thought Goffman's thesis was baloney, and said so. Basing his argument on his own experience, he insisted that all inmates carry a great deal of behavioral baggage into prison and retain it during their stay.

John later led the seminar group in a lively discussion of his "no stripping" thesis. I suggested that he write a paper on the subject. He agreed, but did not have time to complete it before the end of the term, when I departed for a year as visiting professor at Cambridge University. During the summer he wrote a rough draft and sent it to me.

Six months later, in January 1961, Irwin graduated from UCLA. He celebrated by using the waiter's tips he had saved to buy a new Volkswagen and tour Europe. He stayed at our Cambridge home for a few days, and we discussed his paper over pints of beer at the local pubs. We decided to publish. When he went off to Spain I revised the paper, cited the relevant literature, gave it a framework, "sociologized" it, and sent it to him. He did some polishing and then returned it. Eventually we got a good first draft, and I shipped it off to some of my friends for comment, but without any indication as to authorship. Goffman, who was very enthusiastic about the draft, said the author clearly had made an "honest" person of the type of inmate we called the "Thief." After more polishing I submitted "Thieves, Convicts and the Inmate Culture" to Howard S. Becker, then editor of *Social Problems*. He suggested some changes, and after I had made them the paper finally appeared (*Social Problems,* 10:142–55, fall, 1962).

Just after our paper was published, I visited Becker in his San Francisco apartment. *Outsiders* had just come out and we discussed its ideas, which were not then perceived as maintaining that there is no deviance without labeling. Later we went to a bookstore and Becker picked up a copy of his book and showed me that the first footnote was a reference to an article of mine on how criminologists limit the kinds of theories that can be developed whenever they ignore the variable character of the process of deciding what shall be called crime and what shall not. Then we turned to a discussion of the Irwin-Cressey paper. He showed me the critique written by Julian B. Roebuck. I decided that the critique was misguided, had some laughs, then proposed that it not be published. Becker seemed to agree with me but he, always the democrat, said that since two assistant editors had recommended publication, he was going to publish. He did. (*Social Problems,* 11:193–200, fall, 1963.)

Sociological investigations of prison culture boomed in the 1960s. Irwin's observation to the effect that prisons import behavior from the outside stood up under empirical test. Although criminologists in the 1970s shifted their interests to police, courts, and deterrence—where the money is—two or three studies showing the validity of the "Irwin-Cressey hypothesis" still appear each year. I have told Irwin that I no longer bother to read these studies because they merely demonstrate the obvious, namely that a "Square John" or "Right Guy" in prison is just being the person he was on the outside. Irwin agreed, but in the last few years has inevitably added that these new studies, like our article, are now irrelevant because the contemporary prison, whose inmate culture we described, is very different from the Big House and the correctional institution. *Prisons in Turmoil* documents this difference, as well as *why* prisons and prison ideology have changed.

Santa Barbara, California   Donald R. Cressey

Preface

This book is, primarily, an attempt to develop an understanding of what goes on in prison; and this means, more than anything else, what happens to prisoners there. First, it examines how they cope with prison, what systems of social order they construct, and how administrators and other policy makers influence these systems. Second, it is an attempt to demonstrate that the distorted conceptions of the prison world and of prisoners previously held or manufactured by prison administrators, guards, politicians, and experts function to serve the interests of these officials (not necessarily the interests of society), and result in pain and unfairness to prisoners.

A huge mistake made by earlier students of the prison was to consider prisons as isolated, unchanging, and uniform. Obviously, administrative policies and other influential social processes are different from place to place and time to time, and the social order that prisoners construct varies. In this book, I separate prisons into three types of social organizations —the Big House, the correctional institution, and the contemporary prison. Although these do not include all prisons, they represent a large number and have been, I think, the *dominant* types throughout the last forty years. I distinguish between them because their confusion in the minds of the public and the sociologist prompts contradictory theories and creates ambiguity. But I do more than distinguish them. I mark off the universe of prisons that comprise these types, set them in their social contexts, and trace the links and continuities between them. I describe the social processes that moved prisons from one stage to another, particularly the demographic shifts of the 1950s as well as the political activities of the 1960s and 1970s, and the response of prison administrators to these activities. Those social processes ushered in the last stage—the violent prison.

Although much of the discussion is historical as I trace the development of the prison, history does not interfere with my primary focus: the social organization of the prison. If putting the historical record in second place causes it to be skimpy here and there, I apologize at the outset.

The books ends with my attempt to clarify the necessary and attainable goals of imprisonment and to offer some principles for changing the prison into a place that punishes but neither treats prisoners unfairly nor destroys them as people.

Acknowledgments

Many people contributed greatly to the actual writing of this book. Jerome Skolnick started me on the project. The Berkeley "study group": Sherri Cavan, Dave Chandler, Troy Duster, Russ Ellis, Dave Vogel, Barbara Heyns, Arlie Hochschild, Terry Lunsford, David Matza, and Henry Miller listened to the original outline and encouraged me to proceed. My wife, Marsha, assisted me at all stages. David Greenberg read and influenced virtually every draft. Michael Snedeker worked closely with me on several chapters. Kenneth Polk, Jim Galvin, Peter Garabedian, and Barbara Owen commented on sections of a draft. Donald Cressey, Lloyd Ohlin, David Ward, and Gresham Sykes read drafts, and their suggestions assisted me tremendously. Sharon Harsha diligently and precisely typed many drafts.

But my indebtedness extends beyond those who contributed directly to the writing. My experiences with hundreds of prisoners, ex-prisoners, and movement people whom I talked to, worked with, and learned from between 1967 and 1979 supplied most of the information, perspective, and inspiration for the undertaking. I mention only those I can pull out of my memory, and apologize to those unmentioned. I must start with Ted Davidson who more than any other "outsider" started the motion which later became the prison movement. Jan Marinessen was there from the beginning and is still there. Most important to me and to the book are all the persons with whom I worked to organize a prisoners' union, particularly Jim Smith, Willie Holder, Patty Holder, Stephanie Reigel,

Connor Nixon, Sheigla Murphy, Michael Snedeker, Sylvia Petrin, Ralph Carroll, Bruce Goldstein, Roney Nunez, Randy Williams, and Willie Brandt. Other movement people who worked with us in the Prisoners' Union and influenced me were Mark Dowie, Fay Stender, Eve Pell, Howard Berman, and Jessica Mitford. Finally, I must mention the working party on criminal justice for the American Friends Service Committee. The eighteen months that I spent in writing *Struggle for Justice* with the other members of the party, especially Caleb Foote, supplied me with a more thorough understanding of the criminal justice system and a philosophy of justice that has been the foundation, not only for this book, but for all my work in criminal justice.

Contents

Introduction

Since I was released from prison twenty years ago, I have had difficulty keeping my attention away from that institution for any length of time. In the first few years I thought less and less about it, occasional flashbacks triggered only by diminishing contacts with prison buddies. Then my academic plans shifted, and I was face to face with the prison again. I was working on a physics degree at UCLA, planning to go on to graduate studies in oceanography (to complement and finance my number one interest, surfing). Physical science courses were becoming more tedious and social science more interesting. I went to talk to Donald Cressey, the chairman of the Sociology and Anthropology Department and a leading criminologist. He advised me to change to sociology and, because of my experiences in crime and prison, to specialize in criminology. In his class during the next semester I was introduced to the sociology of the prison, particularly to some new theories about the inmate social system. I considered the theories, tested them against information that I could dig out of my memory, and discovered that they did not fit. Extended discussions with Professor Cressey eventually led us to interview many ex-convicts and revise the current theories.

Later, in graduate school at Berkeley I moved along in the broader stream of sociology. Except for an occasional news story about racial violence that brought back memories, my interest in prisons began to fade again. When I had completed all the Ph.D. requirements except the dissertation, I was asked by Sheldon Messinger, a student of the prison, to join a large study of parole that was being conducted by the institute he administered. My part was the career of the felon, and I was back to studying the prison again.

From then on there was no leaving it. While conducting research, particularly at San Quentin, the inhumanity and un-fairness of prison gnawed at me. By then I was much better equipped to fully comprehend these qualities—to me the most salient aspects of imprisonment. They became important parts of my analysis and of the book, *The Felon,* which came out of my study, and compelled me to begin working with others, free citizens and prisoners, to change some of the more flagrant in-justices. This occurred in 1968, two years before the incident at Soledad Prison that began the prison movement. When the movement gained energy, it quickly overtook and almost ran over the few of us working on the prison issue. We scurried along, trying to keep up with the rapidly changing events and issues; and when the movement ended, almost as suddenly as it started, we were left wondering what had happened. By then I was too deeply involved in the prison, and there was no pulling out.

Part of my involvement was professional. I had earned a reputation as a criminologist with special expertise in the prison. This reputation and the attendant professional credentials drew me to many assemblies where prison issues were aired and into prisons as a project director and consultant on many studies and evaluations. I have kept abreast of the sociology of the prison and even helped shape it.

However, it is not my professional attachment that keeps drawing me back to the prison. As a sociologist, I have even tried to move into other areas. What draws me back is, above all, a deep curiosity or, better, a fascination that overrides my hate and fear of prison, both of which are intense (my re-curring nightmare is finding myself back there, serving another sentence for robbery). Whenever I receive a bit of information about a new incident—a rash of stabbings, a hunger strike, or a shooting on the yard—or an event—a prisoner receives an advanced college degree, San Quentin establishes conjugal visit-ing, or a drama group from a New York prison presents a play at the Lincoln Center—I begin wondering what is really going on and what the consequences will be. My training as a sociologist, refined in graduate school, is to be a participant-observer—dipping into a social world and soaking in the collective acting, talking, and thinking. When I have done this at a prison, or in any other setting, I have often discovered that what is going on is different from news accounts, official claims, and social scientists' published studies. At a prison I usually discover that what is going on infuriates me because it is unfair and dehumanizing to prisoners. My training in sociology also makes me sensitive to the inevitable connection between the popular and official misunderstandings and the injustices and inhumanity. "Radical" sociology persuades me that the connection is not accidental; instead, officials purposely embrace or generate distorted versions of reality for their self-interests, and their self-serving actions based on these distorted realities produce the injustices and inhumanity.

My other strong interest in prisons involves radical change. Here is a dilemma. I hate prisons; that is, I hate what happens to convicts in prison (my people, I suppose). But, unlike many with whom I work for change, I find the simple solution—abolishing prisons—unfeasible. I cannot convince myself that society will ever stop punishing people for serious crime and that there is a sufficiently punitive alternative that is not fraught with other problems as serious or more serious than those attached to the prison. I am convinced that we are stuck with the prison, at least for the future that we can anticipate. My position is that we must understand exactly what we intend to accomplish by imprisonment and what happens in prison, and we must stop doing all the unnecessary things that degrade, embitter, cripple, and dehumanize prisoners.

In much of this book I focus on events in California. The major reason is that most of my experience with prisons and prison-related events has been in California. This bias, however, is somewhat justified, because California has been so prominent in setting the trends that have spread across the country. After World War II, California led the nation in the movement toward rehabilitation. The racial difficulties and other divisions that shattered the calm in the new rehabilitative prisons occurred first and most intensely in California. The prison movement began and was centered in California. Most of the planning for community corrections was by California correctional experts. And, finally, California led the country into the present era of prisoner violence.

1
The Big House
THE GREAT AMERICAN PRISON

Most of our ideas about men's prisons are mistaken because they fix on a type of prison — the Big House — that has virtually disappeared during the last twenty-five years. A dominant type of prison in this century, the Big House, emerged, spread, and prevailed, then generated images and illusions and, with considerable help from Hollywood, displayed these to the general society. It caught and held the attention of both the public and sociology. Its images and illusions linger on, surrounding contemporary prisons like a fog and blurring our sight. We must clear the air of false visions, distinguish the Big House as a type, and then move toward an analysis of succeeding types of prisons.

The Big House developed during a long and important phase in the varying history of the prison in the United States.[1] This phase began early in this century and lasted into the 1940s or 1950s and even into the present in some states. Long before

---

[1] I am skipping over a lot of interesting history of prisons in the United States, because my intention here is to develop an understanding of the contemporary prison and not to construct a new history of prisons. Images of the Big House have mixed into our thinking about modern prisons, and its traditions and patterns linger on. This is somewhat true of earlier phases (no social trait ever completely disappears), but the Big House constitutes a long and dominant phase and is, therefore, a logical starting place. Also, there exist many studies of this type of prison and few of earlier phases. For a more complete history of earlier phases, see Harry E. Barnes, *The Evolution of Penology in*

1

this era, the prison had outgrown its infancy as a penitentiary, where the prison planners intended that prisoners be kept in quiet solitude, reflecting penitently on their sins in order that they might cleanse and transform themselves. It also had passed through a half century during which prisoners spent their time in "hard labor," working in prison rock quarries or in profit-making industrial and agricultural enterprises. Eventually, federal legislation and union power forced most convict labor out of the public sector. More recently, prisons in the East, Midwest, and West were touched (most lightly, some belatedly, and a few not at all) by the humanitarian reforms of the "progressive era." [2] Cruel corporal punishment such as flogging, beating, water torture, shackling of inmates to cell walls or hanging them by their thumbs, entombment in small cribs, and long solitary confinement as well as extreme corruption in the appointment of personnel and in the administration of the prison were largely eliminated. The Big House phase followed these reforms.

Although Big Houses appeared in most states, there were many notable exceptions. Many state prison systems never emerged from cruelty and corruption.[3] In a few states, guards unofficially but regularly used brutality and even executions to con-

---

Pennsylvania (Indianapolis: Bobbs-Merrill, 1927); Gustave de Beaumont and Alexis de Tocqueville, *On the Penitentiary System* (Carbondale, Ill.: Southern Illinois University Press, 1964); and David J. Rothman, *The Discovery of the Asylum* (Boston: Little, Brown, 1971).

[2] Descriptions of these "clean-ups" and praise for them appear in several biographies and autobiographies of the reform wardens. See Clinton Duffy and Jean Jennings, *The San Quentin Story* (Westport, Conn.: Greenwood Press, 1968); Gladys Erickson, *Ragen of Joliet* (New York: Dutton, 1957); Frank Tannenbaum, *Osborne of Sing Sing* (Chapel Hill: University of North Carolina Press, 1933). James Jacobs in his study of Stateville, describes the clean-up in more detail and with more sociological analysis: *Stateville* (Chicago: University of Chicago Press, 1977).

[3] The authors of *An Eye for An Eye*, three of whom were convicts, describe the Indiana Penitentiary during the 1960s as an extremely cruel prison. Undoubtedly, several midwestern and southern state prisons have continued with excessive corporal punishment up to the present time. See H. Jack Griswold, Mike Misenheimer, Art Powers, and Ed Tromanhauser, *An Eye for An Eye* (New York: Holt, Rinehart and Winston, 1970).

2

trol prisoners.[4] Some prison administrations continued to engage prisoners in very hard labor throughout the first half of the twentieth century. Even in the eastern, midwestern, and western states where the Big House predominated, there were many residues of earlier phases; silence systems endured through the 1940s. But in most states outside the South, there emerged a type of prison that was relatively free of corporal punishment and that did not engage most prisoners in hard labor.[5] This prison predominated until the "rehabilitative ideal," a new theory of reform, altered penology and the correctional institution appeared. Since the Big House has been the source of most of our ideas about prisons, I shall construct a composite picture of it and then consider some of the exceptions to the type. This will help us to understand its modern progeny.

PHYSICAL DESCRIPTION

The Big House was a walled prison with large cell blocks that contained stacks of three or more tiers of one- or two-man cells. On the average, it held 2,500 men.[6] Sometimes a single cell block housed over 1,000 prisoners in six tiers of cells. Most of these prisons were built over many decades and had a mixture of old and new cell blocks. Some of the older cell blocks were quite primitive. Donald Clemmer, who studied a midwestern prison in the mid-1930s, describes an older one:

> In general, *A* house is a miserable domicile. The toilet buckets, in spite of daily care and disinfecting, lend a putrid

[4] After he was appointed warden of Tucker Farm in Arkansas, Thomas Murton began searching for bodies, which, it was rumored, were buried on the grounds. He found many bodies of executed convicts. He was fired when he continued to demand an investigation. See Thomas Murton, *Accomplices to the Crime* (New York: Grove Press, 1969).

[5] In 1940, only 44% of the prisoners in state and federal prisons were engaged in productive labor (Sutherland and Cressey, *Principles of Criminology,* 6th ed. [New York: Lippincott, 1960] p. 318). When we consider that many states, particularly in the South, engaged most prisoners in labor, the Big House prisons in the East, Midwest, and West must have had more than 60% in idleness.

[6] Donald Clemmer noted that Menard, the prison that he studied in the late 1930s, had a population of 2,300, which varied only 200 from the average of fifty-one major correctional institutions (*The Prison Community* [New York: Holt, Rinehart and Winston, 1958], p. xv).

3

odor. The small windows and the antiquated ventilating system do little to cleanse the atmosphere from 420 toilet cans and 850 male bodies which are not frequently bathed. In summer, the walls collect moisture. On cold winter nights, the air is warm and stuffy, as the few guards on duty object to opening the windows completely as the cold air would make them uncomfortable. The mattresses are generally lumpy. The 25-watt bulbs are so weak that a yellowish gloom pervades the cellhouse and reading is difficult. More than any other place in the prison, one gets the impression of caged animals in cramped quarters.[7]

Many of the cell blocks were newer. Their cells had toilets and small sinks, and they were ventilated, heated, clean, and slightly more spacious. In many Big Houses, convicts were permitted to add furnishings and decorations to their cells, and many cells had rugs on the floors, paintings on the walls, and other pieces of furniture that fit into the small space between the bunks and the cell wall. When Joseph Ragen was appointed warden of Stateville, Illinois, in 1935, he made his first tour of the prison and noted

> Many cells dolled up with curtains concealing cell doors and more frilly curtains over the barred window.
>
> . . .
>
> "Bigshots" have curtains plus overstuffed chairs, chests of drawers and dressers in cells."[8]

Overall, however, cell blocks were harsh worlds of steel and concrete, of unbearable heat and stench in the summer and chilling cold in the winter, of cramped quarters, and of constant droning, shouting, and clanking noise.

The other prominent physical features of the Big House were the yard, the wall, the mess hall, the administration building, the shops, and the industries. The yard, formed by cell blocks and the wall, was a drab place. Victor Nelson, who served time in the 1920s, described the yard of an eastern prison:

[7] Ibid., pp. 73–74.
[8] Erickson, *Ragen of Joliet,* p. 44.

> Four o'clock. Yard time. Recreation. We go from the stuffy shop to the colorless yard. In it is no blade of grass, no tree, no bit of freshness or brilliance. Gray walls, dusty gravel, dirt and asphalt hardness. We walk about, or during our first few months or years, manage to throw a ball back and forth and in some degree exercise our bodies. The longer we stay here, the less we do. At last we merely walk at a funeral pace or lean against a wall and talk.[9]

Better-appointed yards had a few recreational facilities: a baseball diamond, perhaps basketball courts, tables and benches, and handball courts, which often were improvised by using the walls of the cell blocks. The mess hall had rows of tables and benches and invariably was too small to seat the entire population at one time. The thick granite wall encircled the place and, with its gun towers, symbolized the meaning of the Big House.

This granite, steel, cement, and asphalt monstrosity stood as the state's most extreme form of punishment, short of the death penalty. It was San Quentin in California, Sing Sing in New York, Stateville in Illinois, Jackson in Michigan, Jefferson City in Missouri, Canon City in Colorado, and so on. It was the place of banishment and punishment to which convicts were "sent up." Its major characteristics were isolation, routine, and monotony. Its mood was mean and grim, perforated here and there by ragged-edged vitality and humor. Individuals and groups persistently, defiantly pursued plans opposing the rules or the wishes of the staff. Roney Nunez, convicted of a crime that he swears he did not commit, fought through the courts for his release. The Stateville administration tired of his constant "writ writing," placed him in the "hole," and finally took away his books and writing materials. Nunez smuggled out a petition to the courts written in his own blood on toilet paper.[10]

A new prisoner who refused to work at Stillwater, Minnesota, was placed in the hole and tear gassed. When he was

[9] Victor Nelson, *Prison Days and Nights* (Boston: Little, Brown, 1933), p. 16.
[10] Nunez described his struggle to me in many conversations during 1970 and 1971.

finally informed that he would not have to work, he stopped his defiance, was soon released from segregation, and caused no more trouble during his sentence.[11] Robert Stroud, the Birdman of Alcatraz, serving life in solitary confinement (mostly at Leavenworth), was constantly thwarted by the administration, even the director of the Federal Bureau of Prisons. But he pursued the interest that he had acquired in the hole and eventually became the world's expert on domestic bird diseases.[12] Groups of prisoners carried on rackets, brewed alcoholic beverages, and planned escapes. One type of prisoner, variously labeled a "thief," "yegg," or "gangster," lived by a rigid code, helped other thieves (whether or not he knew them), and would die before he would betray someone else. Victor Nelson was impressed by the gangster's integrity of this type:

> Having spent several years in daily contact with the gangster, I have had ample opportunity for observing the way in which he lives up to his narrow code. Without for an instant wishing to glorify him or make him glamorous (which he is not), I nevertheless have to record that he is, of all criminals, the man who most nearly lives up to a code of conduct which he believes right (from his twisted point of view). I have personally known gangsters who went to prison for long terms when, by revealing the truth, they could have shifted blame where it rightfully belonged (on other members of the tribe who luckily evaded arrest).[13]

Big House comedy had sharp, twisted edges. Two old prison jokes, which sent the group of convicts into derisive laughter when I heard them, demonstrate the humor's cutting quality.

> When I was doing time in Salem [the Oregon State Penitentiary], they put me in with this guy who threw epileptic

[11] David Ward supplied me with this anecdote in conversations in June 1978. Actually, the events occurred in the late 1960s, but Stillwater, as a few other prisons, maintained its Big House characteristics long into the age of correctional institution.

[12] For a complete story of Stroud's defiance, see Thomas Gaddis, *The Birdman of Alcatraz* (New York: Random House, 1955).

[13] *Prison Days and Nights,* p. 120.

6

fits. When he threw one, he flopped around on the floor of the cell. I just turned over on my bunk and faced the wall. But there was this hot water pipe running along the floor and the wall and he used to burn himself. He finally went to the sergeant and asked for a cell change. He told him he wanted to cell with someone who would keep him from burning himself when he threw a wingding. The sergeant comes down to the cell and asks me why I won't help this guy. I say, "Man, I do my number. Let him do his."

These two guys are celling together and they both got a lot of time to do. So one night, one of them comes up with this plan. He says to the other guy, "Listen, man, we got a lot of time ahead and we ain't gonna get no sex, unless we fuck these punks around here and I don't want to fuck with these punks. So, why don't we be smart. We can trade off. One night I'll fuck you and then the next night you can fuck me. Now we won't tell nobody and we won't be punks, just sensible."

After thinking it over, the other guy agrees. The con who brought up the plan says that he gets to go first because it's his plan. So, he fucks his cell partner that night. The next evening after lockup, nothing is said for awhile and finally the second con says to his cell partner, who is laying on his bunk reading, "Okay, man, it's my turn tonight." The other con turns to him and says, "Don't rap to me, punk."

Half humorously, half bitterly, prisoners sliced at each other, the guards, the administration, and the world. The prison "dozens," a verbal exchange exposing each other's vulnerable points, most often related to homosexuality, ground on and on.

Two convicts approach a third, who is known by one of them. One introduces the third to his companion, "Tony, this is Charlie," and then adds in an afterthought, "He's my kid." Charlie quickly retorts, "I got your kid hanging, you punk." [14]

Some prisoners dedicated their prison and criminal careers to the creation of such humor, and the skilled were celebrities in the Big House. The following story, involving one of Califor-

[14] This is just one of thousands of exchanges using a similar punch line.

nia's famous comedians, displays his wit and dedication to comedy.

> One night Paul is reading on his bunk and he calls down to his cell partner reading below, "Hey, Beebee, listen to this poem. It's really heavy."
>
> Beebee answers, "No, man, I don't want to hear it. Don't read it to me."
>
> "Come on, man, you'll dig it."
>
> "No, man, I don't feel like being read to. Don't read it to me."
>
> They go back and forth like this and finally Paul, over the objections of Beebee, reads the poem. The next evening at lockup while they are waiting to get in their cell, Paul notices that Beebee has a big book under his arm.
>
> "What's that book, Beebee?"
>
> "*War and Peace*, man."
>
> "Man, that's a long motherfucker. You gonna read all that?"
>
> "Ya, I'm gonna read it all."
>
> When they are both settled on their bunks, Beebee calls up to Paul, "Hey, man, listen to this passage." He then starts to read *War and Peace* from the beginning. Seven days later, after not being able to get Beebee to stop reading aloud whenever they were in the cell together, Paul gets a cell change.

SOCIAL ORGANIZATION

The Big House was, like all prisons, a place where convicts lived and constructed a world. This world had divisions and strata, special informal rules and meanings, and its own set of enterprises. Some of the patterns and divisions were built upon external characteristics. The prisoners came from both the city and the country. In Clemmer's study in the 1930s it was about half and half.[15] By and large, they were the poorer and less educated persons, those from the wrong side of the tracks. Many of them were drifters, persons who floated from state to state, looking for work and, when they failed to find it, stealing and then brushing against "the law." About half previously had been in a prison or reform school.[16] The most frequent

[15] *The Prison Community,* p. 7.
[16] Ibid., p. 57.

8

criminal type was the thief, a criminal who searched for the "big score" — a safe burglary or armed robbery. But most of the prisoners never came close to a big score, and those who were serving a sentence for theft, which was over half the population, were typically convicted of very minor crimes. Clemmer noted that most prisoners were "amateurish and occasional offenders. Most typical of burglars are those who break into a house or store and carry away loot or money seldom exceeding eighty dollars — and not those who tunnel under a street and steal sixty thousand dollars worth of gems from a jewelry store." [17]

Many prisoners were black or other nonwhite races, but most in the Big Houses outside the South were white. Racial prejudice, discrimination, and segregation prevailed. Blacks (and sometimes other nonwhite prisoners) were housed in special sections, in special cell blocks, or at least with cell partners of the same race; and blacks held menial jobs. By rule or informal patterns, blacks and whites sat in separate sections in the mess hall. In fact, in all facets of prison life, patterns of segregation and distance were maintained.

White prisoners kept blacks and, to some extent, other nonwhites "in their place." They did not accept them as equals in the informal social life of the prison and directed constant hate and occasional violence at them. In a novel about a riot in a Big House, Frank Elli, an ex-convict, has accurately depicted the tenuous situation of blacks in this type of prison. While surveying the prison on the first day of the riot, Cully, a white leader, stops to talk to a group of blacks whom he knows.

> He glimpsed at a familiar face and stopped in front of the cell. Railhead Simpson, a slow-moving heavyweight whom he had decisioned twice and knocked out once in the main event on the last three holiday boxing shows, was pacing the floor. The other three Negroes in the cell were sitting on one of the lower bunks.
> "What's happenin' out there man?" Railhead asked.
> "Why don't you come out and see for yourself?"
> "Too many rednecks lookin' for trouble."
> "Don't believe that crap you hear on the radio."

[17] Ibid., p. 56.

"I got eyes, man. I see 'em walkin' past here — all loaded down with weapons. They're lookin' for trouble, all right."

"Not with you guys. Why should they be lookin' for trouble with you guys?"

Railhead grinned. "It's the skin, man. They don't like the color." He glanced at one of his cell partners. "Ask Charlie there. Coupla them boys that broke outta The Hole this mornin' stopped here awhile ago to tell him about it. They mad 'cause he got a white gal comin' to visit him."

"I been in two before," Charlie said. "Only this one gonna be worse. If them studs that broke outta The Hole get high on raisinjack, they gonna be lookin' for blood. And if it's like them other two I was in, we the ones they gonna come lookin' for."

The bull-shouldered Negro sitting next to Charlie snorted and said, "We ready for 'em, though."

Cully shrugged and walked away. What could he say? If a rumble started, the poor bastards wouldn't have a chance.[18]

According to the formal routine, the prisoners rose early; hurriedly ate breakfast; returned to their cells for one of the four or five daily counts; proceeded to work, school, or the yard for a day of idleness; hurriedly ate lunch; counted; went back to work, school, or idleness; hurriedly ate dinner; and returned to their cells for the night. After count, they read, wrote letters or literary works, pursued hobbies, talked to other prisoners, listened to the radio on their ear phones (when this innovation reached the prison), and then went to sleep when the lights were turned off. Clemmer supplies us with the typical schedule of a summer weekday:

Arising Bell and Count	5:30 A.M.
Guard Change	6:00 A.M.
Breakfast (long line)	6:30 A.M.
Breakfast (short line)	7:15 A.M.
March to Work (long line)	7:15 A.M.
Sick Call	7:30 A.M.
March to Work (short line)	7:45 A.M.
Dinner (short line)	10:45 A.M.
Dinner (long line)	11:30 A.M.

[18] Frank Elli, *The Riot* (New York: Coward, McCann, 1966), p. 87.

Return to Work	1:00 P.M.
Supper (short line)	3:30 P.M.
Supper (long line)	4:30 P.M.
Evening Count and Whistle	5:00 to 5:30 P.M.
Guard Change	6:00 P.M.
Warning Bell	8:45 P.M.
Lights Out	9:00 P.M.[19]

This routine was punctuated by the weekends with their sports events — a baseball game, perhaps against an outside team, or a fight card of convict boxers — and their occasional visits and by parole board hearings, which, along with the sentence itself, constituted the broad frame within which each prisoner "did time."

This was the formal, or more visible, routine. Within this general outline a complex, subtle, informal prisoner world with several subworlds was also operating. It pivoted around the convict code, a prison adaptation of the thieves' code. Thieves were not the majority, but they were the most frequent criminal type, and their strong commitment to thieves' values, their communication network — which extended through the thieves' world, inside and out — and their loyalty to other thieves gave them the upper hand in prison. Jack Black, a self-proclaimed thief, described his first entry into prison and revealed the status of the thief in the prison world, the patterns of cooperation between thieves, and certain key aspects of the thieves' code that had been established in prison.

> Shorty was one of the patricians of the prison, a "box man" doing time for bank burglary. "I'll put you in with the right people, kid. You're folks yourself or you wouldn't have been with Smiler."
>
> I had no friends in the place. But the fact that I had been with Smiler, that I had kept my mouth shut and that Shorty had come forward to help me gave me a certain fixed status in the prison that nothing could shake but some act of my own. I was naturally pleased to find myself taken up by the "best people," as Shorty and his friends called themselves, and accepted as one of them.
>
> Shorty now took me into the prison where we found the

[19] *The Prison Community,* p. 63.

head trustee who was one of the "best, people" himself, a thoroughgoing bum for the road. The term "bum" is not used here in any cheap or disparaging sense. In those days, it meant any kind of a traveling thief. It has long since fallen into disuse. The Yegg of today was the bum of twenty years ago.

"This party," said Shorty, "is one of the 'Johnson' family." (The bums called themselves "Johnsons" probably because they were so numerous). "He's good people and I want to get him fixed up for a cell with the right folks." [20]

The central rule in the thieves' code was "thou shalt not snitch." In prison, thieves converted this to the dual norm of "do not rat on another prisoner" and "do your own time." Thieves also were obliged by their code to be cool and tough, that is, to maintain respect and dignity; not to show weakness; to help other thieves; and to leave most other prisoners alone. Their code dominated the Big House and generally it could be translated into these rules: Do not inform, do not openly interact or cooperate with the guards or the administration, and do your own time. These rules helped to produce a gap of hostility and unfriendliness between prisoners and guards, a hierarchy of prisoners, a system of mutual aid among a minority of prisoners, and patterns of exploitation among others.

The prisoners divided themselves into a variety of special types. In addition to the yeggs, "Johnsons," "people," "right guys," or "regulars" — thieves and persons whom they accepted as trustworthy — there were several types more indigenous to the prison. There were prison "politicians," "merchants," and "gamblers," who were involved in supplying, exchanging, and controlling prison resources and commodities. There were prison "queens," who openly presented themselves as homosexuals, and "punks," who were considered to have been "turned out" — that is, made into homosexuals by other prisoners or by the prison experience. There was a variety of prison "toughs," persons who were deeply and openly hostile to the prison administration, the conventional society, and most other prisoners and who displayed a readiness to employ violence

[20] Jack Black, *You Can't Win* (New York: Macmillan, 1927), pp. 104–5.

against others. These types ranged from the less predictable and less social "crazies" to the more predictable and clique-oriented "hard rocks" or "tush hogs." There was the "character," who continuously created humorous derision through his dress, language, story-telling ability, or general behavior. There were the "masses," who broke into the subtypes of "assholes" or "hoosiers," lower- and working-class persons having little or no criminal skill and earning low respect, and "square johns," persons who were not viewed as criminals by the rest of the population and were oriented to conventional society.[21] There was a variety of "dingbats" who were considered to be crazy, but harmless. Finally, there were "rapos," persons serving sentences for sexual acts such as incest and child molesting, which were repulsive to most prisoners, and "stool pigeons," "rats," or "snitches," who supplied information about other prisoners to authorities.

These types were arranged in a hierarchy of prestige, power, and privilege. At the top of the stack were the right guys, through their propensity to cooperate with each other, their prestige as thieves, and their presentation of coolness and toughness. Clemmer described the elite of the prison in the following manner: "In the class which we have termed the 'elite,' are the more intelligent, urbanized, sophisticated offenders who, for the most part, do not toady to officials and who set themselves apart, and have their relations chiefly with each other." [22] Very close to the top were the merchants, politicians, and gamblers. They occupied this high position because they largely controlled the scarce prison resources. Characters, when they were accomplished, were awarded a special position with considerable respect and popularity, but not much direct power. Down the ladder were the toughs, who had to be respected because they were a constant threat. The cliques of hard rocks occasionally hurt or killed someone, though seldom anyone with prestige and power. The crazies, who were often very dangerous, were treated with extreme caution, but were avoided and excluded as much as possible. In the middle were

[21] "Hoosier" had this meaning in states other than Indiana.
[22] *The Prison Community,* p. 107.

13

the masses who were ignored by the leaders, stayed out of the prison's informal world, and restricted their social activities to small friendship groups or remained "loners." Below them were the queens, punks, rats, and rapos, the latter being at the very bottom of the pile. On the outside of all informal prisoner activities were the dingbats, who were ignored by all.

Most prisoners followed one of three prison careers. The most frequent was that of just doing time. This was the style of the thief and of most other prisoners who shared the thief's primary concern of getting out of prison with maximum dispatch and minimum pain. Doing time meant, above all, avoiding trouble that would place a prisoner in danger or lengthen or intensify his punishment. But in addition, doing time involved avoiding "hard time." To avoid hard time, prisoners stayed active in sports, hobbies, or reading; secured as many luxuries as possible without bringing on trouble; and formed a group of close friends with whom to share resources and leisure hours and to rely on for help and protection.

Thieves who established this style generally confined their group associations to other thieves. Since they had prestige and power in the prison world, however, they occasionally entered into general prisoner affairs, particularly when they were trying to secure luxuries or favors for themselves or friends. Most of the masses followed the pattern of doing time established by thieves, but their friendship groups tended not to be so closely knit and they tended not to enter into the *general* prison social activities.[23]

Some prisoners, particularly the indigenous prison types, oriented themselves more completely to the prison and tended to construct a total existence there. Donald Cressey and I once described the style of adaptation of convicts who

> seek positions of power, influence and sources of information, whether these men are called "shots," "politicians," "merchants," "hoods," "toughs," "gorillas," or something else. A job as secretary to the Captain or Warden, for example, gives an aspiring prisoner information and consequent power, and

[23] Clemmer's descriptions of primary group and semi-primary group affiliations suggest that many of the primary groups were composed of more criminally oriented men (Ibid., pp. 123–28).

14

enables him to influence the assignment or regulation of other inmates. In the same way, a job which allows the incumbent to participate in a racket, such as clerk in the kitchen store-room where he can steal and sell food, is highly desirable to a man oriented to the convict subculture. With a steady income of cigarettes, ordinarily the prisoner's medium of exchange, he may assert a great deal of influence and purchase these things which are symbols of status among persons oriented to the convict subculture. Even if there is not a well-developed medium of exchange, he can barter goods acquired in his position for equally desirable goods possessed by other convicts. These include information and such things as specially starched, pressed and tailored prison clothing, fancy belts, belt buckles or billfolds, special shoes or any other type of dress which will set him apart and will indicate that the prisoner has both the influence to get the goods and the influence necessary to keep them and display them despite prison rules which outlaw doing so.[24]

Many of the persons who occupied these roles and made a world out of prison — that is, followed the strategy sometimes referred to by prisoners as "jailing" — were individuals who had long experiences with jails and prisons beginning in their early teens or even earlier. Actually, they were more familiar with prison than with outside social worlds. Claude Brown, raised in Harlem, runs into a prison friend who had served many sentences.

"Yeah, Sonny. The time I did in Woodburn, the times I did on the Rock, that was college, man. Believe me, it was college. I did four years in Woodburn. And I guess I've done a total of about two years on the Rock in about the last six years. Every time I went there, I learned a little more. When I go to jail now, Sonny, I live, man. I'm right at home. That's the good part of it. If you look at it, Sonny, a cat like me is just cut out to be in jail.

"It could never hurt me, 'cause I never had what the good folks call a home and all that kind of shit to begin with. So when I went to jail, the first time I went away, when I went to Warwick, I made my own home. It was all right. Shit,

[24] John Irwin and Donald Cressey, "Thieves, Convicts and the Inmate Culture," *Social Problems,* Fall 1963, p. 149.

I learned how to live. Now when I go back to the joint, anywhere I go, I know some people. If I go to any of the jails in New York, or if I go to a slam in Jersey even, I still run into a lot of cats I know. It's almost like a family." [25]

One last strategy followed by a small number of prisoners I labeled "gleaning" in a later study of the California prison system.[26] An old style, it must be included in the description of the Big House.[27] Gleaning involved taking advantage of any resource available to better themselves, to improve their minds, or to obtain skills that would be useful on the outside. In trying to improve themselves, prisoners in Big Houses read, sought formal education through the prison's elementary and high schools (when these existed) and university correspondence courses, and learned trades in the few vocational training programs or in prison job assignments.[28] In addition, they tried to improve themselves in other ways — by increasing social skills and physical appearance. Generally, in gleaning, prisoners attempted to equip themselves for life after prison.

Improvisation In addition to living by the code and stratifying themselves, convicts filled the days with systems of special prison activities. They responded to their situation of scarcity and deprivation by gathering whatever materials were available in the prison and improvising substitutes for many luxuries taken for granted outside. Brewing "pruno" or "raisinjack" is

[25] Claude Brown, *Manchild in the Promised Land* (New York: Macmillan, 1965), p. 412.

[26] John Irwin, *The Felon* (Englewood Cliffs, N.J.: Prentice-Hall, 1970), pp. 76–79.

[27] Evidence that prisoners gleaned in Big Houses is contained in this note on Victor Nelson's prison career: "On March 20, 1924, Nelson was sentenced to serve five years in the Auburn State Prison on the charge of robbery and assault. While in the institution, he took several extension courses at Columbia University on writing and secretarial correspondence" (*Prison Days and Nights,* p. xiv).

[28] In the first half of this century, high school education was increasingly available to prisoners. In a few prisons, correspondence courses from state or private universities could be taken. After World War II, university opportunities increased, and in the 1960s many college programs inside prisons were introduced. See Marjorie J. Seashore et al. *Prisoner Education: Project New Gate and Other College Programs* (New York: Praeger, 1976).

a good example. Some prisoners persistently accumulated sugar, fruit, grains, or potatoes and yeast, hid these ingredients, and then waited anywhere from three days to several weeks, depending on the quality of the hiding place and the patience of the prison brewers. Often the hiding places were very elaborate. Pruno factories have been located in the plumbing in cells and in portable factories disguised as familiar containers, which were moved from place to place. The outcome of all this preparation was a foul-tasting, highly impure, but intoxicating beverage.

Donald Cressey supplied this description of another improvisation, the "glim box":

> It was a snuff box filled with cotton fluff. On top of the fluff was a piece of flint and a piece of string with a small metal disc attached to it in the way kids used to attach buttons to a double length of string so they would twirl. You took the disc and string from the box, twirled it. Then, holding one end of the string in your left hand and the other in your teeth, you spun the metal disc. With your right hand, you made the disc scrape the flint in the box of puff. Presto! The cotton would catch fire. It didn't flame; it glowed. A practiced convict could light a cigarette as fast with a glim box as a man on the street could do it with his fancy lighter.[29]

"Stingers," used to heat water, were another prison invention. The simplest and most common stinger consisted of two small plates of metal (about 1 inch by 3 inches) attached to two wires and separated by a thin, nonconductive material. The wires were plugged into a wall outlet or the socket of the cell light and the stinger was immersed in water, causing it to heat up rapidly.

A few prisoners constructed weapons, particularly "shivs" (prison improvised knives), from a variety of materials available in the prison, such as kitchen knives, metal from the shops, and toothbrushes. Once in a while, they manufactured guns. Today most old prisons have on display a large board to which are nailed dozens, even hundreds of prisoner-improvised weap-

---

[29] Cressey also described to me an elaborate, improvised hot plate that a prisoner pridefully had given him.

ons. The warden or other guides enjoy showing visitors this board to convince them of the danger posed by prisoners.

Occasionally, the improvisation became more ambitious. In the late 1930s a group of prisoners in San Quentin ordered photoengraving equipment for the prison's print shop and began counterfeiting $10 bills. When they were discovered, they had already produced $12,000 and had begun smuggling bills out to friends who had left the prison on parole.[30]

Improvisation had a double value. The first and most obvious was that it supplied the prisoners with commodities that reduced their deprivation. But also important was the satisfaction that prisoners gained in knowing that they were attempting and often succeeding in beating the system.

To a great extent, Big House homosexual patterns were a form of prison improvisation. With no possibility for heterosexual contacts, some prisoners performed homosexual acts as "inserters," although they would not do this on the outside. In addition, many young, weaker, less initiated, and perhaps effeminate prisoners were tricked or forced into the role of "insertee" (that is, they were turned out). Often they were trapped in this role by the knowledge that they had succumbed in the past, and after years of performing as a punk, they developed homosexual identities and continued as homosexuals even after release. Finally, some prisoners, particularly prisoners who were thoroughly immersed in the informal prisoner world — that is, who jailed — performed the role of "wolf" or "jocker." A few of these individuals, after an extended period of continued homosexual activities (ostensibly as the inserter, but actually as both the inserter and insertee in many cases), developed a preference for homosexual relationships and continued in their masculine homosexual role on the outside.

Fantasy Prisoners also confronted their deprivation and restricted freedom by fantasizing. Many of the fantasies were developed in private:

> One cannot rest. One can merely escape from the existing drabness. One can merely lie down on the bed and drift off

[30] See Duffy and Jennings, *The San Quentin Story,* pp. 54–55.

into the dream world; into memories of the past, visions of the future; neither of which is satisfactory except in retrospect or anticipation. One lies in a stupor, shutting out the undignified, unappetizing dullness; deliberately or unconsciously running away from life. This is a bad habit to get into, this flying from reality; but it is a habit into which practically all of us get, mildly or terribly, depending entirely on the length of our sentences, our ages, our intensities of awareness.[31]

But many were constructed in groups:

We always talk. During the cell hours, we store up facts, reflections, broodings so that our minds are overflowing. And every chance to get to unburden them, we avail ourselves of it. We talk *at* each other. We do not converse; we deliver monologues in which we get rid of the stored up bubblings. We try to live through words and self-dramatization. Our essential need is for actual tangible living, which we cannot have; so we try to live by pretending to live in tall stories based on how we'd like to live, how we long to live.[32]

Being removed from the outside world, the prisoners developed distortions of outside realities in both individual and group fantasies. Distortions of women, sexual relationships, and future life possibilities were blended together into a fantasy rendition of the free world. Certain dominant qualities that were distillations of various criminal and prisoner value systems constituted a general framework for this rendition. These qualities became very important to many individual prisoners, because the groups that sustained the values in their collective fantasies became reference groups that judged their progress after they left prison. At least, those who had departed experienced the prisoner groups in this way; consequently, the fantasies often had a powerful impact on prisoners' postprison life.

Some of the dominant qualities that operated in the group fantasies and remained as salient values in the postprison careers of many prisoners were richness of sexual activities;

[31] Nelson, *Prison Days and Nights,* p. 14.
[32] Ibid., p. 16.

"sharpness" (some association with illegal or marginally legal financial enterprises), and autonomy. Negative qualities were "slave" traits — laborious, unskilled, menial, dirty, monotonous, and subservient work — and "policeman" traits. These values, backed up by one's cronies in the prison, endured as strong influences on the prisoner for years after his release.

Stupefaction   When I was in the Los Angeles County Jail in 1952, waiting to be sentenced to prison, I met a "four-time loser" who was going back to Folsom, the state's long-term Big House. He advised me, "Don't let them send you to Folsom. It's the easiest place to do time but, man, you leave something there you never get back." He was alluding to Folsom's impact on prisoners' mentality, which prisoners referred to as "going stir." I think the term *stupefaction* catches the sense of this expression. The dictionary defines *stupefaction* as the "state of being stupefied; insensibility of mind or feeling." Serving time in a Big House meant being pressed into a slow-paced, rigid routine; cut off from outside contacts and social worlds; denied most ordinary human pleasures and stimulations; and constantly forced to contain anger and hostility. Many persons were able to maintain their spirit under these conditions, and some were even vitalized by the challenge. But most prisoners were somewhat stupefied by it. They learned to blunt their feelings, turn inward, construct fantasy worlds for themselves, and generally throttle their intellectual, emotional, and physical life. In the extreme they fell into a stupor. Victor Nelson describes an old con:

> A trustee in a suit of striped overalls was standing with his arms folded lazily against the handle of the rake, his head resting dejectedly on his arms, his whole attitude that of a man who had worked all day and was very tired although it was only about nine o'clock of a cool spring morning. He seemed almost in a coma. There was an expression of utter indifference on his face and his eyes were glazed with absent-mindedness. He was, although I did not know it then, a living example of the total, final, devastating effect of imprisonment upon the human being.[33]

[33] Ibid., p. 219.

The Big House did not reform prisoners or teach many persons crime. It embittered many. It stupefied thousands.

THE BULLS

The "bull," "screw," or "hack" — the prison guard — was the other key figure in the Big House. Regrettably, we have less information about his behavior than about the prisoners'; what we have is a stereotypical image. In one of the rare, but recent, studies of the guard, its authors point out that "what others have said about guards is mostly by way of lament over their meager education, poor training, provincial world view and sometimes sadistic personality traits." [34] This characterization is probably fairly accurate. Guards did tend to come from rural backgrounds and to be low paid (Clemmer notes that in the 1930s the guards at Menard received $112.50 a month, the lowest salary in the institution).[35] The lack of special training was certainly true, the "provincial world view" can be assumed, but the occasional "sadistic personality traits" are speculation. The major difficulty with this characterization, however, is that it does not reveal anything about the guard's routine, the special world view that guards developed, or the particular skills that emerged in their unique work world. I shall attempt to fill in some of the blanks here in order to complete this picture of the Big House's social order.

An analysis of the guard's routine must start with the recognition that it was the guard who was constantly in direct contact with the prisoners, had to oversee their activities, and was held responsible for rule infractions, fights, disturbances, and escapes. Moreover, he was trying to prevent these actions among prisoners who were living in an extremely reduced situation, were systematically hostile toward guards and the prison administration, and were often committed to deviant enterprises. Consequently, many prisoners broke the rules, and some of them were strongly motivated to fight each other, attempt to escape, and even riot occasionally. Further compounding the difficulty was the fact that bulls had insufficient

[34] James Jacobs and H. G. Retsky, "Prison Guard," *Urban Life,* Winter 1975, p. 5.
[35] *The Prison Community,* p. 63.

immediate raw power (methods of direct force) at their disposal. They did have a reserve in the state's resources — additional police, state militia, and the army — but these were extremely costly. They could use many internal direct control devices, such as isolation and "segregation" (permanent or nearly permanent lockup situations), but these lose their efficacy when used too often against too many. On the guards' side was the general tendency of most prisoners to do their time as peacefully and quickly as possible. Rule infractions, fights, escapes, and participation in riots could be converted to longer sentences, the loss of "good time," and additional sentences.

But these aids would have been insufficient in themselves. To avoid calling on the state's back-up systems of force and to avoid the troublesome use of the internal punishment systems, the guards, with the open encouragement or tacit approval of the administration, developed informal, sometimes officially unethical systems of control. One that has been emphasized by critics of the prison was brutality. Although some bulls in Big Houses regularly used brutal control devices, such as beatings, this was probably one of the most exaggerated and less successful control strategies. When guards did employ corporal punishment, more often they were expressing their own sadism or exaggerating the prevailing attitude toward prisoners — that prisoners were subhuman.[36]

The more common and successful informal control strategies were the personal agreement and corrupt favoritism. In the first case, guards reached explicit or tacit agreements with prisoners in which the latter would refrain from rule breaking in return for some favor or special dispensation. A prisoner at Menard described this type of agreement:

> As an illustration, I would like to refer to an incident that happened to me. I was caught violating the rule of smoking in the yard. Through the influence of one of the deputies, the guard did not have me punished providing I promised

[36] The prison generates and sustains this belief. It is useful in buffering the staff from troublesome feelings of compassion that they might experience when constantly confronting persons living in deprivation and suffering from reduced freedom. But this prevailing belief also offered a justification for brutality.

not to do it again. I gave my promise and kept it for two years, even though this particular guard had left the service in the meantime. The guard who took his place proved to be a sadist, issuing orders of his own making to certain men and which he thought might act in some way as punishment for them but which were inconsequential to the interests of the institution and were utterly disregarded by other guards.

I was very careful not to violate any of his orders while he was on duty, but on his relief day, I did violate one of them and took some bananas to the dining room to eat with cream peaches (canned) for my supper. The next day, he was on duty and one of his "helpers" (stool pigeon) told him what I had done. Immediately, he threatened to send me to the solitary. He did not because he knew such an order would not be considered by the deputy warden. A few weeks later, he caught some of the men smoking and though I was not with them, he also placed the same charge against me and I was punished for something I had not done. *More than the punishment, I hated the fact that the deputy who had used his influence on my behalf before thought I had broken my word.* (Emphasis added.)[37]

Rather than originating in a particular act, such as the one described above, the agreement might be built up over time. Some guards, through a general policy of living up to agreements, earned a reputation for fairness and were more successful in encouraging conformity among prisoners. This worked because most prisoners appreciated fairness: "Most men are lovers of fair play and will respect the guard who shoots square with all, though they will have little respect for the guard who will let them openly violate the rules even if they themselves are the ones favored."[38]

In the case of corrupt favoritism, guards granted special privileges to key prisoners in return for their support in maintaining order. The arrangement of favoritism usually grew without any verbal agreements, in a process by which the prisoners would take certain calculated liberties and, when the guard did not take action against them, they would continue the illicit practice. The liberties were such things as taking

[37] *The Prison Community,* pp. 189–90.
[38] Ibid., p. 189.

23

more food for oneself, one's friends, or one's "clients;" placing oneself, one's friends, or one's clients on special "unlocks" for evening recreational activities; arranging cell changes; and "squashing" disciplinary actions. The tradeoff was assistance in maintaining order in the prison. Inmates did this by keeping their own violations within acceptable limits; by supporting the dominant value system, revolving around "do your own time" (which indirectly encouraged conformity), and by applying direct force through threats or actual violence to control prisoners who threatened to disrupt the prison routine and thereby to disrupt the privileged person's special arrangement.

THE RIOT

By and large, strategies of control planned by administrators or practiced by guards worked. The Big House was relatively peaceful. However, it was an unstable peace, maintained in spite of considerable tension. Alfred Hassler, imprisoned as a conscientious objector during World War II, quickly sensed the tension below the surface calm.

> I am finding prison a curious combination of unrelenting tension and acute boredom. The boredom comes from the lack of stimulating things to do, of course; the tension rises out of the collective tension of more than a thousand convicts. On the surface, life here appears to run almost placidly but one needs to go only a very little beneath the surface to find the whirlpools and eddies of anger and frustration. The muttering of discontent and rebellion goes on constantly: the *sotto voce* sneer whenever we pass an official or guard, the glare carefully calculated to express contempt without arousing overt retaliation, the tempers that rise so swiftly to the breaking point. [39]

From time to time, the calm was shattered by small disturbances or large riots. The big riots came in series: 1912–15, 1927–31, 1939–40, and 1950–53. Some of the earlier riots were precipitated by or resulted in mass escape attempts. After the early 1930s, when the FBI and its national record-keeping

[39] Alfred Hassler, *Diary of a Self-Made Convict* (Chicago: Henry Regnery, 1954) pp. 70–71.

activities made escape less fruitful and appealing, most riots were set off spontaneously; after a short period of destruction and violence, hostages were taken and demands made. Some of the larger riots were very murderous and destructive. Vernon Fox, in a comprehensive study of riots in prisons in the United States, included these two in his descriptions.

At California's Folsom Prison on Monday, November 24, 1927, 1,200 to 2,000 inmates fought National Guardsmen. Seven hostages were held. Police circled the prison, 400 National Guardsmen surrounded the building which prisoners defended, tanks were brought in, National Guard airplanes were in action over the scene, one-pound artillery was set up and a Southern Pacific Railway switch engine trained flood lights on the building. The troops fired round after round. By the time Governor Young arrived and ordered the attacks to cease, nine inmates had been killed, with 31 wounded, three of whom were expected to die; two guards had been killed outright, three were wounded, one of whom was expected to die. An aged officer died from excitement. Governor Young's action prevented what could have gone down in history as an infamous and wanton massacre. The inmates were prevented from getting to the kitchen and their lack of food placed time on the side of the prison officials. The inmates were starved out.

In Colorado, on Friday, October 3, 1929, 150 inmates, three of whom were murderers, obtained four guns and barricaded themselves in cell-house No. 3, holding seven guards hostage. Prison officers attacked the cell-house, and the inmates felled three officers in the first rush, killing them immediately. They demanded that the prison gates be swung open and that they be allowed to escape. If their demands were not met, they threatened to kill a hostage each hour on the hour as long as their demands were ignored. The administration demanded unconditional surrender.

The body of Guard J. J. Elles, the hangman, was the first to be thrown from the cell-house. Austin MacCormick was quoted in 1952 as having said that their heads were sent out on platters, but I was unable to substantiate it. Armed guards had been able to isolate the riot to the cell-house. National Guardsmen were called, bringing in one airplane and several 3-inch field pieces. Warden Francis E. Crawford was shot seriously, but recovered. The Catholic chaplain, Father O'Neil, set the charge of dynamite at the cell-house and exploded it, after which the cell-house was sprayed with machine-gun fire. The prisoners retreated to the undamaged part of the cell-house and continued their fight. The militia advanced, but the prisoners drove them back. Governor Adams endorsed the manner in which the riot was being handled. As their ammunition ran out, inmate leader Danny Daniels shot his lieutenants and then shot himself. The toll was seven guards killed, five inmates killed, $500,000 in property damage — a new record and an escape prevented.[40]

Many riots followed changes in administrative routines that upset the delicate balance between prisoner leaders and other prisoners or resulted in loss of privileges or increases in punishment and deprivation. The pattern of riots suggests contagion: a riot in one state inspired riots in others. But riots were mostly spontaneous and unpredictable. Most Big Houses were in a constant state of fragile peace, the heavy tension being balanced precariously against everyone's (including the prisoners') fear of riots. But the delicate balance could be upset by a variety of events or changes: if a guard broke up a fight and hauled the fighters off to the hole, other prisoners might jeer and then riot; or a group of gorillas or "hard noses" might break out of segregation and send the prison into a frenzy of destruction. Although small events set them off and tension was constant, riots were exceptions to the monotonous calm of the Big House.

THE ADMINISTRATION

The official administrators included the warden and his assistants, the business manager, the head cook, the chief of maintenance, the chief of industries, and the captain and his lieutenants. Their duties were primarily (1) to maintain order (that is, keep down internal disruption and violence and prevent escapes), (2) to supply the prisoners with their life necessities (usually on a very skimpy budget), and (3) to manage the prison industries, which, after the restrictions on the use of

[40] Vernon Fox, *Violence Behind Bars* (Westport, Conn.: Greenwood Press, 1956), pp. 22, 26–27.

prison labor, were limited to the production of commodities consumed within state institutions — furniture, clothing, and food — and items sold by the state, such as license plates.

Informally, in most Big Houses a persistent conflict prevailed, producing factions in most administrations, influencing the strategies and careers of many administrators (particularly wardens), and resulting in regular reshuffling of administrations. This was the conflict between the use of humane or of punitive prison routines. The factors that stimulated this conflict were located internally and externally. Inherent in the problems of controlling prisoners (many of whom were violent individuals and escape risks) and in the social organization of the prison (which was an isolated, relatively autonomous, hierarchial, and authoritarian organization, very much like the military) was a strong tendency to move toward more and more forceful and cruel forms of social control. In addition, there was occasional pressure from the less informed and more punitive sectors of the public to keep prisoners under control and not to mollycoddle them. On the side of humane practices were persistent pressures from very active and respected reformers, such as Austin MacCormick, and from reform organizations, such as the American Friends Service Committee and the John Howard Society, and from the expanding and spreading humane philosophy of the liberal tradition in the United States. Consequently, most states in the East, North, and West went through liberal phases during which a governor backed prison reform and appointed a reform warden. Men like Clinton Duffy, Thomas Osborne, and Joseph Ragen pushed the prisons toward humanity in their tenure as wardens. Between these periods, penal practice would swing back toward punishment and cruelty and sometimes toward corruption. The overall movement, though slow, was toward less and less overt brutality and punishment. However, the struggle between the two opposing forces was always present in the Big Houses and greatly influenced the structure of the administration and the careers of individuals.

In the next era, this struggle crystallized within the formal structure of the prison when two branches were established: one for "care and treatment," which handled rehabilitative

27

services, and one for "custody," which managed control matters. This did not remove the tension, but elevated it to a more complex (and confusing) theoretical level.

EXCEPTIONS TO THE BIG HOUSE

Although this composite picture fits many, perhaps a majority, of the prisons in the United States during the first half of the twentieth century, there were many departures. For instance, many prisons in the South had a majority of black prisoners or were totally segregated.[41] The formal administrative structure, the relationships between prisoners and between prisoners and guards, and the informal social worlds that evolved under these special conditions may have been very different. In addition, many states operated extensive agricultural enterprises with the use of convict labor. Tucker Farm, Arkansas's prison farm, and the Huntsville complex in Texas are examples. The use of convicts to oversee other convicts, the extreme cruelty, and the very hard work in these prisons made them different from the Big Houses that I have described. In Florida and other southern states, most prisoners worked in chain gangs on state projects, mainly roads. Again, the work was hard and the cruelty extreme. Finally, each state had a population of women convicts, which it kept separate. In larger states, there were special women's prisons; in smaller states, special sections were set up in the male prisons. Later studies of women's prisons have revealed that they are quite distinct in social structure.[42]

Despite the existence of these deviant types, the Big House was dominant and provided the source of most popular images and sociological theories. But as we proceed, we must keep in mind that even in this era of relative homogeneity there were many exceptions that were ignored when a sociology of imprisonment was developed.

[41] We have no studies of these. For a rare description of a southern prison, see H. Patterson and E. Conrad, *Scotsboro Boy* (New York: Garden City Press, 1952).

[42] See Rose Giallombardo, *Society of Women* (New York: John Wiley, 1966); David Ward and Gene Kassebaum, *Women's Prison* (Chicago: Aldine, 1965); and Esther Hefferman, *Making It in Prison* (New York: John Wiley, 1972).

SOCIOLOGICAL THEORIES OF THE BIG HOUSE

The Big House was the source of images and illusions that continue to obscure the contemporary prison. Some of these images and illusions were created by sociologists who began investigating the prison in the 1930s and have since become the authorities on life there. (Even Hollywood, the society's leading image maker, consults sociologists when it makes a new movie about prisons.) Consequently, to clear our vision, we must sift the sociological ideas on prisons.

In their early excursions into the strange land of the Big House, sociologists shared several biases. First was their class and ethnic bias. The late C. Wright Mills noted that the early "social pathologists" (sociologists who studied social disorganization and deviance) had rural and Wasp backgrounds and that their small-town, Protestant morality influenced their research and conclusions.[43] The same is true of those who studied prisons. They were unfamiliar with the lower classes, particularly urban lower classes, and they were deeply imbued with rural, Wasp morality.

In addition, they were sociologists. This meant that they carried with them the latest set of sociological concepts, a sociological perspective, or, as Thomas Kuhn has called it, a paradigm.[44] In making this claim, I am not suggesting that this paradigm completely distorted reality or that it was possible for them to do otherwise. Reality is experienced only through paradigms or perspectives, and all abstract theories are more or less useful or valid. This is an unavoidable limitation of abstract thinking, scientific analysis, and the human enterprise in general.

We must be aware, however, that a particular set of abstract ideas or a general perspective usually is shaped by other influences, in addition to the reality to which it is being applied, and that biased selection and distortion of data or observations take place. Consequently, we must remain sensitive to the potential sources of bias and attempt to make the theories

[43] C. W. Mills, "The Professional Ideology of Social Pathologists", *American Journal of Sociology,* Sept. 1943, pp. 165–80.

[44] Thomas Kuhn, *The Structure of Scientific Revolutions* (Chicago: University of Chicago Press, 1962).

or perspectives explicit in order to increase our understanding of any phenomenon.

The first sociologists who approached the Big House and developed the early theories saw it as a universal type. Clemmer reveals this bias in his introduction to *The Prison Community* when he argues that Menard was much like all prisons in the United States: "Our prison is fairly typical in respect to discipline, labor, and the various practices found in most other adult correctional institutions. It has been described by a distinguished penologist who has inspected every American penitentiary as "just another place where men do time." [45] This is not completely true, and it becomes less true as we move through the 1950s and into the 1960s. We shall see how the early sociologists' failure to consider the exceptions led them to develop a theory of prisoner social organization that ignores differences in prisoner population.

Clemmer's Study of Menard For all intents and purposes, the series of sociological studies began with Donald Clemmer's study of Menard, an older maximum-security prison located in the southern part of Illinois. This study, from which I have been quoting so liberally, was conducted in the late 1930s, and Clemmer was within the sphere of the Chicago school of sociology that dominated the discipline in that era. Consequently, Clemmer carried into the prison two of the school's pet concepts — the primary group and culture — and its ethnographic tradition. Like the students of Robert Park at Chicago, who discovered the unique cultures carried by hoboes, taxi dancers, jack rollers, gang members, slum dwellers, and professional thieves, Clemmer located a special prisoner culture comprised of the

> habits, behavior systems, traditions, history, customs, folkways, codes, the laws and rules which guide the inmates and their ideas, opinions and attitudes toward or against homos, family, education, work, recreations, government, prisons, police, judges, other inmates, wardens, ministers, doctors, guards, ballplayers, clubs, guns, cells, buckets, gravy, beans, walls, lamps, rain, clouds, clothes, machinery, hammers,

[45] *The Prison Community*, p. xv.

rocks, caps, bibles, books, radios, monies, stealing, murder, rape, sex, love, honesty, martyrdom, and so on.[46]

He suggested that this unique culture produced a social order peculiar to the prison and that prisoners became "prisonized" into this culture, which disrupted their reentry into the outside society and sometimes deepened "their criminality and antisociality."

In analyzing informal group life, Clemmer began with the primary group concept that was so popular in sociology in that period. Other observers had reported that prisoners formed highly integrated groups, and he set out to determine if this were true. His research indicated that slightly over half the prisoner population were members of "primary" or "semi-primary" groups. He characterized the primary group member in the following manner:

> This is the man who is one of a group of three or more men who are all very close friends. They share each other's luxuries and secrets and have accepted or are willing to accept, punishment one for the other. The "clique man" is so closely associated with this group that he thinks in terms of "we" rather than "I" and he acts as the group acts. The clique has some permanence.[47]

The semi-primary group member

> is the man who is friendly with a certain small group of men but who does not entirely subject himself to the wishes and acts of the group as a whole. He would share his luxuries, tell some of his secrets, but would not go "all the way" for those with whom he is friendly. While he is particularly friendly with one group, he also mixes freely with a number of other men and is at least friendly with these others.[48]

This is consistent with my description of Big House patterns except that I would relate the grouping tendencies to the different prisoner types. Thieves or right guys and the clique-oriented toughs had a greater tendency to form the groups that he labels primary, while the "masses," merchants, politicians, and others

[46] Ibid., pp. 294–95.
[47] Ibid., p. 118.
[48] Ibid., p. 118.

in jailing groups are those whom he labels semi-primary. The masses' and "jailers' " lack of commitment to a common sub-culture or their exploitative adaptation to prison tended to prevent a more complete commitment to any clique.

Clemmer did not limit the analysis to culture and primary group. In fact, he produced a full ethnography of prison life. He described the hierarchy of prisoners, the fantasizing, the sexual and other leisure patterns. In addition, he produced a rather complete glossary of terms and described many of the subtle, unique meanings within the prisoners' culture.

I must mention two weaknesses in Clemmer's analysis. The first is his failure to identify the subcultural systems that were carried into the prison, particularly that of the thief, which was so influential in the development of the prisoner code and the establishment of the prisoner hierarchy. Second, he did not recognize the exploitative, corrupt relationship that politicians, merchants, and other prison "big shots" formed with the administration. However, in spite of these shortcomings and in spite of the middle-class moral cast that dulls or distorts some of his analysis, it is still the most complete study of the prison.

The Big House as a Social System   Clemmer's study was exploratory, descriptive, and, like most early sociology of crime and deviance, heavily moralistic. After World War II a few sociologists attempted to turn the study of prison into a pure (that is, value-free) scientific enterprise and to explain the unique prison social structure and prisoner culture by applying the emergent sociological theory or paradigm — the social system. In 1951, Talcott Parsons published *The Social System* and, with several other social scientists, *Toward a General Theory of Action*. These books marked the full adaptation and expansion of British social anthropology's functionalism into sociology. The impact was far-reaching. It is no exaggeration that this paradigm conquered and then dominated sociology for the next fifteen years. Its influences extended to the sociology of the prison. In fact, the prison was ideally suited for system or functionalist studies because, unlike the complex broader society, it was relatively small, contained, cohesive, and homogeneous. It appeared to parallel the isolated tribal societies that were the subject of the first functional analyses.

The system or functional analyses of the prison began with Gresham Sykes's study of the New Jersey State Prison in the middle 1950s.[49] However, two preceding ethnographies, though not as complete as Sykes's study, supplied him with essential material for his theory of the prison. The first was a short research venture by Hans Reimer in the 1930s; he entered the prison as a prisoner and discovered two types — the politician and the right guy — who were leaders in the prison world.[50] Later, Clarence Schrag, in a study of the maximum-custody prison in Walla Walla, Washington, expanded this classification of prisoner types or roles to include square johns, "outlaws," and "dings."[51] First Sykes and then Sykes and Messinger, following the direction of Parsons and the East Coast sociologists, tied all these and similar prison "argot" roles into a social system that was functionally integrated: it had parts that performed some function for the whole system and that existed for this reason.[52]

According to Sykes and Messinger and other sociologists who joined them in developing this functional analysis of the prison, the social system of the prison was unique, because the situation to which it adapted was unique. Its uniqueness stems from two separate sets of problems, those of the prisoners and those of the administration. The latter had the primary and difficult problem of maintaining control over a potentially obstreperous and rebellious prisoner population that greatly outnumbered the staff. Moreover, the administration had to maintain control with insufficient raw force. The pris-

[49] Gresham Sykes, *The Society of Captives* (Princeton: Princeton University Press, 1958).

[50] Hans Reimer, "Socialization in the Prison," *Proceedings of the Sixty-Seventh Annual Congress of the American Prison Association* (1937), pp. 151–55.

[51] Clarence Schrag, "Social Types in a Prison Community" (Master's thesis, University of Washington, 1944).

[52] Sykes, *The Society of Captives,* and Gresham Sykes and Sheldon Messinger, *Inmate Social System,* Theoretical Studies in Social Organization of the Prison (Social Science Research Council, 1960).

oners, on the other hand, had to withstand the pains of imprisonment, indignity, deprivation and had to live side by side with other deviants, many of whom were repulsive or dangerous.

The functionally integrated social system that emerged as a response to these special problems was accommodative; certain prisoner leaders were given special privileges, such as those which accompany key positions in the prison, in return for enforcing a peaceful, informal social order. (I examined these jobs and relationships earlier in my discussion of the corrupt arrangement.) This exploitative and accommodative arrangement between the prisoner leaders and the administration was implicit and appeared to be one of antagonism, because the prisoner code served as a screen hiding the true quality of the relationship. The appearance of antagonism not only made the accommodative relationship palatable, but also bolstered the wounded dignity of many prisoners.

According to the theory, the various prisoner types were all acting out roles in the accommodative system by dividing up the scarce commodities and privileges and by covertly or implicitly helping the administration maintain control. They helped maintain control by enforcing the general style suggested by the motto of "do your own time," which, as interpreted by these sociologists, meant "do not interfere with my arrangement." In effect, what Sykes and Messinger did was to hinge their entire explanation of the social types and social order on the corrupt arrangement that I described earlier.

In doing this, however, they were faced with a fundamental theoretical problem. A basic assumption was that this special social system emerged as an adaptation to the peculiar problems in the prison situation — the pains of imprisonment and the need to maintain control with insufficient formal power. The system that developed was one in which leaders emerged as they fit into the accommodative relationship. The prisoner code was also a special value system that developed to hold this system of roles together. The theoretical problem is that this indigenous system, unlike that of primitive tribes, was bombarded with new adults who arrived with full orientations, cultures of their own, and power and prestige in outside social worlds. The functional theorists solved this by arguing that entering prisoners had their former cultural identities and social positions neutralized or blotted out by two mechanisms. First, on entering the prison, they were subjected to degrading and disorganizing experiences that tended to erase their former orientations. Second, they were relegated to the lowly status of the "fish," a position from which they had to rise by learning the convict code, accepting the prison status hierarchy, and working themselves into the accommodative system.

Sociology of the Prison Comes of Age   During 1956 and 1957, Gresham Sykes and several other persons who were engaged in research on prisons met regularly in an ongoing conference on prisons sponsored by the Social Science Research Council. This conference established the study of the prison as a legitimate area in sociology and the functional interpretation of the prison social organization as the dominant theory. The full-blown version of the functional analysis of the prison appeared in a highly influential publication entitled *Theoretical Studies in Social Organization of the Prison,* which was the product of the conference and endured as the bible of prison theory for many years. It represented an important step. The door was opened wide for sociological studies of the prison. However, these researchers achieved sociological legitimacy or respectability through conformity: they went along with the general sociological trend toward functional analysis and, in so doing, squeezed the complex and varied prison phenomena into a narrow theoretical mold. (The momentum of functionalism is demonstrated by the fact that at least two of the sociologists who contributed — Lloyd Ohlin and Donald Cressey — had not been functionalists, but fell in with the others and accepted the functional interpretation.) They selected one type of relationship in the Big House, the corrupt arrangement between some prison big shots and the administration, and built their entire explanation of the informal prison social world around it. They ignored and thereby obscured other influences, such as the pre-prison orientations of many prisoners. In addition, they assumed that all prisons had the same system problems and developed essentially the same type of social system. This hid variation.

35

The theory was somewhat invalid for the prison from which it was derived and for which it was best suited. Its invalidity was increasing at the time of the conference. By the end of the 1950s, most states were moving toward the next phase — the correctional institution and its heavy emphasis on rehabilitation. The participants in the conference were aware of this development. Several articles in *Theoretical Studies* focused on the difficulties of accomplishing rehabilitative goals in the older prison, and a few had been working to shift prisons toward more rehabilitation.[53]

It is time to consider the next phase, during which prisons change considerably. But aspects of the Big House linger on. I shall try to trace the continuities while examining the new patterns.

---

[53] The narrowness of the functional model even damaged their rehabilitative intentions. Persons who accepted the functional interpretation planned and attempted to implement treatment programs aimed at inhibiting the development of the type of prisoner culture that, the theory suggested, prevailed in Big Houses. They tried to establish anticriminal social systems and, in doing this, ignored other relevant adaptive strategies, particularly gleaning and preprison orientations that made it difficult or impossible for some individuals to participate in treatment-oriented group practices.

2
The Correctional Institution

After World War II, many states replaced Big Houses with correctional institutions, which, when they were newly constructed, looked different, were organized differently, housed different types of prisoners, and nurtured different prison social worlds. Importantly, they had a different effect on prisoners. They spread and became the dominant type of prison in the 1950s, if not in numbers, at least in the minds of penologists.[1] And, like Big Houses, their images live on, blurring our view of contemporary prisons. Consequently, we must distinguish this type of prison to understand the modern violent prison. The correctional institution's emergence was related to broad changes in our society. Briefly, the postwar United States — prosperous, urbanized, and mobile — confronted a new set of pressing social problems. Hard times, natural disasters (floods, droughts, and tornadoes), epidemics, illiteracy, and the "dangerous classes," had been updated to or replaced by poverty,

[1] My conclusions on the spread of the correctional institution are based on a variety of sources. The first is all my conversations, formal and informal, with prisoners and ex-prisoners through the years. In them I obtained considerable information about the spread of rehabilitation and the changes in prisons that it precipitated. Then in the late 1960s and early 1970s, established as a sociologist, I was able to visit and study many prisons as a consultant or director on research projects (in such places as Saint Cloud, Minnesota; Santa Fe, New Mexico; Ashland, Kentucky; Jackson, Michigan; Salem, Oregon; Easthan, Texas; Lompoc, California; Stateville, Illinois; Rockview, Pennsylvania; Atlanta, Georgia; and El Reno, Oklahoma) and to learn about the past influence of rehabilitation on these institutions. The writings of prisoners

mental health, family disorganization, race relations, juvenile delinquency, and urban crime. Americans faced these with a fundamentally altered posture. The Great Depression and World War II had moved them from their isolationist and individualist position, and they accepted, even demanded, government intervention into conditions that they believed should and could be changed.

Along with all organs of government, agencies whose official function was intervention into domestic social problems grew, gained power, and proliferated. Peopling these agencies and leading the large social services expansion were old and new professionals: physicians, psychiatrists, psychologists, social workers, urban planners, sociologists, and a new group of specialists in penology. The latter group — a growing body of college-educated employees and administrators of prisons, parole, and probation and a few academic penologists whom I will hereafter refer to collectively as "correctionalists" — went after the apparently mushrooming crime problem.[2] These

---

and ex-prisoners from many states supports my conclusions. For example, Mike Misenheimer, one of the convict authors of *An Eye for An Eye,* writes about the routine in the Indiana State Prison in 1959: "In the meantime, I received the full benefit of the prison's treatment personnel. I was given a battery of tests which occupied a week of my time. Then I lay in a cell in the Admission & Orientation Section for three months waiting for the results of the tests to be determined so the classification committee could assign me to a job" (H. Jack Griswold, Mike Misenheimer, Art Powers, and Ed Tromanhauser, *An Eye for An Eye* [New York: Holt, Rinehart and Winston, 1970], p. 32). Finally, other studies of prisons confirm the spread. Even in the highly disciplined Stateville, Joseph Ragen made some changes in the spirit of the new era of penology. James Jacobs describes the changes: "In the mid-1950s, greater societal acceptance of the legitimacy of prison reform moved Ragen to redefine his system of total control as "rehabilitation." . . . The change in the philosophical justification of the same prison system is explained by the increasing prominence being given to prison reform by professional administrators and academics after World War II and following the wave of prison riots in the early 1950s. If Stateville was to maintain its preeminence, then its basis of order would have to claim legitimacy within the vocabulary of the mainstream of "enlightened" opinion about the purpose of prison" (*Stateville* [Chicago: University of Chicago Press, 1977], p. 45).

[2] It is not clear if crime was increasing between 1945 and 1965. Although the FBI's *Uniform Crime Reports* reflect an increase, this can be explained by shifts in reporting. The homicide rates, probably

correctionalists were convinced and were able to convince many state governments and interested segments of the general population that they could reduce crime by curing criminals of their criminality.

A growing number of persons working in penology had come to accept this idea since the last century, when new "social scientists" (men like Karl Marx, Emile Durkheim, Cesare Lombroso, and Sigmund Freud), emulating successful and celebrated physical scientists, began searching for the *causes* of human behavior. The social scientists were seeking forces similar to those that propelled and guided the stars, planets, objects on earth, and complex workings of the human body. These forces could be empirically observed and operated independently of human will. They searched in various realms or levels — the psychological, biological, and sociological — and amassed a large body of social scientific theories that purported to explain, or identify the causes of, human behavior. The innovative penologists kept abreast of the developments in the new social sciences and began constructing a philosophy of penology based on the concept that criminal behavior was caused by identifiable and changeable forces. This led them to the conclusion that the primary purpose of imprisonment should be "rehabilitation," a new form of reformation based on scientific methods. This new penology is generally referred to as the rehabilitative ideal. One of its earliest critics identifies its essential characteristics.

> The rehabilitative ideal is itself a complex of ideas which, perhaps, defies completely precise statement. The essential points, however, can be articulated. It is assumed, first, that human behavior is the product of antecedent causes. These causes can be identified as part of the physical universe and it is the obligation of the scientist to discover and to describe them with all possible exactitude. Knowledge of the antecedents of human behavior makes possible an approach to the scientific control of human behavior. Finally, and of primary significance for the purposes at hand, it is assumed that

the most reliable indicator of real crime rates, declined through these years. However, the nation believed Hoover's annual pronouncements about new crime waves.

measures employed to treat the convicted offender should serve a therapeutic function, that such measures should be designed to effect changes in the behavior of the convicted person in the interests of his own happiness, health, and satisfactions and in the interest of social defense.[3]

The nation's leading penologists agreed as early as 1870, when they formed the National Prison Association, to establish rehabilitation as the primary purpose of prisons and to alter prison routines in order to implement rehabilitation (particularly to introduce indeterminate sentencing).[4] At that time, however, the society was not ready for what appeared to be a nonpunitive approach to crime. Until World War II and the changes described above had occurred, the architects of rehabilitation experimented in juvenile institutions like Elmira, New York, where Zebulon Brockway introduced a full rehabilitative program, and they slipped bits and pieces of rehabilitation into Big Houses — for example, a more elaborate classification system and a small department of rehabilitation. After the war, receiving an okay from the public and various state governments and an infusion of more funds and more college-trained employees, the innovators in penology created the new prison, the correctional institution. In some states, such as Wisconsin and Minnesota, this meant reorganizing the staff structures and introducing new programs into old prisons, but in others, such as California and New York, it also meant constructing many new facilities. In both cases, the correctionalists organized the prisons around three procedures: indeterminate sentencing, classification, and the treatment that they had been developing for decades.

THE INDETERMINATE SENTENCE SYSTEM

According to the early planners of the rehabilitative prison, prison administrators should have the discretionary power to

[3] Francis A. Allen, "Criminal Justice, Legal Values and the Rehabilitative Ideal," *Journal of Criminal Law, Criminology and Police Science,* September–October 1959, pp. 226–27.

[4] *The Report of the Proceedings of the First Annual Meeting of the National Prison Association* (1870) is a defense of rehabilitation and indeterminate sentencing. Several papers on the subject and the set of principles adopted by the association reflect this.

release the prisoner when the administrators or their correctional experts determine that he is cured of criminality. Many early supporters of the rehabilitative ideal, such as Karl Menninger, advocated sentences of zero to life for all offenders so that correctional professionals could concentrate on treating criminals and releasing them when their illness (criminality) was cured. In actuality, no prison system in the United States or any other place achieved this extreme, but California, after thirty-five years of developing an indeterminate sentence routine through legislation and administrative policies, came the closest. After 1950, the Adult Authority — the official name of the California parole board — exercised the power to determine an individual's sentence within statutory limits for a particular crime, to set a parole date before this sentence was finished, and, at any time until the fixed sentence was completed, to restore the sentence back to its statutory maximum or any other length within the margins. It exercised these powers with no requirements for due process or review of decisions. The statutory limits in California — for example, one to ten years for grand larceny, one to fifteen for forgery and second-degree burglary, one to life for second-degree robbery, and five to life for first-degree robbery — gave the Adult Authority large margins within which to exercise their discretion.

Under this system, prisoners remained unsure of how much time they would eventually serve until they completed their sentence. While in prison, they appeared before the Adult Authority annually until the Adult Authority set their release date, invariably within six months of their last board appearance. While individuals were on parole or awaited release, the Adult Authority could refix their sentences back to the maximum and reactivate the process of annual board appearances for violations of the rules of the prison or conditions of parole.

Board appearances were the most important milestones in the inmates' imprisonment, and the Adult Authority had full power over their lives. According to the ideal, parole boards should use this power to release prisoners when they were rehabilitated. This presupposed, however, that the correctionalists had procedures for identifying and changing criminal characteristics, which they did not, and that parole boards had procedures for determining when these changes had occurred, which they did not. It also presupposed that rehabilitation of the offender was parole boards' major concern, which it was not. Even in the early planning stages the advocates of indeterminate sentencing intended the discretionary powers to be used to control prisoners and detain indefinitely those who were viewed as dangerous by various authorities (district attorneys, police chiefs, and influential citizens). Zebulon Brockway's early description of the benefits of indeterminate sentencing reveals his defense of these other purposes as well as rehabilitation.

> The perfected reformatory will be the receptacle and refinery of antisocial humans who are held in custody under discretional indeterminateness for the purpose of public protection. Legal and sentimental inhibitions of necessary coercion for the obdurate, intractable element of the institution population will be removed and freedom given for the wide use of unimpassioned, useful, forceful measures. Frequent relapses to crime of prisoners discharged from these reformatories will be visited upon the management as are penalties for official malfeasance. The change will be, in short, a change from the reign of sentiment swerved by the feelings to a passionless scientific procedure pursuing welfare.[5]

In addition, although they never admitted this, the advocates of indeterminate sentence systems understood and appreciated that its discretionary powers permitted them to give shorter sentences, or even no sentences, to influence individuals. So, in actual practice, while professing to balance the seriousness of a crime and rehabilitative criteria, parole boards used their discretionary powers to enforce conformity to prison rules and parole routines, avoid criticism from outside authorities and citizens, award higher social status, and express personal prejudice and whim. The eventual effect of this confusing, hypocritical, discriminatory sentencing procedure on prisoners is one of the subjects of the next chapter.

[5] *Fifty Years of Prison Service* (New York: Charities Publication Committee, 1912).

CLASSIFICATION

An ideal correctional institution primarily organized to rehabilitate prisoners would require an elaborate, systematic diagnostic and planning process that determined the nature of the individual's criminality and prescribed a cure. Through the decades before the 1950s, the creators of the rehabilitative approach steadily developed more complex classification systems, ostensibly to accomplish these ends. Theoretically, the finished version that they incorporated in the new postwar correctional institutions operated as follows. First, a team of professionals — psychologists, case workers, sociologists, vocational counselors, and psychiatrists — tested the criminal, interviewed him, and gathered life history information. Then a team of these correctionalists formed an initial classification committee and reviewed the tests and evaluations, planned the prisoner's therapeutic routine, assigned him to a particular prison, and recommended particular rehabilitative programs for him. In the final stage, classification committees at particular prisons periodically reviewed the prisoner's progress, recommended changes in programs, and sometimes transferred him to another prison.

The classification committees in the first correctional institutions tended to follow this ideal in appearance, but they actually operated quite differently. First, the social sciences never supplied them with valid diagnostic methods and effective cures for criminality. Second, the committees never abandoned control and other management concerns, which classification systems had acquired in the decades when they operated in Big Houses. As Sutherland and Cressey pointed out, treatment was the least important consideration in the classification process:

> Probably most classification committees base their decisions on considerations of custody, convenience, discipline, and treatment, in that order. Thus, it may be decided that a particular inmate must be handled as a maximum security risk and if, for example, psychiatric services are not available to maximum risk prisoners, then that decision will mean that

the psychiatric help will not be available to the inmate in question, no matter what his treatment needs.[6]

TREATMENT

A variety of effective treatment strategies would complete the ideal correctional institution. As stressed above, none were discovered. What actually existed in the correctional institutions in the 1950s was care and treatment. An administrative branch that coexisted with the custody branch, planned and administered three types of treatment programs — therapeutic, academic, and vocational — and generated reports on prisoners' progress for the institutional classification committees and the parole board.

The most common therapeutic program was group counseling, which, because it was led by staff persons with little or no training in clinical procedures, was a weak version of group therapy. Originally, the plan was to hire psychiatrists and clinical psychologists, but the pay was too small and the working conditions too undesirable to attract those professionals. Some persons with social work training, who were willing to work for the lower salaries, filled in some of the gaps, but in states such as California, where dozens of group leaders were needed, even their numbers were too small. So staff persons with no formal training in psychology led many, if not most, groups in correctional institutions.[7] Most prisoners participated in group counseling programs, because they were led to believe by parole board members and the treatment staff that they would not be granted a parole unless they participated. Also, they believed that unacceptable traits or attitudes revealed in the sessions would be reported by the staffers, and this would reduce their chances of being paroled early. In addition, many prisoners had a strong distaste for discussing sensitive, personal issues and disparaged other prisoners for doing so. The result was that group counseling sessions were invariably very

[6] Edwin H. Sutherland and Donald R. Cressey, *Criminology,* 10th ed. (Philadelphia: Lippincott, 1970), p. 540.
[7] For a complete description of the training of group counselors, the group counseling sessions, and the role of group counseling in a correctional institution, see Gene Kassebaum and David Ward, *Prison Treatment and Parole Survival* (New York: John Wiley, 1971).

bland. Few prisoners took them seriously or participated sincerely or vigorously. Malcolm Braly, who grew up in California prisons during the heyday of the correctional institution, captured the essence of most prison group counseling sessions:

> He found his group already gathered, sitting in the usual symbolic circle. The therapist, a Dr. Erlenmeyer, occupied what was intended as just one more chair, but the group automatically polarized wherever he seated himself. He was dressed entirely in shades of brown, and his shirt was darker than his coat. His glasses were tinted a pale tan, and his full head of hair seemed soft and dusty.
>
> "You're late, Paul," he said, in a tone that didn't admit the obvious quality of his remark. His voice was opaque.
>
> "I lost track of the day," Juleson said.
>
> This hung in the air for a moment like a palpable lie, then settled into the heavy silence. The group had nothing going. No one, as they said, was coming out with anything. Juleson settled around in his chair, careful not to look at Erlenmeyer, who might try to make him feel responsible for this wasteful silence. Once Erlenmeyer had stressed how therapy was working on them even while they sat dumb, as sometimes happened, for the hour. But he didn't like their silences. . . .
>
> Finally, Erlenmeyer cleared his throat to ask, "Why do you suppose Paul is late so often?"
>
> They looked at each other to see if anyone were going to attempt an answer. Bernard only shrugged; he didn't care. After a moment, Zekekowski said quietly, "He's got better sense than the rest of us." [8]

Not all group sessions were this shallow, and a few prisoners received individual treatment from psychiatrists or psychologists. Toward the end of the 1950s, the more persistent correctionalists experimented with "milieu therapy" by attempting to convert prisons or units within prisons into "therapeutic communities." [9] More recently, contemporary correctionalists

[8] *On the Yard* (Boston: Little, Brown, 1967), pp. 103–4.

[9] One of the more ambitious attempts at milieu therapy is reported in Elliot Studt, Sheldon L. Messinger, and Thomas P. Wilson, *C-Unit: Search for Community in Prison* (New York: Russell Sage Foundation, 1968). This report describes the failure of the experiment, which was corrupted by traditional custodial forces that persist in the prison enterprise.

have introduced more intense therapeutic forms, such as "behavior modification" and "attack therapy." However, group counseling, which is inexpensive and easier to implement, was the dominant form of therapy when correctional institutions were at their peak.

The academic and vocational education programs had more substance than the therapy treatment programs. All the innovative correctional institutions had formed elementary and high school programs in the 1950s, and many had formed links with universities and were making correspondence courses available to some prisoners. All correctional institutions attempted vocational training. In California during the 1950s, those who desired and were able to enter the programs (there were fewer openings than prisoners) could receive training in cooking, baking, butchering, dry cleaning, shoe repair, sewing machine repair, auto mechanics, auto body and fender repair, small motor repair, sheet metal, machining, printing, plumbing, painting, welding, and nursing. All these training programs had inherent weaknesses, and they seldom fully equipped a prisoner for a position in the trade. One of these weaknesses was that some training programs, such as baking and cooking, were appendages of prison housekeeping enterprises and were insufficiently related to outside vocational enterprises. In other cases, the equipment, the techniques, and the knowledge of the instructor were obsolete.

Indeterminate sentences, classification, and treatment were the actualization of the rehabilitative ideal in correctional institutions. As the descriptions indicate, they fell short of the ideal. The reasons for this are varied. In spite of the intentions and efforts of the most sincere visionaries of rehabilitation, they were never able to realize their plans.[10] The public and most government policy makers continued to demand that prisons first accomplish their other assigned tasks: punishment, control, and restraint of prisoners. In addition, the new correctional institutions were not created in a vacuum but planned in ongoing prison systems which had long tradi-

[10] See Daniel Glaser, *The Effectiveness of a Prison and Parole System* (Indianapolis: Bobbs-Merrill, 1964), for a description and analysis of the failure of vocational training and education programs.

tions, administrative hierarchies, divisions, informal social worlds, and special subcultures among the old staff. The new correctionalists were never able to rid the prison systems of the old regime, though often they tried; and the old timers, many of whom were highly antagonistic to the new routines, resisted change, struggled to maintain as much control as possible, and were always successful in forcing an accommodation between old and new patterns. So correctional institutions were never totally, or even mainly, organized to rehabilitate prisoners. Nevertheless, an entirely new prison resulted from the rehabilitative ideal and through its rhetoric, which correctionalists used to defend new programs and disguise other purposes, achieved a temporary unity in the ranks. This type of prison spread throughout the United States, replacing many, perhaps most, Big Houses. In many ways it was a great improvement, and some correctionalists still look on it as the best we can hope for. However, it contained many unnecessary inhumanities, injustices, and idiocies, though for many years these were less visible. Eventually, its own flaws and certain external social changes destroyed it (or at least damaged it beyond repair).

To complete the description of the correctional institution, I shall focus on Soledad, which was opened in 1952, which was planned and operated as an exemplary correctional institution, and in which I served five years during its golden age. All correctional institutions, certainly, had some unique features, but Soledad during the 1950s is a superior example of the type.

SOLEDAD: THE FORMAL STRUCTURE

Soledad prison was part of California's very large investment in the new penology. The state emerged from World War II with a rapidly expanding population, an apparently rising crime rate, relatively full state coffers, and a liberal citizenry. In a few years the state allocated massive sums for higher education, highway construction, and prisons. In the 1950s, in addition to two new "guidance centers," the state constructed six new men's prisons, a new women's prison, and a special narcotics treatment center. Soledad, the first of the men's prisons to be completed after the war, was planned, constructed, and operated as one of the essential parts in a large rehabilitative correctional organization. It was labeled California Training Facility and was intended as the prison for younger, medium-risk, more trainable prisoners.

Soledad's physical structure radically departs from that of the Big Houses. It has no granite wall; instead, circling the prison is a high fence with gun towers situated every few hundred feet and nestled in the corners. The nine cell blocks stem off a long hall. Two relatively pleasant dining rooms with tile floors and octagonal oak tables, a spacious library, a well-equipped hospital, a laundry, an education building, a gym, several shops, and the administration building connect to this hall. In fact, the entire prison community operates in and around the hall, and prisoners can (and many of them do) live day after day without ever going outside.

Each cell block (called a "wing") had a "day room" jutting off the side at the ground level, and all the inside walls in the prison were painted in pastel colors — pale blue, pale green, light yellow, and tan. All cell blocks originally had one-man cells, though many were assigned two occupants later. All cells except those in one small wing used for new prisoners and for segregation and isolation (O wing) had solid doors with a small, screened inspection window. The cells in all cell blocks (except O wing) were in three tiers around the outside of the wings, so each cell had an outside window. Instead of bars, the windows had small panes with heavy metal moldings. All cells originally had a bunk, a desk, and a chair. The close security cells also had a sink and toilet. In the five medium-security cell blocks, the prisoners carried keys to their own cells. A row of cells could be locked by a guard's setting a locking bar, but in the 1950s, except for regular counts and special lockdowns, prisoners in medium-security wings entered and left the cells at their own discretion.

The formal routine at Soledad was more relaxed than in most Big Houses. On a weekday the lights came on at 7:00 A.M., but there was no bell nor whistle. The individual "wing officers" released their cell blocks one at a time for breakfast. A prisoner could eat or could sleep another hour before work. The food was slightly better than average prison fare, which

48

is slightly inferior to average institution fare and ranks well below state hospitals and the armed services. One pleasant aspect of the dining routine was that prisoners were allowed to linger for ten or twenty minutes and drink unlimited amounts of coffee. After breakfast, prisoners reported to their work or school assignment. Before lunch there was a count, during which all prisoners had to be in their cells or at a designated place where guards counted them, then lunch, a return to work or school, and another count before dinner. During the day the cell blocks were open, and prisoners could roam freely from their blocks, through the hall, to the large yard and its few recreational facilities, and to the library or gym. After dinner the wing officer kept the front door to the cell block locked except at scheduled unlocks for school, gym, library, and, during the summer, "night yard."

On the weekends, prisoners were idle, except for kitchen and a few hospital and maintenance workers. The cell blocks, gym, yard, and library remained open all day. Although they could visit on any day, most visitors came on weekends. The visiting room had clusters of padded chairs around coffee tables, and prisoners could sit close to and even touch their visitors, a relatively pleasant visiting arrangement. On Sunday the high-light of the week occurred: two showings of a three- or four-year-old Hollywood movie.

A few rules were perceived by prisoners as unnecessary, arbitrary, and irksome — rules such as, "no standing on tiers" or "prisoners must walk double file on one side of the hall." But in general, Soledad had a more relaxed and pleasant formal routine than most prisons.

The rehabilitative aspect of Soledad was prominent. As its official name implied, it offered a broad selection of voca-tional training programs. It also had a good elementary and high school program, through which a prisoner could receive a diploma from the local outside school district. Rounding out rehabilitation was the group counseling program in which the Adult Authority, classification committees, and prisoners' coun-selors coerced prisoners to participate (if they did not, they were warned that they would not receive a parole). One psy-chiatrist treated some individuals, but usually only the few whom the Adult Authority referred for special reasons, such as a history of violent or sex crimes. The counseling groups met once a week, and the majority of inmates attended them. In the second half of the 1950s, the treatment staff introduced more intensive counseling programs in which the groups met daily. But weekly group counseling led by relatively untrained guards and other staff members was the total therapy component for most prisoners.

Informal Life   Soledad, like all correctional institutions, developed different group structures, intergroup relationships, and informal systems of social control from those in Big Houses. Some of these differences were a result of changes in the prisoner population, the most important being the shift in ethnic and racial balance. In California the percentages of non-white prisoners had been increasing steadily and, by 1950, had passed 40 percent: about 25 percent Chicano and 15 percent black. This shift towards nonwhite prisoners was occurring in most large eastern, midwestern, and western prison systems. The era of total white dominance in Big Houses was rapidly approaching an end.

More and more Tejanos — Mexicans raised in Texas — were coming to California and its prisons. The Tejanos were different from Los Angeles's Chicanos, who made up the largest group of Mexicans. More Tejanos were drug addicts; in fact, they introduced heroin to the Los Angeles Chicanos. They spoke more Spanish and Calo, the Spanish slang that developed in the United States, and were generally less Americanized. The two groups did not like each other, kept apart in jail, and sometimes fought.

All the Chicanos had experienced extreme prejudice throughout their lives, particularly in the public schools, and were somewhat hostile toward white prisoners. However, many Los Angeles Chicanos had associated with whites, particularly white criminals with whom they had engaged in crime. Heroin, which was spreading from the Tejanos through the Los Angeles Mexican neighborhoods and then into some white neighborhoods, intermixed Chicanos and Anglos even more. While some white prisoners disliked Chicanos, in general they feared and respected them, because whites believed that Chicanos would quickly employ violence when insulted or threatened. Consequently, between the two ethnic groups there was enmity, mixed with respect on the part of whites, but many individuals from both groups crossed over this barrier and maintained friendly relationships.

Black prisoners also divided into two groups: persons raised in Los Angeles or the San Francisco Bay Area and others who had migrated to California from the South and Southwest. Here, too, were prejudice and hostility between whites and blacks, but there were many whites and blacks who had intermixed and cooperated in criminal activities. This was more likely to have occurred between urban blacks and whites. So again, there was a gap between the two racial groups, but considerable crossing over the gap. The gap between Chicanos and blacks was wider, because Chicanos were more deeply prejudiced and hostile than whites were toward blacks.

Still over half of Soledad's population in the 1950s was white. Most white prisoners were working-class and lower-class youths raised in Los Angeles, San Diego, and the San Francisco Bay Area. There was a smaller group of whites from the small cities and towns in California: Fresno, Bakersfield, Modesto, and Stockton. Even though most whites in the prison were descendants of migrants from Kansas, Missouri, Illinois, Oklahoma, Arkansas, and Texas, the heartland of the United States, the prisoners from the smaller towns carried many more rural traditions and were labeled "Okie" in the prisons. The remainder of the white prisoners were a conglomeration of middle-class persons, drifters, servicemen, and state raised youths (individuals who had been raised by state agencies, including the California Youth Authority).

Members of all these different ethnic segments tended to form separate groups and social worlds in Soledad. This differentiation was further complicated by the divisions based on criminal orientations, which were more numerous than in past eras. The thieves described in chapter 1 were present, but their numbers were diminishing. This system of theft had been carried to California from the East and Midwest, but it was not crossing racial lines and was being replaced by drug addiction among whites. The thieves present in Soledad were very cliquish, practiced mutual aid, did not trust other prisoners, but were respected by them. However, they were not able to dominate the informal world as they had in Big Houses.

A new deviant subculture, that of the "dope fiend" (heroin addict), was spreading in California and became very prominent in the California prisons during the 1950s. Drug addiction brought to Los Angeles by the Tejanos had metastasized in the late 1940s and early 1950s, and most of the Chicanos and a large number of the young, working-class and lower-class white and black prisoners from Los Angeles, San Diego, San Francisco, and Oakland carried the patterns of this special subculture. In the era of the Big House, other prisoners, particularly thieves, did not trust dope fiends, because they believed that drug addicts were weak and would inform under pressure. But in Soledad and other California prisons in the 1950s, dope fiends were the emergent group, had respect, and, in fact, were rather snobbish. While in prison, perhaps in compensation for their individualistic, antisocial, passive, and often rapacious lifestyle while addicted, they were very affable, sociable, active, and verbal. At work and leisure they tended to form small cliques and spend their time telling drug stories. Many of them were involved in intellectual and artistic activities.

A smaller group of "weed heads" or "grasshoppers" (marijuana users) were present in Soledad. This was before the psychedelic movement and weed heads were urban lower-class or working-class white, Chicano, and black youths who participated in a cultlike subculture; whose carriers lived in "far-out pads," wore "sharp threads," rode around in "groovy shorts," listened to "cool" jazz, sipped exotic liqueurs or wine coolers, and generally were "cool." In prison, weed heads continued to be cool and cliquish. Other prisoners, particularly dope fiends, thought they were silly and stayed away from them. William Burroughs, a junkie, captured the coolness of the "tea heads" and other deviants' disdain for them:

> Tea heads are not like junkies. A junkie hands you the money, takes his junk and cuts. But tea heads don't do things that way. They expect the peddler to light them up and sit around talking for half an hour to sell two dollars worth of weed. If you come right to the point, they say you

52

are a "bring down." In fact, a peddler should not come right out and say he is a peddler. No, he just scores for a few good "cats" and "chicks" because he is viperish. Everyone knows that he himself is the connection, but it is bad form to say so. God knows why. To me, tea heads are unfathomable.[11]

Most black prisoners who had engaged in systematic theft were not thieves, but "hustlers." Segregation and prejudice cut blacks off from the older tradition of theft. When they migrated to the northern, midwestern, and western cities, blacks developed their own system of thievery, which was fashioned after patterns of early white con men — flimflammers — who toured the United States in the late nineteenth and early twentieth centuries. These flimflammers victimized all categories of rural people and imparted the styles of "short con" to blacks. In the cities, many blacks built on these original lessons and became hustlers. In general, hustling meant making money through one's wits and conversation rather than through force or threat. It involved short con games such as "greasy pig," "three card monte," and "the pigeon drop" rackets such as the numbers, and pimping.

Like the other types of criminals, hustlers formed their own groups. Conversation was a major part of their style of theft, and conversation — "shucking and jiving," bragging about hustling, pimping, and the sporting life — was their major prison activity. An ex-convict describes the activities of a black prisoner: "he was off into that bag — Iceberg Slim [a famous pimp who wrote a successful paperback description of pimping] and all that — wearing their Cadillacs around the big yard." [12]

A special deviant orientation shared by at least 10 percent of the population at Soledad was that of the state-raised youth. Many prisoners had acquired this special orientation in the youth prisons; it involved the propensity to form tightly knit cliques, a willingness to threaten and actually to engage in violence for protection or for increases in power, prestige, and

[11] *Junkie* (New York: Ace Books, 1953), p. 31.
[12] *Popeye* (Pamphlet distributed by Peoples' Court Comrades, San Francisco, 1975), p. 6.

privilege, and a preference for prison patterns and styles as opposed to those on the outside. Many state-raised youths formed gangs in adult prisons, stole from and bullied other prisoners, and participated in the prison sexual world of jockers, queens, and punks.

Most prisoners were not committed "criminals." At least a quarter of the young people in prison in the 1950s were working- and lower-class people who had been "hanging out" in their neighborhoods or drifting around the country, looking for work and a niche for themselves. They had been involved in crime only irregularly and haphazardly, and usually it was very unsophisticated crime. They were often confused about the world and their place in it and saw themselves as "fuck-ups" or losers.[13] (The tattoo reading "Born to lose" on the hand or chest of these persons was very common.[14]) These fuck-ups were the masses in the prison. In the Big Houses they were the hoosiers and in Soledad the assholes, and they were pushed aside and demeaned by other criminals. However, Soledad was a more heterogeneous prison, and the disparagement and exclusion were not as intense or complete. So fuck-ups occasionally rose to positions of power (to the extent that these existed), joined groups of other criminally oriented prisoners, and even began to identify themselves as dope fiends, heads, or hustlers. Thieves were more careful about associating with assholes, but on occasion one might befriend and tutor an inexperienced young person.

In addition to fuck-ups, there were many prisoners, mostly white, who had committed only one felony or a few serious crimes and did not consider themselves, nor were they considered by others, as criminals. Other prisoners referred to them as square johns and ignored them unless they wanted to take advantage of their knowledge or skills. (Many of these square johns were better educated, and a few of them were professionals). In general, however, they were ignored, and

[13] In his characterization of Perry Smith in the book *In Cold Blood* (New York: Random House, 1965), the story of the homicide of a farm family by two recently released convicts, Truman Capote has captured this type of criminal.

[14] Perry Smith had "Born to Lose" tatooed on his arm.

they kept to themselves. They either served their time as isolates or formed very small friendship groups with other square johns.

This subcultural mix of prisoners resisted the establishment of a single overriding convict code or the emergence of a single group of leaders. The old convict code did not have the unanimity and force that it had in the Big House. The number of thieves who formerly established and maintained this code was too small, and other criminals — hustlers, dope fiends, heads — with other codes of conduct competed for status and power in the informal realm.

The administrative regime influenced by the rehabilitative ideal inhibited the development of the exploitative, accommodative system, described by Sykes and Messinger, in which politicians' power depended on their control over certain enterprises, allowing them to make important decisions and obtain scarce material, and on their monopoly on information.[15] In this era of professionalism, the staff was much more deeply involved in the day-to-day running of the prison. There was a partially successful attempt to prevent convicts from controlling the prison, and much more information flowed between staff and prisoners. Unlike his counterpart in most Big Houses, a captain's clerk could not autonomously transfer prisoners from one cell to another, squash disciplinary reports, transfer disliked guards to the night watch in a distant gun tower, or place friends on extra movie unlocks. Similarly, the storeroom clerk could not confiscate 20 percent of the prison's coffee, sugar, and dried fruit supply for his and his friends' use or for "wheeling and dealing." These prisoners could manipulate the routine slightly or skim off some commodities, but not enough to elevate them to the levels of power possessed by politicians or merchants in the Big Houses.

Despite the absence of these order-promoting processes, Soledad was still a very peaceful and orderly institution during most of the 1950s. The general mood among prisoners was

[15] Richard McCleery analyzes the decline of the old prison social order when treatment is introduced in *Communication Patterns as Bases of Systems of Authority,* Theoretical Studies in Social Organization of the Prison (Social Science Research Council, 1960).

tolerance and relative friendliness. The races were somewhat hostile toward each other and followed informal patterns of segregation, but there was commingling between all races and many prisoners maintained close friendships with members of other racial groups. During my five years at Soledad there were only a few knife fights, two murders, and one suicide.

Soledad's Ambience   To a great extent, the peace and order at Soledad were the result of a relatively optimistic, tolerant, and agreeable mood. Part of this mood stemmed from the enthusiasm for the new penal routine that the prisoners, entering or returning to prison, experienced in those early years. Most of us who came through the Chino Guidance Center and then moved into Soledad had been raised in the neighborhoods around Los Angeles, where we were involved in a variety of criminal subcultures. Consequently, we had received considerable information about the "joints" before coming to prison. We knew approximately how much time convicts served for a particular crime and how to conduct ourselves in prison: "don't rap to bulls," "don't get friendly with or accept gifts from older cons," "play it cool," and "do your time." The Chino Guidance Center threw us off track. It was a new institution with physical features similar to Soledad's. It had pastel-colored cell blocks named Cyprus and Madrone and guards who had been selected for the guidance center because of their ability to relate to prisoners. We were bombarded with sophisticated tests administered by young, congenial, "college types." We were examined thoroughly by dentists and physicians. For six weeks we attended daily three-hour sessions with one of the college types. During the rest of the day we played basketball, sat in the sun, worked out, or engaged in other recreation while we recovered from our profoundly deleterious "dead time" period in the county jail.

In this relatively agreeable environment, we became convinced that the staff members were sincere and were trying to help us. It was implied or stated that they would locate our psychological problems, vocational deficiencies, and physical defects and would fix them. The guidance center staff promised (mostly by implication) and we believed that they were going to make new people out of us.

56

The enthusiasm and the new hope continued into the early years of Soledad and the other correctional institutions. We believed then that the new penal approach was producing a much more humane prison routine. We experienced the new attitudes of many staff persons as a positive outcome of the new era. Although there were many old-school guards, there were many new guards with college experience and a new attitude toward prisons and prisoners. Many of the old guards were even converted or drawn into the new attitude by the new penology, and they tended to see themselves as rehabilitative agents or at least as more humane "correctional officers," as their new job title read.

The physical environment was not as harsh as in older prisons. The one-man cells, modern heating system, dining room, visiting room, gym, and so on were marked improvements over Big Houses. Rules and rule enforcement were not as strict; there was more freedom of movement; and the relationships among prisoners and between staff and prisoners were more tolerant and friendly than in Big Houses.

The staff's tolerance for and the other prisoners' enjoyment of Yahoo, as the prisoners labeled him, tells a great deal about Soledad's mood. Yahoo was a very large and muscular black prisoner who, from the moment he arrived at the prison, displayed extremely bizarre behavior patterns and never mixed with other prisoners. While in O wing waiting to be released to the main population, he shocked all other prisoners by jumping from the third tier and, after rolling over to absorb the fall, leaping to his feet and briskly walking away. Then he would not bathe and eventually was placed in segregation. When released from segregation, he fell into a pattern that he followed every day. At unlock for meals, with a large friendly smile on his face, Yahoo walked quickly down the walk in front of the cells and dove down each flight of stairs separating the tiers, doing a somersault each time and passing everyone. He walked briskly out of the cell block, almost at a run down the center of the hall (which was against the rules, for prisoners were supposed to walk no more than two abreast on the right side of the hall), and even the guards moved out of his way. Walking past the other prisoners waiting in the chow line,

Yahoo stalled at each food item until the prisoner serving the item heaped several portions on his tray and, imitating a truck backing into a parking place, proceeded to a corner of the dining room where he ate his huge meal alone with his back to the other prisoners. Then after the meal he walked briskly to the yard, again down the middle of the hall. On reaching the yard, he ran around it several times very fast *backwards*. Then he stood in one corner of the yard, facing the cluster of houses in which the warden and several other staff members lived and made loud, unique sounds for about a half an hour (this was the habit that earned him the name Yahoo). He broke this routine only slightly from time to time until he was released. (There was another rumor that he was finally transferred to a mental institution.) The amazing fact was that once all had decided that Yahoo was not dangerous, everyone tolerated or even enjoyed this bizarre routine.

There were other, not quite so extreme characters in Soledad, and the humor was generally more prominent and less cutting than in Big Houses. This was a reflection of the relatively tolerant and friendly ambience in Soledad. It was considered by most prisoners in the early and mid-1950s to be a good joint. Prisoners did not want to risk a transfer to the harsher prisons in the state.

Tips and Cliques   The peace and order at Soledad also resulted from a system of "tips" and cliques. Tips were extended social networks or crowds that were loosely held together by shared subcultural orientations or preprison acquaintances. Most of the tips were intraracial, and they were overlapping and connected. Consequently, an individual could be involved in more than one tip and usually was related to other tips that connected with his own. For example, I was a member of a large network of Los Angeles young people who had been involved in theft and heroin. My Los Angeles thieves–dope fiends tip was connected to a similar tip of San Francisco thieves–dope fiends through ties established in the youth prisons. There were tips of persons who had experienced the youth prisons together, lived in the same town or neighborhood ("home boys"), and engaged in the same criminal activities. A sense of affinity and loyalty existed between members of a tip. A member may not have known other members well, but common membership in the network automatically established some rapport and obligations and increased the possibility of friendship.

Prisoners formed smaller cliques within or across tips. These cliques were almost identical to the primary and semi-primary groups described by Clemmer in his study of Menard. Clique members worked, celled, hung around the tier, yard, and day room, ate, and engaged in the same leisure activities together. The basis of organization varied greatly. Sometimes they formed out of small groups of prisoners who became acquainted at work or in the cell blocks. More often, they developed among persons who shared interest in some activity in prison, preprison experiences, subcultural orientations, and, thereby, tip membership. When clique members were also members of the same tip, the cliques were more cooperative, stable, and cohesive.

Most cliques were constantly transforming. Members were paroled, were transferred, or shifted friendships and interests. Former clique members continued to experience ties of friendships, and this extended friendship bonds outside existing cliques. These clique friendship ties and the ties to other tip members who were interconnected with the cliques established overlapping and extensive bonds of communciation, friendship, and obligation through which cooperative enterprises were accomplished and conflict reduced. For instance, contraband and scarce commodities were distributed through the networks, a function demonstrated by the following story:

> I wanted to get my teeth fixed but there was a long list to get into the dentist's office and some asshole who controlled the list wanted a carton of cigarettes to move you up. I wasn't about to pay so I asked Willy, one of my close friends, to talk to one of his old partners, McDaniels, who had just got assigned to the dental office. I had met McDaniels and he was all right and knew I was all right so he got me into see the dentist the next day.

Many disputes were avoided by indirect negotiations through the tips and cliques. Another story reveals this process:

Me and this Chicano dude got into it at work and it got pretty hairy. After we called each other a sack of mother fuckers, he told me I better have my stuff [knife] next time we meet. I split and went around locating a shiv, but I also swung by and talked to a Chicano who I did time with in Lancaster. We were still tight and I thought he might know this other dude and be able to straighten it out without us getting it on. I told him what had happened and asked him who this other Chicano was in a way to kind of let him know that I would be happy to have it cooled. Well, it worked and in a few hours I got the word that everything was all right and why didn't we just forget it.[16]

In the absence of more effective social organization, the tip and clique networks established ties and bridged gaps between prisoners, even between races, serving to promote peace and cooperation among prisoners. This system is similar to the clan, extended family, or totem organizations that served as ordering systems among primitive peoples before the establishment of larger, overreaching social organizations.

THE REHABILITATIVE IDEAL AND ORDER

The rehabilitative philosophy and its actualizations directly promoted social order. Many of us accepted the altered self-conception contained in the new criminology that underpinned the ideal. We began to believe that we were sick, and we started searching for cures. Many of us adopted Sigmund Freud as our prophet, and we read and reread the *Basic Writings* as well as the works of the lesser prophets: Adler, Jung, Horney, and Fromm. Some of us became self-proclaimed experts in psycho-analysis and spent many hours analyzing each other. (Freudian interpretations provided us with new material for the old game of the dozens.)

Accepting this conception of ourselves as sick directed our attention inward and away from social and prison circumstances. It inhibited us from defining our situation as unfair and from developing critical, perhaps collective, attitudes

[16] These stories about events in the 1950s were told to me by two prisoners whom I interviewed in San Quentin in 1967.

60

toward the society and the prison administration. We were divided psychologically by focusing on our own personalities and searching for cures of our individual pathologies.

In attempting to cure ourselves, we involved ourselves in the programs that grew out of the rehabilitative ideal. The formal policy in Soledad was that every prisoner had to have a full-time work, school, or vocational training assignment. The classification committees and the Adult Authority encouraged prisoners to pursue either academic or vocational training. Prisoners were required by policy to continue school until they tested at the fifth-grade level. A few prisoners refused to work or attend school or vocational training programs, but they were usually transferred or placed in segregation. Most prisoners were busy at work or school whether or not they believed in the rehabilitative ideal, and this promoted peace and stability.

The most effective order-promoting aspect of the rehabilitative ideal was more direct. With the indeterminate sentence system and with release decisions made by a parole board that used conformity to the prison routine as a principal indicator of rehabilitation and refused to review a prisoner who had received any serious disciplinary reports within six months, the message was clear: You conform or you will not be paroled. Most prisoners responded to the message.

However, even from the outset there were a few prisoners who were not persuaded to engage seriously in the rehabilitative programs, were not deterred by the threat of the indeterminate sentence system, and continued to get into trouble. This created a special problem for the administration, which was trying to implement the new, ostensibly nonpunitive routine. They solved it by opening up "adjustment centers" in each prison. The adjustment centers were segregation units where prisoners were held for indefinite periods with reduced privileges and virtually no mobility. The rationale for the units was that some prisoners needed more intensive therapy in a more controlled situation. In fact, no intensive therapy was ever delivered, and the adjustment centers were simply segregation units where troublesome prisoners could be placed summarily and indefinitely. By the end of the decade, the state could segregate a thousand prisoners in these units. The combination of these and the rehabilitative ideal with all its ramifications kept the peace for ten years.

THE SEEDS OF DISRUPTION

Later this peace was shattered by at least two developments that began in the 1950s in Soledad as well as other correctional institutions. First, black prisoners were increasing in numbers and assertiveness. They steadily moved away from their acceptance of the Jim Crow arrangement that prevailed in prison and began to assume equality in the prison informal world. As stressed above, many black prisoners crossed racial lines, maintained friendships with whites and Chicanos, and participated fully in all aspects of prison life. During most of the 1950s, the racially prejudiced white and Chicano prisoners disapproved of this, but rarely demonstrated their disapproval and prejudice. However, when black prisoners became more assertive and finally militant, racial hostilities intensified and set off an era of extreme racial violence, which disrupted the patterns of order based on tips and cliques.

Second, many prisoners in California and other states with correctional institutions eventually soured on rehabilitation and its artifacts. After years of embracing rehabilitation's basic tenets, submitting themselves to treatment strategies, and then leaving prison with new hope for a better future, they discovered and reported back that their outside lives had not changed. Malcolm Braly, who witnessed the disillusionment in California prisons during these years, humorously describes the plight of the rehabilitated prisoner.

> Much later, it was his disfiguring ears that were altered first. One of the pioneer prison psychologists developed a theory that inmates who suffered such comic deformities formed compensatory mechanisms, of which their various felonies were merely symptoms, and their rehabilitation needn't be sweated out in the stone quarry, making little ones out of big ones, when it could be found under the knife of a cosmetic surgeon.
>
> Society Red was scheduled, with a dozen others, for plastic

surgery, which it was hoped would leave him free to be as honest as anyone else. Surely too modest a goal to tax more than lightly the magical skills of a plastic surgeon, but then his time was donated, and he had apparently tried some technique he didn't care to risk on a cash customer, because when the bandages were removed Red's ears were greatly altered, but it was difficult to characterize the difference as an improvement. One ear pinched to his skull as if stapled there, and the other still flew at approximately half-mast, but he figured if they'd sliced his ears clean off it would still be a small price to pay to be rid of something so full of meanness and trickeration as that compensatory mechanism which had forced him to steal, not for wheels, women or money, but only as some sorry-assed symptom.

When he next made parole, he quickly discovered that his cosmetic ears cut no ice. The bitches, as he put it, still wouldn't let him score on their drawers, but continued to deal way around him as if they sensed some violent far-out freakishness thrashing around in his hectic yellow eyes.[17]

After prisoners were convinced that treatment programs did not work (by the appearance of persons who had participated fully in the treatment programs streaming back to prison with new crimes or violations of parole), hope shaded to cynicism and then turned to bitterness. The disillusioned increasingly shifted their focus from their individual pathologies to their life situation. They realized that under the guise of rehabilitation the correctionalists had gained considerable power over them and were using this power to coerce prisoners into "phony" treatment programs and "chickenshit" prison routines. In addition, they realized that parole boards arbitrarily, whimsically, and discriminatorily were giving many prisoners longer sentences and bringing them back to prison for violations of parole conditions that most prisoners believed to be impossible.

Rehabilitation inadvertently contributed to mounting criticism of itself by promoting a prison intelligentsia. Partly because of the expanded possibilities and the encouragement stemming from rehabilitation, more and more prisoners began

[17] *On the Yard,* pp. 10–11.

educating themselves. Once we freed ourselves from the narrow conceptions contained in the rehabilitative philosophy, we began reading more and more serious literature. Most of us came from the working and lower-classes and had received very poor, if any, high school education. Our narrow life experience before and after school did nothing to expand our understanding. But in prison in the 1950s, with time on our hands, the availability of books, and the stimulation of the self-improvement message contained in the rehabilitative philosophy, we began to read. At first, we did not know how or what to read, so we read books on reading. Then when we acquired a preliminary sense of the classics, we plowed through them. Malcolm X expressed it well: "No university would ask any student to devour literature as I did when this new world opened to me, of being able to read and *understand*." [18] Most of us started with history, then turned to other areas: philosophy, literature, psychology, economics, semantics, and even mysticism. After several years of intense reading, we developed a relatively firm foundation in world knowledge. It was constructed under peculiar circumstances and in isolation from large intellectual enterprises; consequently, it was somewhat uneven and twisted here and there. But it was broad and mostly solid.

With this new perspective, we saw through things: our culture, society, the prison system, even our beloved criminal careers. They were all stripped of their original meanings, and what we saw made all of us critical and some of us bitter and cyncial. Art Powers, one of the convict authors of *An Eye for An Eye,* described the conversion of Etheridge Knight:

> From that day, Knight devoted every ounce of his energies toward getting out of prison. He read books like they were going out of style and applied himself in many areas — philosophy, art, science, and religion. In five years, he covered a wide field and he found a bit of Etheridge Knight in all of them. He found a sense of worth, a yardstick of measurement for himself. In his discovery, he became an articulate spokesman for the prison Negro population. He gained a reputation, which, in an unguarded moment, he let slip that

[18] *The Autobiography of Malcolm X* (New York: Macmillan, 1965), p. 173.

he valued highly. He became the Negro voice for "telling it like it is." [19]

Our new understandings guided us in different directions. After being released, some of us "dropped out" and became bohemians or students. Others, particularly many blacks, became activists. Still others, finding no satisfying avenues of expression for their new perspective, returned to old criminal pursuits. But all of us, in different ways, continued to work on a criticism of the "system" and to spread this criticism. This eventually contributed heavily to the great disillusionment with and the eventual dismantling of the rehabilitative ideal. Racial conflict and the sense of injustice that followed this dismantling tore the correctional institution apart.

[19] P. 96.

3
Division

Prison social order has always been fragile and teetered on the edge. The upheavals that jolted our society in the late 1950s and 1960s toppled this order in many prisons, just as they disrupted many other brittle-shelled social organizations and institutions. When it fell, however, it was not completely shattered, and prisoners themselves tried to stop the disintegration, mend the cracks, and pull the scattered pieces back together. "All the king's men," in this case the administration, reacted to the prisoners' efforts with fear and vengeance and finished the demolition. The violent turmoil that followed and still exists is a product of all three phases: the division within the prisoner society, the prisoners' "revolution," and the administrative reaction.

THE BLACK PRISONER MOVEMENT

Division began when black prisoners increased in number and shifted their posture in prisons. The latter change was linked to the civil rights and black movements outside, but it also had very unique qualities. For instance, the civil rights phase was never very important in prison. The tactics of the civil rights protestors were too gentle to catch the imagination of black prisoners, and the central issue, unequal treatment under the law, was not as apparently salient in prison. All convicts, to a greater degree than free citizens, were equally treated and mistreated under the law. Other aspects of the black movement, such as "black is beautiful" and black separatism, were more important in prison than on the outside.

Black Is Beautiful   After World War II, the large migrations of southern blacks into northern and western cities, and some measure of educational and occupational progress, black Americans began to develop a new, unique sense of worth based on intrinsic qualities of the American Negro. Black author Claude Brown described the new identity and its spread.

> In the fifties, when "baby" came around, it seemed to be the prelude to a whole new era in Harlem. It was the introduction to the era of black reflection. A fever started spreading. Perhaps, the strong rising of the Muslim movement is something that helped to sustain or even usher in this era.
>
> I remember that in the early fifties, cats would stand on the corner and talk, just shooting the stuff, all the street-corner philosophers. Sometimes, it was a common topic — cats talking about gray chicks — and somebody might say something like, "Man, what can anybody see in a gray chick, when colored chicks are so fine; they got so much soul." This was the coming of the "soul" thing too.
>
> "Soul" had started coming out of the churches and the nightclubs into the streets. Everybody started talking about "soul" as though it were something that they could see on people or a distinct characteristic of colored folks. . . .
>
> Everybody was really digging themselves and thinking and saying in their behavior, in every action, "Wow! Man, it's a beautiful thing to be colored." Everyone was saying, "Oh, the beauty of me! Look at me. I'm colored. And look at us. Aren't we beautiful?" [1]

This new pride fixed on two separate qualities that blacks (and many whites) in the United States believed were related to the Negro race: "soul" and masculinity. Soul involves being more spontaneous, having the capacity to relate to others with more ease, and having special expressive abilities, particularly as revealed in music. Masculinity depends on various qualities, especially athletic and sexual prowess.

[1] *Manchild in the Promised Land* (New York: Macmillan, 1965) p. 166.

Many of the early carriers of these new definitions — black "hip" hustlers, dope fiends, and musicians — were coming to the prisons in the late 1940s and early 1950s and spreading the new "black is beautiful" idea among black prisoners. Although this new set of definitions was not basically hostile, it irked the more prejudiced whites who were comfortable only with a humble, unassuming black man. However, many whites accepted the new black identity and, in fact, adulated and emulated it. In particular, white weed heads and dope fiends, many of whom had had a great deal of direct or indirect contact with black music and black hip culture, felt a strong affinity for this new viewpoint.

Black Separatism   Black separatism proceeded along with this new identity. Outside, the Black Muslims emerged as the major separatist organization, and it found its way into the prisons in the mid-1950s. Malcolm X, who more than any other individual personified this development, describes the growth of the Muslim faith in prison.

> You let this caged-up black man start thinking, the same way I did when I first heard Elijah Muhammad's teachings, let him start thinking how with better breaks when he was young and ambitious he might have been a lawyer, a doctor, a scientist, anything. You let this caged-up black man start realizing, as I did, how from the first landing of the first slave ship, the millions of black men in America have been like sheep in a den of wolves. That's why black prisoners become Muslims so fast when Elijah Muhammad's teaching filter into their cages by way of other Muslim convicts. "The white man is the devil" is a perfect echo of that black convict's lifelong experience.[2]

Black Muslim prisoners recruited other black prisoners, and the organization grew throughout the 1950s. They continued a nonviolent, separatist direction and clashed with the administrations only over restrictions on their religious practices. They attempted to receive the Muslim newspaper, *Muhammad Speaks,* and copies of the Quran, hold meetings, meet

[2] *The Autobiography of Malcolm X* (New York: Macmillan, 1965), p. 183.

with outside representatives of the organization, be served pork-free meals, and be segregated in the prison. All administrations stubbornly resisted these requests and acted systematically to suppress the organization, which they perceived as a threat to the prison peace and their legitimacy. The Muslims were tenacious. They formed groups of highly committed, disciplined black prisoners who shaved their heads, kept themselves impeccably neat, maintained a cold but polite attitude to other prisoners, refused to eat pork, congregated together wherever possible, and listened to other Muslims deliver the teachings of Elijah Muhammad. Although their rhetoric was hostile, the Muslims precipitated little violence. They were occasionally involved in violence, but it was usually initiated by someone else, perhaps guards firing at a group of Muslims or a group of Muslims and other prisoners. Eldridge Cleaver describes the aftermath of one such shooting and reveals the essentially nonviolent posture of Muslims.

> After the death of Brother Booker T. X, who was shot dead by a San Quentin guard and who at the time had been my cell partner and the inmate Minister of the Muslims at San Quentin, my leadership had been publicly endorsed by Elijah Muhammad's west coast representative, Minister John Shabazz of Muhammad's Los Angeles Mosque. This was done because of the explosive conditions in San Quentin at the time. Muslim officials wanted to avert any Muslim-initiated violence, which had become a distinct possibility in the aftermath of Brother Booker's death. I was instructed to impose iron discipline upon the San Quentin Mosque, which had continued to exist despite the unending efforts of prison authorities to stamp it out.[3]

However, Elijah Muhammad's teaching continued to condemn and vilify whites and white society. This antagonized, threatened, and frightened white prisoners and the administrators. The administrators tried to thwart and suppress the organization. In many prisons, rules against belonging to the organization were introduced. In fact, in one prison a rule prohibiting more than two black prisoners congregating was

[3] *Soul on Ice* (New York: McGraw-Hill, 1968), p. 63.

adopted. The Muslims carried their fight to the courts and finally, in 1965, won the right to exist as a religious organization in the prison.

By the time they won their major court victories, the Muslims were losing their momentum in California prisons. Malcolm X had left the outside organization in 1963 and was later assassinated. The split, his subsequent broader political vision, and his homicide, which many believed was perpetrated by the Muslim organization, turned many California Muslim prisoners away from the organization. Some of them followed Malcolm X's route to a more radical political orientation. Cleaver discusses his conversion after the assassination.

> What provoked the assassins to murder? Did it bother them that Malcolm was elevating our struggle into the international arena through his campaign to carry it before the United Nations? Well, by murdering him they only hastened the process because we certainly are going to take our cause before a sympathetic world. Did it bother the assassins that Malcolm denounced the racist straightjacket demonology of Elijah Muhammad? Well, we certainly do denounce it and will continue to do so. Did it bother the assassins that Malcolm taught us to defend ourselves? We shall not remain a defenseless prey to the murderer, to the sniper and the bomber. Insofar as Malcolm spoke the truth, the truth will triumph and prevail and his name shall live; and insofar as those who opposed him lied, to that extent will their names become curses. Because truth crushed to earth shall rise again.[4]

In California ex-Muslims and other black prisoners followed a variety of black nationalist courses until the Black Panther Party exploded into prominence on the outside and supplied black prisoners with a new, dynamic black nationalistic organization. In this last phase of separatism, the black prisoners who identified with the Black Panthers or participated in similar organizations were more politically radical and more prone to violence. At least they were much more prepared, theoretically and actually, to respond with counterviolence to threats.

[4] Ibid., pp. 65–66.

70

Black Rage   Recently, Charles Silberman analyzed the eruption of black violence after the mid-1960s.

> Over the last fifteen years, white Americans have discovered how deep is the store of anger and hatred that three and a half centuries of humiliation have built up in black Americans, and how quickly that anger can explode into violence. The potential for violence always has been present. "To be a Negro in this country and to be relatively conscious," James Baldwin has written, "is to be in a rage almost all the time." Black Americans had to invent ways of channeling their anger and controlling their hate; they had to create non-suicidal forms of courage. Had they not done so, the United States would have gone up in smoke long ago. What has happened in the last fifteen years, in good measure, is that the cultural devices that kept black violence under control have not yet emerged.[5]

In prison, black rage against whites and white society was magnified. Early in his conversion to black radicalism, Cleaver endured a "nervous breakdown" from the intensity of his rage.

> Two days later, I had a "nervous breakdown." For several days, I ranted and raved against the white race, against white women in particular, against white America in general. When I came to myself, I was locked in a padded cell with not the vaguest memory of how I got there. All I could recall was an eternity of pacing back and forth in the cell, preaching to the unhearing walls.[6]

George Jackson, the celebrated black prisoner leader who was shot in San Quentin, wrote eloquently about his rage.

> This monster — the monster they've engendered in me will return to torment its maker, from the grave, the pit, the profoundest pit. Hurl me into the next existence, the descent into hell won't turn me. I'll crawl back to dog his trail forever. They won't defeat my revenge, never, never. I'm part of a righteous people who anger slowly, but rage undamned. We'll gather at his door in such a number that the rumbling of our

[5] Charles Silberman, *Criminal Violence, Criminal Justice* (New York: Random House, 1978), pp. 134–35.
[6] *Soul on Ice*, pp. 23–24.

feet will make the earth tremble. I'm going to charge them for this twenty-eight years without gratification. I'm going to charge them reparations in blood. I'm going to charge them like a maddened, wounded, rogue male elephant — ears flared, trunk raised, trumpet blaring. I'll do my dance in his chest, and the only thing he'll ever see in my eyes is a dagger to pierce his cruel heart. This is one nigger who is positively displeased. I'll never forgive, I'll never forget, and if I'm guilty of anything at all it's of not leaning on them hard enough. War without terms.[7]

RACIAL VIOLENCE

As black prisoners developed their new identities, experienced new levels of rage, and steadily asserted themselves more and more in the prison public life, racial hostilities and eventually racial violence increased. In Soledad in the early 1960s, a series of racial attacks occurred, and the prison became known to California prisoners as the Gladiator School: "this was, primarily, because of the never ending race war and general personal violence which destroyed any illusions about CTF-Central being an institution of rehabilitation."[8]

From Soledad the violence spread to San Quentin and then to Folsom. An ex-Folsom prisoner described a random attack that occurred in 1967.

> Four or five black convicts, most of them young lowriders who had been transferred from San Quentin for causing trouble there, were coming across the yard knifing dudes. They were out to get some "honkies." They were coming right at me and I didn't see them but an old black Folsom con who knew me pretty good yelled at me to look out. He also yelled to them that I was all right and I got passed over. They killed one oriental dude and another old white convict.[9]

Informal Segregation   Some degree of formal and informal segregation had been practiced even in the enlightened era of rehabilitation. At least black and white prisoners were not

[7] *Soledad Brother* (New York: Bantam Books, 1970), pp. 164–65.
[8] Micha Maguire, "Racism II," in Robert Minton, Jr., ed., *Inside* (New York: Random House, 1971), p. 84.
[9] Interview, San Francisco, June 1976.

72

allowed to cell together. After 1960, the mounting hostility and violence between black and other prisoners resulted in rigid informal patterns of segregation. Black and white prisoners stopped commingling in public places. The dining rooms, movies, day rooms, waiting lines, and informal gatherings were almost completely segregated, not by institution rules, but by prisoners themselves. George Jackson describes his attempts to break the pattern and demonstrates their rigidity.

> I don't know where you got the tale of me attempting to integrate a movie area. It is a bit off but it could have come from the events of that week I spent in J unit. The blacks had to sit in the rear of the TV room on hard, armless, backless benches while the Mexicans and whites sat up front on cushioned chairs and benches with backrests!!!! Now, check this, if one of those punks was in his cell or the shower, no one could sit in his seat and certainly no black dare sit there. I'm serious!!!! All of this taking place in front of a uniform and a large bold print sign in English and Spanish that read "No Saving of Seats Allowed!!!"
>
> The first three nights, I went in to catch the news I stood in the front, looking down the room at the old slave for some sign of support. Old slave ignored me, eyes darting. He wants to go home, so do I, but I don't want to leave anything behind. Since my father didn't bequeath me much to begin with, any further losses leave me with nothing. I sat right in the front the fourth night but I couldn't watch TV. I had to watch my back, the cop walked up and looked at me like I had lost my mind. The cons tolerated me (215 pounds and apparently a lunatic) for three days. On the fourth (or seventh day out) night of setting they attacked me. They *locked me up* afterward, and sent me back to San Quentin to stay.[10]

Besides the patterns of segregation, this passage reveals the alliance between whites and Chicanos that endured through this period of mounting racial hostility. It also reveals that blacks in Tracy (a California adult prison) were in the less favorable position at that time because they were outnumbered by Chicanos and whites. In other prisons, where these new

[10] *Soledad Brother,* pp. 162–63.

patterns of segregation were setting in and where the percentage of blacks was close to or greater than half, it was usually more equitable. When they were the majority, they often claimed the best areas and whites had to accept inferior facilities.

The Unraveling Social Order The web of social order described in the preceding chapter, a web composed of extended ties of tip and clique membership, was cleaved through by the racial violence. It had had racial tears, but there were still many connections between the races. Now the gap became almost complete. A prisoner who returned to the California prisons in the mid-1960s stated in an interview,

> When I got back to the joint, I ran into one of my old partners, a black dude who I was tight with. Right away, he told me that we had to cool it 'cause we'd bring down a lot of shit if we hung out together. Now this dude and I had stole together. We were tight but we couldn't sit together in the dining room or the show. Or hang around at all. If we did, some Nazis would start leaning on me and some low-riding black dudes on him. So, we kept our distance and only talked once in awhile.[11]

Older convicts who were respected by other prisoners could break the rules of segregation from time to time, but not on a regular basis. There was always the threat of violence if one continued to mingle too much with members of the other race.

The tip and clique system depended greatly on racial disputes' being mediated though the network. After racial hatred reached a high level, this became less likely, if possible at all. Consequently, the extended overlapping tip network atrophied, and the cliques increasingly became organized for their members' protection. Victor Dillon, a prisoner at Soledad in the late 1960s, described the prison clique in the following manner:

> Physical security is quite important in prison society, partly because of the racial friction. On the one hand, you have the blacks. On the other, the whites and in the middle of all this, you have the Mexicans and others. If one clique member of good

[11] Interview, San Francisco, April 1977.

74

standing is offended by a member of a clique of another race, woe be to the members of that race until the clique is satisfied. The individual in the clique feels secure in the knowledge that he has "friends" to back him up.[12]

The Rise of Lowriders   As the racial hostilities and violence mounted and the tip and clique network unraveled, "lowriders" ascended into prominence. The term *lowrider,* borrowed from the outside and originally applied to young hoods who rode around in their cars, slouched down in their seats, is a derogatory label pinned on young hoodlums, many of them state-raised, who formed cliques, hung around the prison yard, and "talked shit," or bragged about their exploits and capabilities. Presenting themselves as tough, they were more violent than the average prisoner. They also stole from other prisoners and were involved in wheeling and dealing to the degree that they could penetrate these enterprises, which tended to be controlled by older prisoners. Other prisoners generally disliked and did not respect them, but feared them somewhat because of their occasional violence. However, their power was minimized by the consensus against them and the fact that there were older, respected prisoners who, it was believed, were ultimately more murderous when pushed and whom, therefore, lowriders respected. However, this changed in the late 1960s, and lowriders were carried to the forefront by the tide of racial hostility.

Even in the era of racial tolerance, lowriders were more racially prejudiced than the general population. Many of their experiences in the youth prisons, which were more racially segregated and hostile, had imbued them with considerable racial hostility. When the racial hostilities broke into the open and the threat of violence rose, the lowriders became open racists. Many white lowrider groups called themselves Nazis and tattooed swastikas on their bodies. Black lowriders also displayed open racism. As other black and white prisoners began to feel increasingly threatened by racial violence, many of them joined or affiliated with racist lowrider groups. Some older and more respected prisoners joined them. Hell's Angels

[12] "Inside the Prison Clique," in Minton, *Inside,* p. 33.

and other white motorcycle riders who had been openly racist on the outside were coming to prison in increased numbers. They joined, and sometimes took over, racist lowrider groups.

Chicano lowrider cliques were also ascending, but not along the same lines, for Chicanos were ambivalent about their racial position. They were more hostile toward blacks than whites and had many close friends among white criminals. There was also a division among them — the Texas–Los Angeles split. Furthermore, there had been warring neighborhood tips or "gangs" in Los Angeles in the 1940s. Drugs had blotted out these neighborhood structures, but latent enmity endured.[13] Thus, during the early 1960s some young Chicanos from particular neighborhoods in Los Angeles were forming more cohesive cliques. Instead of focusing on racial hatred and violence, they fixed on drugs and started fighting each other to obtain drugs and to control drug trafficking. The development of Chicano violent cliques exploded into prominence in the 1970s after the prisoner movement. (This development will be examined more thoroughly in chapter 6.)

The racial violence and the expanding lowrider activities involved only a minority of the prison population. Most prisoners, as always, did their time and attempted to stay out of trouble. This became much more difficult, however, because the threat of violence, even random violence, increased. To maximize safety, persons had to watch themselves carefully, stay away from other racial groups, and withdraw from prison public life as much as possible. More prisoners isolated themselves or restricted their activities to small friendship groups.

REUNIFICATION

New Perspectives　Toward the end of the 1960s in California and other states, many prisoners began redefining their relationships to each other, the prison, the system (the criminal justice system), and the society in a more politically radical fashion. Many black leaders became Marxists, most Chicanos developed a Chicano political identity, and most whites, though

---

[13] See Joan W. Moore, *Homeboys* (Philadelphia: Temple University Press, 1978) for full description of the Los Angeles Chicano gangs, their hostile relationships, and their swing into heroin addiction.

not becoming radical, developed a sense of injustice about their legal status. The spread of these more radical perspectives stalled the drift toward racial segregation, hostility, and violence and supplied a basis for a new unity among prisoners. This led to the explosive prison political movement in which outside political organizations focused on prisons and prisoners and directed many of the movement activities. But in the earlier precursory stage, prisoners worked toward shared political goals and unity, with very little help from outsiders, demonstrating the potential for a new form of social organization in the apparently disintegrating, hostile prisoner world.

Black Prisoners and Marxism After the phases described above, the separatism and rage, many black prisoner leaders were heavily influenced by Marxist perspectives, abandoned hostile separatism, and began cooperating with white radicals. Beginning in 1967, Eldridge Cleaver, a black prisoner leader and former Muslim, wrote *Soul on Ice,* which states a radical, but not separatist position; became friends with Paul Jacobs, a central San Francisco Bay Area white radical; joined the staff of *Ramparts,* a radical magazine, on his release; and then accepted the candidacy of the Peace and Freedom Party (a multiracial radical party) for the 1968 presidential campaign. George Jackson, earlier a rabid white hater, shifted to Marxism and began interacting with white radicals. This shift was not exclusive to California. For example, at this time Etheridge Knight, a self-educated black poet, wrote from the Indiana state prison: "in the meantime, what is going to happen to these young men here who might have been hewers of wood or climbers of high mountains? Well, they will wait, milling about with sparks dancing in their eyes until the storm breaks, until the built-in contradictions of this racist, exploitative system burst through its already cracking seams." [14] Although racial hostility simmered below their new radical perspective, in the late 1960s many of the heads of black prisoner organizations and other respected black prisoners were ready to cooperate with whites to achieve shared political goals.

[14] Etheridge Knight, ed., *Black Voices from Prison* (New York: Pathfinder Press, 1970), p. 10.

The Chicano Movement   In the late 1960s, Chicanos in California prisons began to cultivate their racial ethnic identity and promote their special interests. In other states, Puerto Ricans, American Indians, and other minority groups were doing the same. California Chicanos had been ambivalent about their Mexican identity and their relationship to Anglos. Then the ideology of racial ethnic identity and pride spread to them and inspired them to assert themselves as Chicanos. They began studying Chicano history and seeking special rights and privileges as Chicanos (such as movies in Spanish and recognition of Mexican holidays). Some of the more militant Chicanos followed the paths earlier traveled by the black militants and developed extreme hostility toward white prisoners. In general, the new Chicano activists did not become separatists. But they did become less hostile toward blacks and less willing to back up whites in their hostilities toward black prisoners.

The Sense of Injustice   Most of the remaining prisoners, particularly the whites, did not follow the more radical directions of the nonwhite activists, but they began adopting the view that they, as a class, were treated unfairly by the law. In earlier periods, individual convicts may have believed that they personally "got a bum deal," but most of them believed that, in general, felons got what they deserved. They were aware that mainly the poor went to prison, but thought that this was their inevitable fate or deserts. The relevant adage circulating among criminals and convicts when I entered these worlds was "when you play, you gotta pay."

This changed in the 1960s. Social scientific studies, penetrating, skeptical, and far-reaching media reporting, and criticisms from the "new left" broadly disseminated the evidence of systematic discrimination in all phases of the criminal justice system and the belief that this was not fair. Most prisoners redefined their legal status, began recognizing instances of injustice, and experienced what legal scholar Edmond Cahn described as "outrage, horror, shock, resentment, and anger" from their sense of injustice.[15]

[15] *The Sense of Injustice* (New York: New York University Press, 1949), p. 24.

They began deeply resenting that big shots not only get away with crime, but are dignified for it: "Beverly Hills is full of all the biggest gangsters living up there on those hills with their plush pools, and the Adult Authority associates with them, ya know." [16] They resented that punishment is delivered mainly to the poor:

> In the past, it has generally been the indigent person who has had to "dance" at the end of a rope or "fry" in the electric chair. As a matter of fact, of all the men condemned to die in the prisons where I [was] serving time, not one of them had even a middle-class background, and certainly none of them were from the upper echelons of society. The reason for this state of affairs is obvious: the man who can afford expensive lawyers to defend him and a battery of psychologists and psychiatrists to testify in his behalf is seldom if ever required to walk that "last mile." Rather, he will frequently be given life in prison (if he's convicted at all). Then after a few years have elapsed and the public has lost interest in his case, he receives executive clemency and is released from prison. [17]

And they resented that the criminal justice system is set up to convict them quickly and move them into prison, because they did not have money for a good defense.[18]

Prisoners in states with indeterminate sentence systems had a more immediate focus. As disillusionment followed after the initial stage of the correctional institution, more and more prisoners were critically examining the operation of the most crucial process in prison, the fixing of their sentence, and were discovering systematic injustices in its operation. When I studied the California prisons in 1967, this was one of the most

[16] Interview, Berkeley, June, 1968.

[17] H. Jack Griswold, Mike Misenheimer, Art Powers, and Ed Fromanhouser, *An Eye for An Eye* (New York: Holt, Rinehart and Winston, 1970), p. 148.

[18] For example, in interviews of a random sample of male defendants in New York in 1962 to 1964, Abraham Blumberg discovered that slightly over half believed that they were innocent and had pleaded guilty because they had been persuaded, manipulated, tricked or coerced by members of the system — attorneys, public defenders, district attorneys, police, and judges. See *Criminal Justice* (Chicago: Quadrangle Books, 1967), p. 90.

important issues among prisoners, and I devoted half a chapter to a description of prisoners' critical analysis of the practices of the Adult Authority. Excerpts from this analysis follow.

Denial of Due Process   The convicts believe that in many cases the Adult Authority actually convicts men for crimes without due process. This occurs in cases where a man is held accountable and made to serve extra time for crimes which were not charged against him and/or crimes for which he was not guilty. It is possible for the Adult Authority to give a person an additional sentence for these crimes because of the leeway which exists in indeterminate sentences.

> S. was convicted for second-degree burglary and served two years. While on parole, he states that his relations with his parole agent were not good even though he was working steadily and conforming to parole regulations. After completing eighteen months on parole, he was arrested two blocks from his home at 11:00 P.M. He was on his way home from a nearby bar where he had just spent two or three hours. The police were looking for someone who had committed a burglary several blocks away about an hour earlier. When they discovered that S. had a record for burglary, he was taken to jail and charged with this crime. When his alibi was established and there was no evidence to connect him with the crime except for his being in the neighborhood, the judge dismissed the charge and admonished the arresting officer.
>
> S.'s parole was cancelled, however, and he was returned to prison. When he appeared before the A.A. for a parole-violation hearing, he was asked if he knew why he had been returned. He replied that he did not. The A.A. member became irritated with him and told him that just because he "beat the charge" in court did not mean that he was not guilty, and that the best thing he could do was to admit that he was guilty. He refused to do this and tried to explain to the member that the judge clearly believed him to be innocent and that he could prove this from the transcript of the preliminary hearing.
>
> S. was denied parole consideration and postponed for another year. The next year, he brought the transcript of this case to the hearing and the member said that he did not want to read it and that it made no difference to him anyway. He was guilty as far as they were concerned. Once again, he

was denied parole and scheduled for another hearing in a year. (Interview, San Quentin, December, 1967.)

Ex Post Facto Enforcement   The United States Constitution states that "no bill of attainder or ex post facto law shall be passed." [19] Lon L. Fuller, in his book *The Morality of Law,* states that:

> A retroactive law is truly a monstrosity. Law has to do with the governance of human conduct by rules. To speak of governing or directing conduct today by rules that will be enacted tomorrow is to talk in blank prose.[20]

In California prisons, many inmates feel that they have confronted this "monstrosity." They believe that the Adult Authority, again applying the wide discretionary powers and manipulating the vast time margins at its disposal, enforces laws retroactively.

> L. served two years for burglary. Shortly after release from prison in 1959, he returned to the use of narcotics. He had used both marijuana and heroin in moderation since his midteens, but never had a narcotics arrest nor was there any indication in his record of heavy involvement in narcotics traffic. In 1959, after becoming addicted he became involved in drug traffic in order to support his habit. Four months later, he was arrested with nine ounces of heroin. He pled guilty to a charge of possession and was given the maximum term allowed — 1 to 10 years. This, however, was imposed consecutively to the sentence — 1 to 15 years — that he was serving, so in effect, he returned to prison with a sentence of 1 to 25, of which he had served a little more than 2 years. After serving 3 years, he felt that there was some chance of having his term fixed and being granted a parole date. (The average time served for opiate convictions of men released in 1965 with one prior jail or prison sentence was 44.1 months.) At this board appearance, the subject of sales was brought up by the A.A. members and it was implied that he was going to serve the time usually given a seller of narcotics.
>
> L. returned to the board with four years and felt that he

[19] Article I, Section IX, Paragraph 3.
[20] *The Morality of Law* (New Haven: Yale University Press, 1964), p. 53.

should be granted a parole at this hearing. The subject of sales was brought up again and at this time L. tried to explain that he was addicted and that his trafficking in drugs was merely a way of maintaining his habit. At this time, an A.A. member told him that the "public has spoken" and now wants narcotics addicts to serve more time. The more stringent laws which were passed 1961 were a mandate from the public to hold narcotics offenders in prison. L. returned that these new laws did not apply to him because he was sentenced in 1959 under the old laws. L. felt that this was retroactive enforcement of the law. L. still has not been released on parole after serving more than eight years. At each board appearance, the subject of sales and the more stringent narcotics laws are brought up. (Interview, San Quentin, December, 1967.)

Cruel and Unusual Punishment The Constitution also prohibits cruel and unusual punishment. However, it does not supply guidelines for defining it. The concept seems necessarily culture-bound. In prisons, cruel and unusual punishment is decided by comparing a particular sentence with "normal" sentences in a general class of crime. When one serves much more than the norm for his particular crime — allowing for the peculiarities of his crime — or when one serves more time for what is generally considered a less serious crime than is normal for a more serious crime, then he usually experiences the sense of injustice from cruel and unusual punishment.

P., a Mexican-American heroin user, has a long history of arrests related to drug use: misdemeanor "marks," paraphernalia arrests and a felony conviction for possession of a small quantity of heroin. In 1960, he was stopped and searched as he was leaving the toilet facility of a skid-row hotel. He was found to be in possession of a hypodermic needle and an eyedropper. An examination of his arms revealed a number of puncture wounds, some fresh. He was booked under a charge of "Suspicion of Narcotic Act, Felony." Under interrogation, P. admitted his addiction, the extent of same, and the fact that he had just prior to arrest "shot-up" a half a gram of heroin. The paraphernalia found in his pocket was forwarded to the forensic chemist who, after testing, stated that the residue scraped from the eyedropper "was a substance containing heroin."

Felony charges of possession of heroin were brought against P. He pled not guilty. There was no narcotic substance in evidence at the trial as the amount found in the eyedropper had been scarcely detectable and all of it was used in the chemist's test. The trial resulted in a guilty verdict. In view of his prior convictions, he was given the maximum sentence of 2 to 20 years.

When last contacted, P. had made five appearances before the Adult Authority, having served more than six years. He would have served seven years when he made his next appearance. In his last appearance, the A.A. told him that his request for parole was premature since he was a recidivist for narcotic offenses. P., who professes that he has never been anything but a "boot-and-shoe-hype" — a drug addict who is involved in petty theft to support his habit — feels that he is being made to serve an extremely long sentence. (Interview, San Quentin, December, 1967.)

Desert   Besides these precepts of justice which are spelled out in the Constitution, there are other conceptions of justice which are part of our Western cultural tradition and about which the convicts are becoming increasingly sensitive now that they are attitudinally in a position to question the morality of the penal system.

A violation of just desert occurs when an individual receives the punishment for the crimes of others or receives extraordinary punishment for his crime because of other contingencies not directly related to his particular crime. Many California convicts feel that they are receiving more than their just desert because of the acts of other persons. They believe that when crimes in the same general class as theirs are committed on the outside and receive undue public attention, they have less chance of receiving a parole. Many have reported that these outside crimes are discussed in the board appearances.

D., an armed robbery offender, appeared before the Adult Authority after serving 4½ years. He felt that because of his crime, the time served, his past record and his institutional record, he should be paroled at this time. However, approximately two months prior to this board appearance an armed robbery had occurred which because of having excessive violence received considerable news media coverage.

83

Furthermore, many statements by law enforcement officers and political leaders had followed which requested harsher treatment of armed robbers. At D.'s board appearance, very little was said about his progress in prison; instead the conversation turned to the recent violent robbery and the attendant publicity given to this crime. D. was not granted a parole at this time and was scheduled to return for another board appearance when he had served 5½ years. Needless to say, D. felt that he was being punished for the acts of other persons. (Interview, San Quentin, December, 1967.) [21]

THE UNITY STRIKES AT SAN QUENTIN

Most black, other nonwhite, and white prisoners still hated each other in 1967, but many, particularly group leaders, had adopted one of the new, more radical perspectives and were willing to cooperate to achieve common goals. In some prisons, key individuals, often leaders of organizations or cliques, began working to organize multiracial prisoner protest activities. The events at San Quentin in 1967 and 1968 reveal the shift in thinking of prisoner leaders and their successful efforts to organize political activities across racial lines.

In January 1967, a guard in the San Quentin dining room tried to take a cup of milk from a prisoner and then gave him a disciplinary report for having the milk. The prisoner's black coworkers resented the officer's action, which they believed was motivated by racial prejudice. When they objected, twelve of them were fired from their assignments. The next day, thirty-one more kitchen workers, most of them black, went on a sympathy strike. The more militant blacks called for a work strike by all black prisoners. Many prejudiced whites defined the incident as one involving only blacks and encouraged white prisoners to stay out of it. The next work day, Monday, January 16, most of the black workers did not report to work. On this day a dense fog settled on San Quentin, and in the fog a few fights occurred between white and black prisoners, resulting in several stabbings and one death. The racial hostilities mounted, and rumors of a large racial confrontation circulated

[21] These paragraphs on the sense of injustice were taken from *The Felon* (Englewood Cliffs, N.J.: Prentice-Hall, 1970), pp. 56–60.

through the prison. On Wednesday, fearing a general riot, the administration diverted all prisoners to the "big yard" after the noon meal. This jammed several thousand prisoners together in one place, and the prisoners, fearing racial violence, congregated in small groups. Some of the more hostile white and black clique members began shouting racial insults to the other groups, and the groups began to separate into two large crowds on opposite sides of the yard — blacks on one side, Chicanos and whites on the other. Prisoners broke up wooden furniture on the yard and received knives and trays passed to them by friends from the dining room, which adjoins the yard. From then on, the groups remained separated, and all available guards and staff were ordered to the gun rails that surround the yard. No riot occurred.

After many hours of shuffling large groups of prisoners from one part of the prison to another, which involved shooting into a crowd and wounding eight prisoners, guards stripped, searched, and locked the prisoners back into their cells. After several weeks of lockdown, searches, abusive treatment by guards, and transfers or segregation of alleged leaders, the prisoners were permitted to return to their normal routine.

In the weeks that followed the near riot, many prisoners, black, white, and Chicano, reevaluated the events and began to believe that the administration and their own racial hostilities had diverted them from protesting a legitimate grievance to engaging in a racial confrontation. Consequently, many of the more respected and resourceful leaders of the white, black, and Chicano groups began communicating and planning unified protest activities. At this time a small group of prisoners with access to a ditto machine composed, reproduced, and circulated a one-page newspaper that they entitled the *Outlaw*. In jest, the lead story in the first edition identified the warden as a homosexual and reported that he had been discovered in a restroom performing fellatio on a prisoner. The administration immediately tried to suppress this underground newspaper. More politically oriented prisoners continued to publish it and to deliver vituperative criticism of the conditions in San Quentin and the indeterminate sentence system. Its contents became more and more political, and the seriousness of being caught with a copy increased. Persons suspected of printing it were transferred and ditto machines were guarded, but it continued to appear, though its circulation was curtailed.

In late 1967 an issue presented a list of grievances and called for a general, nonviolent strike for a date in January 1968. This strike did not occur. Persons who were attempting to organize it believed that the poor circulation of the contraband *Outlaw* and the resultant lack of consensus on the strike issues and the date caused this failure.[22] To overcome these problems, the organizers produced another *Outlaw,* which restated the grievances and called for another strike. This time they requested support from outside radical groups and individuals and smuggled out a copy to the *Berkeley Barb,* a widely read Bay Area counterculture newspaper. The *Barb* printed the news of the strike and the list of demands and called for support for the impending strike. Some individuals and groups on the outside organized support for the strikers, and news of the approaching strike was announced twice in the *Barb* and was broadcast over the local major television network news programs. Now there was no confusion among San Quentin prisoners. The fact of their strike and its date was being announced to them over the 6:00 P.M. news, which many of them watched. On the day of the strike, two well-known Bay Area rock bands and several hundred supporters appeared at the outside gate of San Quentin. Only a few prisoners actually followed the plan and stayed in their cells that morning, but after others became aware of the outside support, which they could hear and see from several locations in San Quentin, the strike picked up momentum. By noon, hundreds of prisoners had returned to their cells and remained there. The administration quickly locked down the prison.

The prison remained on partial lockup (only prisoners assigned to maintenance work were released) for a week, dur-

[22] Actually, strikes rarely occur by plan. Prisoners are very reluctant to strike or riot because they believe that the consequences are severe and they are fearful of being singled out for punishment if only a small number of prisoners actually are involved. They more often follow along in the case of an unplanned disturbance once it has started and it becomes apparent that large numbers are involved.

ing which the warden met with prisoner leaders and agreed to allow a committee of prisoners to conduct a study of prisoner grievances. It would be delivered to him, to the head of the department, and, the prisoners understood, to certain legislators who had been interested in prison reform. After the prisoners were released, the prisoner committee undertook their work with energy and care. They surveyed the prison population for grievances, codified them, and embellished the report with a relatively complex analysis of the injustices, contradictions, and failures in the California correctional and indeterminate sentence systems.[23] The warden received the report, but did not deliver it to legislators or take any other atcion. When it appeared to the prisoners that nothing was going to change as a result of their efforts, they began to organize another strike, using the same strategies as those used in the February strike. They published another *Outlaw* calling for an August Unity Day nonviolent strike, requested support from outside, and smuggled the *Outlaw* to the *Berkeley Barb*. Again an outside group of supporters was formed, and several hundred demonstrators and a rock band appeared on Saturday, August 8, 1968. This time, the vast majority of the prisoners followed the strike plan in the morning, and, in fact, they spontaneously extended it through the weekend.

CONCLUDING REMARKS

The San Quentin unity strikes mark a turning point in the developments inside U.S. prisons. After these events, more and more prisoners throughout the country began redefining their legal and social status, adopting political ideologies, and becoming involved in various forms of political activities. New outside organizations formed, and existing ones refocused to work to reform or eliminate the prison. The general public raised the prison issue to the top of its list of concerns. Political activists and radical political organizations shifted their attention to the prison and generated the prison movement.

The criticisms emanating from prisoners, the prison move-

[23] This report, "A Convict Report on the Major Grievances of the Prison Population with Suggested Solutions," is printed in Robert Minton, *Inside* (New York: Random House, 1971) pp. 209–325.

ment organizations, and the public inspired criminologists and sociologists to rethink their ideas on prisons and prisoners and quickly to devise new solutions to the prison crisis. Prison administrators and guards, the primary recipients of the criticisms, fumed and then finally responded with vengeance.

In other words, the developments inside prison, among prisoners who initially were helped and influenced only slightly by outsiders, set off processes that then dominated prison events for several years. Increasingly, outsiders and outside organizations made the decisions on the prison movement strategies. Academic criminologists planned massive overhauls of the criminal justice system, which mainly flowed from their own perspectives.[24] Finally, prison administrators with strong backing from conservative legislators, governors, and the public (who had lost their sympathy for prisoners) put a stop to all the political activities in prison. When we interpret the horror which remains in prison, we must understand the impact of the external processes and remember what was developing among prisoners themselves, before prisons became such a large political issue and all control of events shifted away from prisoners.

[24] David Ward has suggested to me that academic criminologists had lost contact with the prison after the mid-1960s. He argues that most sociologists were white and not well received by hostile black, Chicano, and native American prisoner spokesmen. Also the Vietnam War and the civil rights protests influenced academics to shift their attention from prisoners and criminals to police and the law.

4
The Revolution

After the unity strikes, a series of prison-related events drew the attention of many people involved in outside civil rights, war protest, and other political activities. Eldridge Cleaver, an ex-convict from California prisons published *Soul on Ice* in 1968. He subsequently rose to stardom in the radical movement and was rearrested after a shootout with the Oakland police. Huey Newton, the leader of the Black Panther Party, went to prison. Previously, he had sprung into national attention by leading a group of armed Black Panthers into the spectators' gallery of the California State Assembly. More and more outside activists became familiar with the conditions inside prisons and the lives of actual prisoners and were attracted to prison issues. They joined a few released prisoners who, instead of attempting to disappear into more or less conventional lifestyles (which most ex-prisoners had always done), became active in organizations working to change prisons or help ex-prisoners. Existing prison reform groups, such as the American Friends Service Committee, and a few new prisoner self-help organizations, such as Seven Steps and the Fortune Society, initiated a new prison reform movement.

Then a series of very violent and notorious events attracted many more radical activists and radical political organizations to prison issues. On January 13, 1970, a Soledad gun-tower guard rapidly fired several shots into a group of adjustment center prisoners, who were fighting during their brief exercise period, and he killed three black prisoners. A two-year period of extreme violence between prisoners (mostly black) and guards followed. Three days after the Soledad homicides, the warden announced over the prison radio that the coroner's jury had ruled that the killings were justified.[1] That evening, a guard was beaten and thrown to his death from the third tier of a close-custody cell block in Soledad. Three black prisoners were charged with the crime. One of them, George Jackson, who had been involved in many racial fights in his eleven years in prison, recently had adopted Marxist-Leninist ideology. He contacted Fay Stender, a San Francisco Bay Area "movement" lawyer. Stender rushed to Jackson's defense, found lawyers for the other "Soledad brothers," and began organizing a defense committee. Stender had many contacts in the Bay Area radical network, and many new left activists followed her swerve into prison issues. Huey Newton's imprisonment and Eldridge Cleaver's defense efforts already were multiplying the ties between political activists and the prison. Also, the war protest movement was losing its momentum, as Nixon's troop withdrawal had diminished public concern over the war. Many new left activists turned to the prison for a new issue to dramatize the injustices in society and to sustain radical political momentum. New radical prisoner support organizations formed, and some existing prison reform or self-help groups, influenced by the infusion of new left activists and radical ideologies, became more radical in their goals and strategies.

While the outside organizational activities accelerated, the violence between prisoners and guards increased, and another guard was murdered at Soledad in July 1970 (before 1970 the

[1] Later, in a civil rights action for the wrongful deaths of the three black prisoners, a Salinas, California, jury found that eight Soledad staff members had willfully and unjustifiably conspired to kill the three prisoners. Ming S. Yee, in extensive interviews, discovered the extreme hostilities that were festering in Soledad's O wing and that resulted in the following actions: (1) the guards released prisoners who were expected to begin fighting, (2) the prisoners fought, (3) the guard, Opie G. Miller, fired five shots and hit three black prisoners in the middle of their torso, and (4) the guards took over thirty minutes to carry the mortally wounded prisoners to the hospital, although it was adjacent to O wing. The prisoners were all dead by then (*The Melancholy History of Soledad Prison* [New York: Harper's Magazine Press, 1973]).

murder of a guard was rare).[2] Seven more black prisoners were charged with the crime. Then Jonathan Jackson, George's seventeen-year-old brother, attempted to free three black San Quentin prisoners from the Marin County Courthouse. Jonathan Jackson, two of the prisoners, and the judge were killed in the shootout. The surviving prisoner, Ruchel Magee, and Angela Davis were charged with crimes related to the escape attempt. In August 1971, George Jackson, two white prisoners, and four guards were killed in what appears to be another escape attempt. Six black and Latino prisoners were charged with murder and other crimes. All these incidents resulted in famous court cases and produced active defense committees.

In the same period, a wave of organized prisoner strikes and other disturbances passed across the country. Prisoners who considered themselves political activists led the strikes and made demands that were aimed at basic structures in the prison, criminal justice system, and society. A prison political movement was underway.

The Backdrop To understand the shape and size of the prison movement, we must consider the period, 1970 to 1975. During these years, the number of U.S. citizens who were profoundly critical of their society in general and several of its arrangements and activities in particular (for example, racism, sexism, and the Vietnam War) was continuing to grow and becoming more vociferous and militant. This large, loose social movement — made up of racial minorities, new left activists, middle-class and middle-aged liberals, and even upper-class "radical chic" patrons — never became a majority (as clearly demonstrated by George McGovern's trouncing by Richard Nixon in the 1972 presidential election). But it constituted a very prominent, active, assertive, sometimes aggressive minority who for several years disrupted the normally even flow of conventional activities, shamed and quieted more conservative and conventional citizens, and, in the minds of

[2] In a summary of prison homicides, Peter C. Buffum concludes that the homicide of staff by prisoners was extremely rare before the mid-1960s, rose slightly afterwards, and then rose sharply in some prisons around 1970. See "Prison Killings and Death Penalty Legislation," *Prison Journal,* Spring–Summer 1973, pp. 49–57.

many, threatened to grow and radically to transform U.S. society. It did not continue to grow, but peaked somewhere between 1970 and 1975 and then subsided, allowing a conservative reaction to follow. When it peaked, the prison was one of its major issues.

This large social movement generated a widespread and critical perspective on prisons that influenced the thinking of many and perhaps most Americans, including prisoners awed by the movement's apparent size and import, which were magnified from the prison vantage point. More concretely, the movement supplied leaders and workers for the multitude of old and new prisoner organizations, lawyers for a new area of law (prison law), and participants and audiences for conferences, rallies, and other staged movement events.

This broader social context in which the movement developed is much more complex than I have made it seem here, but my concern is prisons and I have merely sketched in the backdrop so I may concentrate on the prison movement.

THE ORGANIZATIONS

Although this political movement's widespread publicity, infectious enthusiasm, and seemingly virtuous goals drew all organizations working on prison issues together and pushed them in a radical direction, the organization remained distinct and had different philosophies, goals, strategies, and memberships.

Self-Help Organizations   The first new organizations to appear in this era of prison history, self-help organizations primarily worked to improve the life circumstances of ex-prisoners. Their upsurge predates the prison movement by several years. Bill Sands, an ex-prisoner of San Quentin, described in his autobiography, *My Shadow Runs Fast,* how he regained an interest in the prison in 1964 after a series of sensational (and unbelievable) ventures.[3] After he received considerable initial

---

[3] Bill Sands in his autobiography claims to have been successful in several adventurous enterprises including mining diamonds and starting an airline in South America. See *My Shadow Runs Fast* (Englewood Cliffs, N.J.: Prentice-Hall, 1964).

financial backing from Clement Stone, a wealthy conservative who donated funds to various causes, he formed a self-help organization based on the approach employed by Alcoholics Anonymous. Seven Steps, which recommends a step-by-step self-improvement career patterned after AA's program, spread across the country and is still one of the biggest self-help organizations. After Seven Steps broke the ground, dozens of similar organizations sprang up: EMPLEO (Chicanos), SATE (blacks), the Fortune Society, and the Church of the New Song.

Self-help groups are fundamentally conservative. They define the problems of the prisoner and ex-prisoner very narrowly, either as problems of the individual (his character or personality) or a problem of being stigmatized as an ex-convict. They avoid recommendations or strategies aimed at effecting broad or fundamental changes in society's structures. During the movement years, members of self-help organizations became involved in more radical approaches, but these were not part of the self-help organizations' official policies, and often these members came into conflict with the larger organizations because of political activities.[4]

However, the self-help groups were significant in the prisoner movement in two different ways. For one, they were the largest prisoner organization. They did draw outside citizens into their organizations and often maintained outside branches, especially when they had funds to pay ex-prisoners to develop opportunities for other ex-prisoners, but most members were inside. Administrations permitted — in fact, often encouraged — self-help organizations as an alternative to other, more political groups; and many prisoners preferred self-help organizations because the prisoners were more interested in self-advancement than political change. These large groups of prisoners, who met regularly and maintained systematic contacts with outsiders, often were mobilized into political actions. They drew many

[4] While we were organizing the Prisoner's Union, several ex-convict employees of the Seven Steps Sacramento office participated in the union's formation. This led to a break between the national organization and the Sacramento office and eventually an official policy prohibiting political activities for Seven Step employees.

persons into the prison arena to help prisoners, and then these outsiders witnessed unanticipated abuses and moved toward more radical forms of action.

Self-help groups were also significant because they offered the first encouragement for the ex-convict to "come out." Formerly, being an "ex-con" in conventional realms was something that one must hide or live down. After Bill Sands and Seven Steps, it became acceptable, even prestigious, to be an ex-convict, and many individuals unabashedly and proudly announced that they were ex-convicts. In fact, a career — that of the professional ex-convict — appeared and was used by many more or less successful imitators of Bill Sands. This opened the door for admitted ex-convicts to a variety of conventional endeavors, including political activities.

Prisoner Rights Groups The prisoner rights groups that began to multiply just before the onslaught of the prison movement inherited an old tradition in the United States: the prison reform tradition, which itself began with prisons in this country and is even blamed for creating prisons.[5] In the 1960s, this tradition underwent basic alterations. In earlier periods, reformers believed that prisoners were fundamentally different than decent, law-abiding citizens. Prisoners were moral or physiological inferiors, and because of this they were psychologically flawed. Out of their sense of humanity, the old prison reform groups worked to eliminate excessive cruelty and to provide opportunities for these inferiors to redeem or remake themselves.

The post-1960 rights groups were influenced by new libertarian viewpoints that spun off the civil rights movement and new academic perspectives on criminals, in which the distinction between the criminal and the noncriminal was fading. They tended to view the felon as a person who was essentially like other citizens, except perhaps for a background of excessive discrimination and reduced life chances. Consequently,

[5] Many students of the prison argue that a group of Philadelphia reformers, including Benjamin Franklin and Benjamin Rush, planned and brought into existence the first prison used for punishment in the United States. The most current analysis of this early period in the history of prisons is David Rothman, *The Discovery of the Asylum* (Boston: Little, Brown, 1971).

the new prisoner rights groups strived to reduce the differences in the legal status and social circumstances of the prisoner and the free person.

This general goal divided into many subsidiary goals, such as elimination of inhumane treatment, expansion of constitutional rights, reduction or removal of barriers to communication between prisoners and outsiders, introduction of meaningful work and fair wages to prisoners, and complete restoration of all citizens' rights and privileges after release from prison. Most rights groups in the 1960s abandoned the goal of rehabilitation, because they believed that rehabilitation inaccurately implied that criminals were different and that the society had the right or expertise to change them. The rights groups agreed that society must do something to convicted felons, but must not strip them of all their rights, punish them excessively, reduce their capacities, or stigmatize them permanently. However, the groups did not agree on what should be done. Their ideas on this subject ranged from short sentences in a humane prison to work in public service while living in the community.

The membership of the rights groups varied. Some, such as the National Prisoners' Rights Associations in Massachusetts and Rhode Island, emerged in a particular prison and had mostly prisoner members; a few, such as the Committee for Prisoners, Humanity and Justice in California, were organized outside by a mixture of ex-prisoners and "squares" and had a small inside following (or none at all); and others, such as the Prisoners' Unions in California, Minnesota, Ohio, and North Carolina, had both inside and outside constituencies. The non-ex-convict supporters tended to be liberal humanitarians, many of whom had been associated with libertarian organizations such as the American Civil Liberties Union, the American Friends Service Committee, and the Unitarian church.

Radical Organizations The primary interest of the third class, the radical groups, was in changing not the prison, but the society in general. To their members the prison issue was not an isolated or primary one, but another manifestation of the oppression of poor and nonwhite people by the exploitative capitalist society. They were attracted to the prison partly because it represented an opportune issue and partly because their early contacts with prisoners convinced some of them that a few prisoners would emerge as leaders in outside radical activities. They had a romantic view of prisoners' general humanity and sincerity. For example, early in her involvement in the prison movement Fay Stender wrote: "I certainly feel that, person for person, prisoners are better human beings than you would find in any random group of people. They are more loving. They have more concern for each other. They have more creative potential." [6]

To many radicals, the preprison and prison experiences of many prisoners laid bare the injustices and contradictions of U.S. society and instilled prisoners with exceptional insights. Several prisoners or ex-prisoners (Eldridge Cleaver and George Jackson being the best known) whose writings revealed a complex analysis of racial and class discrimination in the United States and a deep commitment to revolutionary values helped to inspire this faith. The radical groups believed that prisoners were political prisoners for the following reasons: they had committed crimes because of unnatural, unjust, and inhumane strains or pathological socialization, which stem from the relationships in a capitalistic society; they were pressured into economic crime as a means of surviving in an economically exploitative capitalist society; they were framed by police for crimes that they did not commit because of political activities; or they were actually conscious perpetrators of political crimes, such as acts committed in protesting the war, racial discrimination, or the capitalist society in general. [7]

Further separating them from the other prisoner support groups was the radical groups' belief that racism was the central issue in justice in the United States. Many, perhaps most, of the new left activists and organizations had previously adopted racism as one of their central issues, and many radicals drawn to the prison issue maintained a mistaken belief that the vast majority of prisoners in the United States were non-

[6] Introduction, in Eve Pell, *Maximum Security* (New York: Dutton, 1972), p. 13.

[7] This definition is similar to that offered by Angela Davis, *If They Come in the Morning* (London: Orbach and Chambers, 1971), p. 51.

white. (Actually, whites were more than half, but their percentage was decreasing.)

Most of the radical groups were organized on the outside and had only a few prisoner members. These were invariably covert, because prison administrators did not knowingly permit radical groups to exist in prison. The outside members were drawn from the new left, which was composed of a small number of committed active members of radical organizations and a larger, less committed segment of part-time activists who drifted in and out of movement activities. When a group had inside members, they were mostly nonwhite. Except for a few white radicals, some of whom had been activists before going to prison, white prisoners shunned and even resented the radical groups. Most white prisoners were conservative in their political beliefs and at least latently racially hostile. They were not drawn to the more radical perspectives and were resentful of the focus of outside radicals on racism and black prisoners.[8] To them, the radical groups' descriptions and interpretations suggested that they, the white prisoners, were nonexistent or experienced lavish privileges in prison. On the other hand, most black prisoners leaned toward revolutionary interpretations, although they were not committed to actual political organizations or activities. Leo Carroll labeled these persons "half-steppers" in his study of Rhode Island prisons in 1972.

> For want of a better term, we may identify the vast majority of the black inmates as "half-steppers." Half-steppers talk the talk of revolution, but do not "walk the walk." Their public behavior manifests an intense commitment to revolution. Their cells are decorated with portraits of revolutionary heroes and posters proclaiming "Power to the People," "The Revolution is Now," "Burn, Baby, Burn," and "Off the Pigs." . . .
>
> The very public and external nature of these affirmations, however, reveals them as self-conscious attempts to collectively claim and support an identity to which they in fact

[8] These conclusions were reached after extended discussions with prisoners and ex-prisoners during the early 1970s. Also, Leo Carroll's study of a Rhode Island prison supports them (*Hacks, Blacks and Cons* [Lexington, Mass.: Lexington Books, 1974]).

are not fully committed. The prison style of the "half-stepper," their actual behavior and private conversations, reflect an importation and enactment of the perspectives of "soul" within the prison. Where the orientation of the "revolutionary" is to the outside and the future, the orientation of the "half-stepper" is to the present and to the opportunities for self-expression within the prison.[9]

OUTSIDE ACTIVITIES

When the prison issue became a movement and drew the attention, support, and participation of thousands of free citizens, most of the control of organized activities shifted to outside persons. With their limited resources, mobility, and means of communication, prisoners could not direct the proliferating groups or plan the myriad activities, most of which were situated outside. Even if the prisoners could have run the movement, many would have chosen not to do so because they were humbled by its apparent size and significance, which were magnified greatly by the mass media's distorted lens. So, most prison movement activities were outside activities led and conducted by free citizens. Since the invasion of outsiders irritated and threatened prison officials so much and precipitated such an enormous and destructive reaction, we must carefully examine what the outsiders actually did.

The Trials   The few trials of celebrated, "political" prisoners that were highly publicized ignited the movement and consumed most of the radical activists energies. The Soledad brothers' defense, which went on for several years, was the first of a series. In each case there was an incident, usually involving violence, and then some prisoners, usually black, were charged with crimes related to the incident. The particular incidents were chosen because the prisoners charged with the crimes were defined as political activists, because the incidents were seen as acts of political protest, or because the selection of defendants was perceived as racially prejudiced and politically motivated.

In each incident, outside activists organized a defense committee, raised funds for the defense, publicized their inter-

[9] Carroll, *Hacks, Blacks, and Cons,* pp. 104–5.

pretations of the incident, and attempted to expand participation in the defense committee's efforts in order to educate the uninformed about prisons, particularly about racism in prisons.

In their interpretations the defense committees emphasized three characteristics of the cases. First, they stressed the background of racial and class discrimination in the lives of the defendants. For instance, one of the defendant's lives is described in the San Quentin Six Defense Committee's pamphlet:

> Willie Tate is twenty-nine years old. He is black. He was born in Selma, Alabama and lived there with his mother and his father, a sergeant in the United States Army until he was six years old. Then the family moved to El Paso, Texas. He couldn't go to school in El Paso because they didn't have kindergarten and first grade for black children.
>
> The Tate family moved to California when Willie was about eight years old, and settled in Fresno. Willie Tate was first arrested when he was fourteen years old. There was an incident. Someone called him a "nigger." He responded appropriately to the insult. The police arrested him. He spent two years in a prison reformatory.[10]

Second, they stressed the harassment that the defendants had experienced and that stemmed from the racial prejudice of the prison staff or from the political activities in which the defendants had been involved. Another defense committee pamphlet reads, "The parole board considers this young man a 'trouble maker.' In one instance, he was placed in solitary — a cell with only a mattress and a hole in the floor — for refusing to be segregated in the back row of the San Quentin television room." [11] Finally, they emphasized the illegal and unethical procedures involved in investigating and prosecuting the cases:

> We do know that a veritable reign of terror descended upon the prisoners in the aftermath of the August 21st events. Survivors were stripped, clubbed, burned with cigarettes, shot, their heads shaved. When Fleeta Drumgo and John Clutchette

[10] *The San Quentin Six* (San Francisco: San Quentin Six Defense Committee n.d.), p. 9.

[11] *Soledad Brothers* (San Francisco: Soledad Brothers Defense Committee n.d.), p. 6.

appeared in court a few days later for a scheduled hearing in the Soledad case, they could hardly walk, and they tore off their shirts in the courtroom exposing the lacerations, welts and burns.[12]

The overall intent of these interpretations was to underscore the existence of unjust practices against poor people and racial minorities, the illegalities practiced by people in power, and, therefore, the general injustice and oppressiveness of the power structure in the United States. The San Quentin Six pamphlet is introduced with the following paragraph:

Anatomy of a frame up
The waves of the Watergate attempt to crush all political opposition do not begin nor end at the doors of the Democratic Party headquarters. They were already present in full force in our communities, in the factories across the country and behind the prison walls. The jails are filled with working people, many of them young, black, Chicano and Latino, Asian, Native American and white — victims of the brutal system of racism, exploitation and oppression; while the real criminals are to be found in the White House, the Pentagon and the Attorney General's office.[13]

The more radical participants in the prison movement concentrated on the trials of the celebrated political prisoners. The defense committees were usually organized by existing radical organizations or by individuals who were members of radical groups. The committees themselves constituted a big part of the radical sector of the movement.

Litigation of Prisoners' Rights The prison movement enticed a sizable group of lawyers into a totally neglected area of law, which became known as prison law. Their work was especially significant, because formerly there was virtually no law defining the rights of prisoners or limiting the powers of prison administrations.[14] The prisons were required by most

---

[12] *The San Quentin Six,* p. 16.

[13] Ibid., p. 2.

[14] "He [the convicted felon] has, as a consequence of his crime, not only forfeited his liberty, but all his personal rights except those which the law in its humanity accords to him. He is for the time being the slave of the State" (*Ruffin* v. *Commonwealth,* 62 Va. 790, 796 [1871]).

states' laws to avoid corporal punishment, keep prisoners alive, and release them according to the statutes on sentencing. With no externally imposed standards of review and almost unlimited discretion, prison officials regulated the prisoners' correspondence and visitation (sometimes denying them completely), governed prisoners' financial affairs, provided or denied medical services, and segregated prisoners in isolation cells under conditions of extreme deprivation. In addition, because of indeterminate sentences, "good time" laws, and parole systems, prison administrators in most states had some or almost complete control over the decision to release within the wide margins set by statutes. What this actually meant was that prison administrators could place prisoners in solitary cells, indefinitely isolate them from everyone but attorneys, and supply them with just enough food, clothing, and medical services to prevent them from perishing. In fact, nothing ever happened to prison administrators if prisoners did perish from ill-treatment. It may be argued that, by and large, prison administrators are not evil men and would not take advantage of their powers in such a manner unless there was some justification, such as extreme recalcitrance on the part of the prisoner. It is true that in most prisons they rarely abused their powers to the extreme, but they could and sometimes did. Moreover, prison administrators, staff, and guards, operating with unchecked powers and negative estimations of prisoners' motives, regularly treated prisoners arbitrarily and inhumanely. Two ex-prisoners described incidents involving exactly this kind of treatment.

I had a bad pain in my stomach and I went to sick line for a few days, but I couldn't get by the fucking MA [medical assistant]. He kept giving me aspirins and wouldn't let me see the doctor. Finally, my ulcer started really bleeding and they had to put me in the hospital. I goddam near died. Man, if you get sick in the slammer, you're fucked. If they don't want to treat you, that is just too bad.

They put me in the hole in Stateville because I kept filing writs. Then they took my law books, my paper, and all my writing material. I finally smuggled out a petition written on toilet paper in my own blood! I'm not lying; you can look it up. The case is in the books.

Whenever prisoners would present claims to the courts, they were traditionally denied on the grounds that courts had no jurisdiction or power over the internal management of prisons. The following language was typical: "The problem is moreover one which involves administrative discretion . . . which as an independent and abstract question is not within the jurisdiction of this court"; [15] "It is not the province of the courts to supervise prison discipline";[16] "Courts do not have the power and it is not their function or responsibility to supervise prisons." [17] The ideas expressed by this language came to be known in the 1960s, when they were under attack, as the "hands-off doctrine." [18]

The litigation by prisoners and prison movement lawyers began changing this. The change, goaded by prisoner unrest, was a slow, spasmodic, almost accidental shift that occurred on many fronts. The progress began in the early 1960s when the Black Muslims won an important series of court victories. The Muslims were trying to exist as a religious group in prisons, but prison officials persisted in trying to deny them any requests and repress them. Litigating from many prisons, the Muslims argued to the courts that the First and Fourteenth Amendments to the Constitution established their right to hold religious services on the same basis as Catholics and Protestants, to receive their newspaper, and to eat a special diet. Courts have traditionally been more sensitive to religious freedom than any of the other rights reserved to the people by the First Amendment, and after a period of struggle and uncer-

[15] *Feyerchak* v. *Hyatt,* 7 F.R.D. 725 (N.E. Pa., 1948).

[16] *Numes* v. *Miller,* 165 F. 2d 986, 987 (9th Cir., 1948).

[17] *Curtis* v. *Jacques,* 130 F. Supp. 920, 921 (W.D., Mich., 1954).

[18] This notion is well summarized in an influential law review article, "Beyond the Ken of the Courts: A Critique of Judicial Refusal to Review the Complaints of Convicts," *Yale Law Journal* 72 (1963): 506. For many decades, courts have grappled with the problem of reviewing decisions made by administrative agencies and have evolved fairly definite standards governing when and how such decisions should be subjected to judicial review. These standards are generally thrown aside when prison cases arise. Judges have shown no hesitation in making themselves experts on core samples of mineral ore or on the mechanisms that underwriters use to finance corporate expansion, but few judges have ever had the stomach for the task of learning about prisons.

tainty they largely agreed with the Muslims. These decisions expanded the constitutional rights available to all prisoners and paved the way for favorable First Amendment decisions in other areas, such as correspondence and receipt of books and magazines.

After the Muslims' court victories, all prisoners' chances of being heard by the courts increased. A series of cases expanded the remedies available under a writ of habeas corpus and removed procedural obstacles to filing such writs in federal court. Prisoners also found it easier to file suits alleging violations of constitutional rights by state officials under Section 1983 of the Civil Rights Act of 1877.

When courts finally listened to prisoners, inhumane conditions were revealed. The most dramatic case was *Holt* v. *Sarver,* concerning the Arkansas prison system.[19] After hearing undisputed testimony showing torture, rape, extortion, and assault to be as common as bed lice and after learning of the discovery of dirt mounds at the edge of the prison filled with decomposing bodies and nameless bones, an appalled federal court judge held the entire state prison system in violation of the Eighth Amendment to the Constitution, which prohibits cruel and unusual punishment. In the face of *Holt* and other only slightly less spectacular cases, judges found it very difficult to assume automatically that prisons in the United States were in the hands of expert administrators.

After the courts abandoned the hands-off doctrine, limited progress was made in changing prisoners' civil and legal status. For example, the courts addressed cruel and unusual punishment, but they sidestepped the basic issue by ruling only that particular instances brought before the court were or were not cruel and unusual and by failing to establish standards that could be used by lawyers in subsequent litigation. Moreover, virtually all these decisions pertained to isolation or segregation situations, and in only one "mainline" situation did the court rule against the prison administration. In this instance, the court ordered Arkansas to cease using prisoner trustees as guards and to begin to establish rehabilitation programs.

[19] 309 F. Supp. 362 (E.D. Ark. 1970).

A little more progress was made in the general area of citizen rights, particularly those guaranteed by the First Amendment (for example, freedom of speech). Prisoners have been granted the right to receive any literature that does not incite to violence or violate statutes regulating mailed material, the right to communicate through the mail without censorship to free citizens and with confidentiality to government functionaries and lawyers, and the right to adequate medical services (the last was never defined, however). But the courts did not venture far into this vast area: it generally limited the prison administrators' powers to make highly arbitrary and irrational decisions, but again did not set down binding standards.

The area in which the most progress was made was the introduction of some due process in judicial or quasi-judicial decision making. (It seems that judges, who live in a world of procedure, are more willing to uphold standards in this area.) Prison administrators and parole boards made a wide variety of decisions that vary the intensity and extend the length of punishment. These included classification decisions, in which the custody and location of imprisonment were decided; disciplinary decisions, in which prisoners could be placed in very punitive situations; and release and parole revocation hearings. Before the 1960s, there were no limits on the administrators' discretionary powers in these decisions. After a long series of court rulings, prisoners gained the right to some limited due process in disciplinary hearings (the rights to be advised of charges, to call witnesses, and to cross-examine hostile witnesses) and fuller rights in parole revocation hearings.

This movement forward by the courts came to a halt in 1974 with the United States Supreme Court's decisions in *Pell* v. *Procunier* and *Wolff* v. *McDonnell* and has gone into reverse with the decisions of *Meachum* v. *Fano* and *North Carolina Prisoners' Union* v. *Jones*.[20] These decisions have marked the resurgence of the hands-off doctrine in a new guise: courts do not deny jurisdiction or claim that the Constitution does

[20] 417 U.S. 817; 418 U.S. 539; 427 U.S. 215 (1976); 433 U.S. 119 (1977).

104

not apply to prisoners, they simply accept conclusions, allegations, and predictions made by prison officials as better evidence than any amount of facts, law, expert testimony, or common sense mustered by prisoners.

In summarizing the progress of the two decades of vigorous litigation in the prison law field, I must emphasize that prisoners still have very few rights and administrators continue to govern arbitrarily. Prisoners do receive more visits from more people, correspond with less restriction, and receive more literature and somewhat better medical treatment than in the past. Moreover, they are not returned to prison with quite such dispatch or lack of due process. But prison administrators and parole boards have actually discovered methods to obey the letter of the law, but not the spirit, or to avoid it entirely and to continue in their old arbitrary directions, despite their bitter complaints that the courts have created serious custody problems for them. Brian Glick, one of the movement lawyers, summed it up well: "Prisoners' rights to minimally decent living conditions, freedom from brutality, fair disciplinary procedures, and racial equality have been even less honored in practice than their rights of access to court." [21]

Actually, the most significant change produced by the litigation is the altered conception of the prisoner. He started as part noncitizen, part nonentity, and part subhuman over whom prison administrators had unlimited power to treat as they saw fit. This status was legally reflected in "civil death" statutes.[22] Now we have progressed to the conception of a prisoner as a citizen in a temporarily reduced legal status. This conceptual alteration, although it has not yet substantially changed the degree of punishment or future life possibilities of prisoners, is another facet of the claim of respectability that prisoners have been increasingly asserting for

[21] "Change Through the Courts," in Erik Olin Wright, *The Politics of Punishment* (New York: Harper & Row, 1973), p. 292. See also David F. Greenberg and Fay Stender, *The Prison as a Lawless Agency, Buffalo Law Review* 21 (1972).

[22] "He is civilites mortuus; and his estate, if he has any, is administered like that of a dead man." *Ruffin* v. *Commonwealth,* at 796.

twenty years. This improved conception of themselves and resultant demands for dignity play a very salient role in precipitating and shaping a reaction to the prisoner movement. It may also eventually play a part in more substantial changes in the management of prisoners.

Prison Conferences   Between 1968 and 1975, support groups and other organizations — churches, universities, and professional associations (probation officers or psychiatrists, for example) — planned and participated in dozens of conferences on prisons. Their central themes included such topics as "correcting corrections," "prisoner rights," "racism in prison," and "abolishing prisons." Usually they presented one or more keynote addresses, sometimes delivered by prison movement celebrities, including Angela Davis, Fay Stender, Jessica Mitford, Ramsey Clark, and William Kunstler. Panel discussions or workshops filled in the remainder of the schedule. The conferences ended with a final session or speech intended to summarize their efforts.

In organizing these conferences, the planners intended (1) to spread information and particular perspectives on prison issues, (2) to generate new insights into problems associated with the prison, (3) to plan strategies to reach agreed-on goals or to solve certain problems associated with the prison, (4) to create new organizations and expand participation in the prison movement, and (5) to convert or pressure decision makers (prison administrators, legislators, prosecutors, and judges) who sometimes attended the conferences.

Some education, organization, and recruitment occurred, but not nearly as much as the planners hoped.[23] What the conferences actually accomplished, more than their intended purposes, was to give the movement the appearance of substance and momentum and to create new or dignify old movement celebrities. Outstanding orators were rewarded with acclaim and leadership. When conferences were well attended, it appeared to all that there was high interest in the prison movement.

[23] I helped plan and participated in many conferences and witnessed very little conversion or follow-up organizational activities precipitated by the conferences.

106

INSIDE ACTIVITIES

While the outside organizations orchestrated the trials, the litigation, and the conferences, prisoners did not stand by idly. In many states they built on the model of the San Quentin Unity Day strikes and conducted a series of prison strikes or rebellions totally different from those of past eras: they were more organized, led by people who defined themselves as political activists, and aimed not at effecting concrete changes in prison routines (increased privileges or better food), but at making basic, far-reaching changes in at least the prison and the criminal justice system and perhaps in the society in general. The patterns in many of these disturbances was as follows. First, a group of prisoners of varying size and racial composition constructed a list of grievances or demands that revealed a far more complex analysis of the prison system and sought much more drastic alterations in the existing relationships and structures than demanded in previous prison disturbances. Second, this core group attempted to bring together and sustain a large coalition of prisoners, including all major racial groups in the prison, which would support the grievances (or demands) and the strategies planned by the organizers. Simultaneously, the organizers attempted to mobilize outside support, usually through prisoner support organizations if any existed in their area. Finally, they attempted to initiate forms of collective action, such as strikes or demonstrations that would force the administration to negotiate with them and would draw attention and sympathy from the public for their situation and grievances.

The nineteen-day strike at Folsom prison was the prototype. In 1968 a few Folsom prisoners tried to organize a sympathy strike for the San Quentin strikers with limited success. During the next two years some of these prisoners continued to plan a strike for Folsom. They developed a list of grievances that, as more and more individuals of different races and points of view became involved, expanded to a manifesto of twenty-nine demands.[24] In the summer of 1970 the organizers set a strike date for November 2, election day in California. They smug-

[24] See Appendix A for this manifesto.

gled out copies of the manifesto and asked for support from the proliferating prisoner support groups. At this time, two main clusters of groups existed: one composed of the more radical groups revolving around the active Soledad Brothers Defense Committee and the other composed of the rights and self-help groups, affiliated through a Coordinating Council of Prisoner Organizations, which was based in San Francisco and formed to bring different prisoner support groups together. The clusters planned and carried through a press conference on the steps of the state capitol and a demonstration outside Folsom's entrance to kick off the November 2 strike.

The strike began on time with a great majority of the prisoners staying in their cells instead of going to work or the yard. The warden, in turn, immediately locked down the prison (he refers to the strike as a nineteen-day lockdown). After the big splash on the first day, the outside groups tried to continue promoting support for the strike by organizing picket lines at the entrance to Folsom, contacting other groups, and describing the strike, the issues, and prisons in general in the mass media, particularly the few radio stations in San Francisco and Sacramento that gave audience to movement causes.

Folsom is located where the Sierras and the San Joaquin Valley join, twenty miles east of Sacramento, which is one hundred miles from San Francisco. The entrance to the grounds, unlike San Quentin's, is at least a mile from the prison itself and is out of sight from all prisoners. So it was difficult to organize outside picket lines and impossible to convey directly an impression of support to the prisoners. They knew about the strike support only through the radio stations, which they tuned into on battery-operated transistor radios. After two weeks, however, the batteries gave out, as did cigarettes and extra food that many prisoners had stored. Enthusiasm wore down, and when the warden circulated an offer to unlock the prison if the prisoners would go back to work, most of them agreed.

Similar strikes occurred in many state and federal prisons. They often started and progressed somewhat differently, but all contained some essential elements of this new type of political demonstration. At Attica, New York, in September 1971, after months of unrest and intense political activities on the part of a few prisoners, hundreds of prisoners went on a short and destructive rampage, secured part of the prison, held hostages, and then followed the pattern of the political demonstration described above. At Lewisburg, Pennsylvania, a federal penitentiary, in February 1972 several hundred prisoners refused to work, elected a strike committee, and then developed a list of demands. From then on, they pursued the political direction. At Leavenworth, Kansas, another federal penitentiary, in July 1973, prisoners in the dining room began rioting, two guards were seized as hostages, a prisoner committee was selected, and the hostages were released. Then the disturbances settled into the political demonstration pattern. At Attica again in September 1976 the prisoners went on strike, but this time they conformed to the total pattern. At Norfolk Prison in Massachusetts on July 30, 1978, after unsuccesfully pursuing a series of grievances with the administration and building a solid support network with outside organizations, the prisoners voted to go on strike. This strike, which lasted until October 1978, epitomizes the pattern. These are a few of the new political demonstrations, and there were many more.[25] They were not isolated incidents, but reverberations of the political eruptions centered in California. California influences went out in the interchange of prisoners from one prison to another and from one state to another; in contacts accomplished through the activities of outside organizers who were able to develop a weak national network; and in news stories of the California prison events carried by the popular media or a growing number of undeground newspapers, such as the *Anvil,* the *Outlaw* (which was mailed to over twenty thousand prisoners at the height of its circulation), *NEPA News,* the *Midnight Special, Penal Digest International, S.C.A.R. Times,* the *Freeworld Times,* and the *Fortune News.* Clear evidence of the interconnections between strikes is re-

[25] There were political demonstrations at Rahway State Prison, New Jersey, and the Nebraska State Penitentiary in 1971. In 1972 there were demonstrations at Patuxent, Maryland; Attica, New York; Walpole, Massachusetts; Terra Haute (federal penitentiary), Indiana; and Stillwater, Minnesota, and in 1973 at Southern Ohio Correctional Facility, Lucasville; Jackson, Michigan; Windsor, Vermont; Indiana State Penitentiary; and Joliet, Illinois.

vealed by the fact that the list of demands delivered to the warden of Attica and director of the New York Department of Corrections in May 1971, before the September riot at Attica, was the Folsom manifesto with a few word changes that were needed to make the demands applicable to the different laws and situation in New York. The strikers at Lewisburg were inspired by the Prisoners Bill of Rights from California. Ben Bagdikian described events at the beginning of the strike.

> Phillips continued. "For the benefit of guys who don't know me, my name is Ron Phillips. I work in the dental lab. I'm tired of the bullshit treatment I'm getting and I'm tired of the bullshit treatment I see my fellow convicts getting. These people don't give a damn about anybody."
>
> Someone shouted, "Rap on, baby!"
>
> "The paper in my hand is the Prisoners Bill of Rights and we do have rights whether the pigs know it or not. The prisoners in California drew up this document." [26]

Violence and Defiance Because of the prison movement, many more prisoners openly defied and physically attacked guards than in any other period in the history of our prisons. In past eras, violence against guards or other staff members was extremely rare. Also, it was less random. When prisoners attacked guards, it invariably followed some hostile interaction between them. During the prison movement, guards were often randomly selected for attack. Defiance — which was always present, but had been more subtle or covert — became open and bold.

James Jacobs, in his study of Stateville, witnessed this new tendency:

> Inmates simply refused to follow orders, refused to work and refused to follow the rules. When a lieutenant was called to "walk" an inmate, he was often confronted with ten or twelve of the inmate's fellow gang members surrounding him, challenging his authority. One Stateville guard explained: "The inmate will say, 'Fuck you, Jack, I'm not going.' Then a group of his gang will gather around him. I'll have to call a lieutenant. Sometimes, one of the leaders will just come over

[26] *Caged* (New York: Harper & Row, 1976), p. 40.

and tell the member to go ahead." The chief guard on one occasion was confronted by a line of inmates in the F house tunnel while he was escorting a gang leader to isolation. The inmates shouted threats. There were calls to "tear it down." The chief guard backed off while his captive returned to the cell house and barricaded himself in his cell.[27]

This defiance, which was mostly by black gang members in Stateville, would not have occurred as frequently or at all without the political activities of the 1960s. These gangs — the Black P Stone Nation, the Devil's Disciples, and the Vice Lords — were influenced directly or indirectly by the civil rights activities and were somewhat politicized. Prisoners in other states, particularly black prisoners, displayed much more hostility and defiance toward prison employees because of the ideas and mood spread by the 1960s political movements, including the prison movement. This defiance at times escalated into violence. For instance, the Attica riot began with a guard's attempting to remove two black prisoners, who were fighting on the yard, and his being stopped by other prisoners watching the fight.

Some of the killings resulted from planned prisoner movement activities. Many of the more radical participants in the movement, inside and outside prison, believed that violence was an inevitable part of the approaching or unfolding revolution and were prepared for it, even encouraged it. In fact, to many activists violence was more than a necessary and evil means to the final goal; it was a self-actualizing and ennobling activity.[28] Many killings were planned or occurred as a direct result of other planned activities, such as escapes. In a few of these incidents, such as the escape attempt at the Marin County Courthouse and the 1972 escape of a Chino prisoner, Ron Beaty, outside activists joined with prisoners in executing the plans. Both forms of violence, the spontaneous and the planned,

[27] *Stateville* (Chicago: University of Chicago Press, 1977), pp. 161–62.

[28] Many sections of the American left were influenced by Frantz Fanon, who argued that violence was not only necessary to overthrow colonialism, but was actually a "cleansing force" (*The Wretched of the Earth* [New York: Grove Press, 1963]).

111

were extremely provocative to administrations and staff. However, the few planned incidents threatened the staff in the extreme, particularly those in which the recipient of the violence was chosen randomly or outside movement activists were involved. These types of incidents were crucial in shaping the intense administrative response to the prison movement.

Demise of the Movement   By 1975 a variety of external and internal problems had intensified, and the prison movement floundered. This era, the Nixon era, was a period of putting the lid back on America. Many of the society's more powerful individuals and groups nervously had watched the developments of the 1960s, finally recoiled, and then coalesced. I cannot delve far into this complex period, but in a glance we can see that a broad reaction was spearheaded by Nixon's open and clandestine operations, but also propelled by most sections of the mass media and by some very influential segments of the eastern liberal-turned-conservative intelligenstia; it helped stop dissent in the United States. This reaction shifted the attention of citizens from the war, civil rights, the plight of the poor, and prisons to crime and the economy. In a survey of 1,991 households, Louis Harris discovered considerable sympathy for striking prisoners in 1972. In response to the question "In the recent take-overs of prisons by inmates, do you think the main reason for the outbreaks is more the result of prison authorities being too easy on inmates?" 58 percent answered that "authorities don't understand the inmates' needs," and only 23 percent responded that "authorities [are] too easy on inmates." [29] By 1975 this sympathy was consumed by fear of crime in the streets, which was fueled by an apparent increase in crime, particularly violent street crime, and by the mass media's persistent presentation of the horrors of contemporary crime in the city. The public support for the prison movement issues dwindled. Attendance at conferences fell off. Reporters failed to respond to press conferences. Donations from the public diminished.

Simultaneously, the small number of private foundations

[29] Reported in Louis Harris's column in the *Chicago Tribune,* February 7, 1972.

that had funded prison projects (the Stearn; Irwin, Sweeny, and Miller; Burden; and Ottinger foundations) followed fads or responded to mounting conservative pressures, and they lowered the prison issue on their lists of priorities. The Nixon government's withdrawal from the "war on poverty" (waged through the Office of Economic Opportunity) and its attack on crime through the Law Enforcement Assistance Agency transferred most government funds from the few organizations and projects sympathetic to or involved in the prison movement to police, departments of corrections, or private organizations that were fighting crime, not helping prisoners.

This combination of loss of funds and public support finished off most groups. All formal organizations need some financial resources to continue, and when the funds diminished, most prisoner movement organizations shrunk or disappeared. The loss of general public support damaged the movement in a more complex manner. First, most political movements require a large pool of marginal sympathizers who participate occasionally in some events, such as demonstrations and conferences. They give to the movement the appearance of size and momentum. When they are not present, many of the active participants, who are there less because of their commitment to beliefs and goals of the movement and more because of the excitement, drift away. This leaves only the hard core, who also become discouraged when the larger support base crumbles.

The strategy adopted by most of the radical groups in the prison movement, that of focusing on the trials of prisoner celebrities, unintentionally aggravated the problem of abandonment. The efforts of many hard-working and sincere volunteers were directed for months, even years, to a particular case, such as that of the San Quentin Six. The intention of the original organizers was to dramatize the situation of the poor and nonwhite people in the United States and in the criminal justice system and, thereby, to radicalize more and more people. The trials did involve people for a length of time, but failed to give them a more permanent, organized activity. When the trials were over, most of the defense committee people drifted away. The defense committees did not continue to work on other prison issues, and little in the way of general improvement in

113

the prison situation resulted from the trial strategy. The main benefit was that many persons who were charged with the celebrated crimes and who probably would have been convicted without the defense committees' efforts were acquitted.

These problems would have been enough to slow or defeat the movement, but it also experienced many internal difficulties that further weakened it and that have general relevance because they parallel the problems that hampered other political movements. Probably the most serious was intergroup conflict, intensified by vindictive animosity, which often produced an incapacity to cooperate in movement events and in a few instances led to divisive and destructive action. This was particularly true in California, the center of the prison movement. Distrust prevented many California groups from cooperating with others, some groups refused to join in collective enterprises with particular groups, and some groups split into hostile factions, which then bitterly attempted to destroy each other. At the height of the movement the central San Francisco Bay Area radical organization, the Prison Law Project, divided into two organizations that remained hostile toward each other and cooperated minimally. When one group was being considered for refunding, members of the other wrote a letter to the funding agency and criticized the other group. The funding agency did not refund the group, and it collapsed. The Prisoners' Union, which I helped organize, suffered a bitter split; and rumors, denunciations, and accusations that followed reduced our effectiveness for several years.

This intergroup conflict had many usual and unusual sources. One of the more usual was a typical group process. In order to survive, organizations invariably develop an *esprit de corps* and inflate the importance of the organization and its goals. This is essential when there is competition over insufficient funds, personnel, and external support, which was always the case in the prison movement. When organizations are also engaged in activities that may involve them in legal difficulties (which was true with some prison movement groups), secrecy intensifies these group dynamics and further isolates groups. These processes led to prisoner support groups' selfishly, uncooperatively, even divisively pursuing their own goals.

114

More importantly, differences in perspectives produced a level of distrust, animosity, and conflict. All three types of groups — self-help, prisoner rights, and radical — were guilty of this. The self-help groups believed that the other groups were not sensitive enough to their goal, the improvement of the life chances of the ex-prisoner, and that the others actually engaged in strategies that damaged the prisoners' life chances or, in the case of the radicals, sought changes in the society that would eliminate material opulence and other aspects of the self-help people's conception of the good life. The rights groups stood between the self-help and radical groups. On the one hand, they disliked the self-help groups because of their extremely individualistic goals.[30] On the other, the rights groups distrusted the radicals because they believed that the radicals were in the prison movement with a larger agenda — revolution — and that the radicals would readily sacrifice the rights groups' goals, the correction of injustices and inhumanities in prison. The radical groups distrusted the others because of their reluctance to concentrate on political and economic issues or to accept more forceful tactics.

In spite of the differences, the self-help and rights groups maintained some willingness to cooperate, at least on activities that were in the public eye, but they tended to distrust the radical groups. The self-help and rights groups believed that the radicals practiced more divisive and violent strategies. In addition, members of self-help and rights groups perceived that the radicals operated with "secret agendas," that is, they planned strategies within their own group and then entered into planning activities with other groups with the intention of manipulating them.[31] They believed that a few radical groups supported, even applauded, the acts of violence committed by prisoners against guards and that some outside radicals conspired to and occasionally engaged in acts of violence themselves. Consequently, the groups in the movement that prac-

[30] I participated in dozens of discussions in which such evaluations of other groups took place.

[31] In one instance, a radical organization asked the Prisoners' Union to join in the planning of a conference. Halfway through the planning process, we discovered that, in private sessions, the radical group had eliminated us from the conference.

ticed more open decision making and did not approve of violence did not trust some of the radicals.

The Higher Morality   The Bay Area radical groups not only alienated many of the self-help and rights groups, but they also developed intense suspicions and hostilities among themselves. This divisive propensity of radical groups, which is not restricted to the prison movement, is devastating to political movements and begs for a special analysis. A key quality of this propensity is self-righteous dogmatism, which so many radical groups acquired. In the prison movement, self-righteous dogmatism had several sources. In general, many participants in the new left movements of the 1960s were self-righteous, because they had been conventional citizens who suddenly discovered systematic inhumanity and injustice in their society. They collectively responded with self-righteous indignation. Also, at this particular juncture many young people were reeling away from earlier movements — civil rights, free speech, hippie, yippie, and war protest movements — which were relatively devoid of political theory, as well as formal social organization. The experience of formlessness had been unsettling; many persons recoiled and then rediscovered ideology. For a while in all radical movements, prestige was won by those who revealed sophistication in radical political theory, and competition over the right interpretation of Marx, Engels, Lenin, and Mao was intense. The new ideologues dogmatically brandished their correct ideologies.

Moreover, many of these new leftists had adopted some of the more materialistic radical theories. In the latter, all human phenomena are produced by social relationship, particularly economic relationships. People's position in the society, especially their role in the productive enterprise, determines their ideas or their "consciousness." The position of the workers in a capitalist country should produce an awareness of the oppression and exploitation that they are experiencing. However, the powerful ownership class deludes the working class with "false consciousness." The radicals who understand this process must work to dispel false consciousness and spread true consciousness. However, forms of false consciousness are like the temptations offered by the devil: they appear every-

116

where, not only among the workers and the more privileged members of the lower class who start identifying with the interests of the upper class, but even among other radical groups, who must be watched for "revisionism." This vulgar determinism, which was embraced by many of the new leftists who recoiled from less well defined earlier movements, also produced dogmatism.

These three sources do not explain some radical groups' extreme self-righteousness. It had emotional roots. Radical groups attracted "romantic moralists" who were deeply repulsed by social injustices that they strongly desired to correct. They also experienced, displayed, and even enjoyed intense emotions of pity, sorrow, rage, and anger in their sincere concern over injustice. These romantic moralists had considerable power in radical organizations because their expression of extreme emotions and their occasional demonstration of a willingness to sacrifice and to take risks inspired the ambivalent and quieted the less committed and less romantic. This occurred because the problems that the romantics bemoaned were seen by persons participating in the groups to be real and serious. Moreover, when the romantic moralists made emotional stands, a fear of dissent ran through groups, particularly when they were large and less structured.[32] The Attica Commission commented on this process, which appeared in the decision making by a prisoner in D yard during the riot.

> As a result, the "decision" [to reject the twenty-eight points] was never more than the initial emotional gesture of ripping up the 28 points and various noises of approval for the rhetoric that followed.
>
> Not only did the inmates lack a decision-making process, but most of them were reluctant to voice their opinions. Fear of dissenting was a theme running through many of the explanations for the rejection of the 28 points voiced by inmates in private interviews.[33]

[32] I witnessed this occurrence many times. On one occasion an individual tried to disagree with a speaker who had just delivered a fiery speech and was vehemently denounced by several emotional members of the audience.

[33] *Attica: The Official Report of the New York State Special Commission on Attica* (New York: Praeger, 1972), pp. 264–65.

The result was that some radical groups were dominated by the more emotional, romantic moralists, who tended to be self-righteous.

Another emotional source of self-righteousness was a dilemma that many utopian radicals experienced. According to the world views of many of the 1960s radicals, all the negative character attributes seen in the United States — selfishness, greed, and lust — are artifacts of our capitalist society. Under pure democratic socialism, humans are or will be unselfish, loving, cooperative, cheerful, honest, self-effacing, and so on. A dilemma often developed for many individuals and groups in the prison movement when they attempted to undo or overcome their own corrupt socialization and to purify themselves. Many of the more dedicated formed special groups or communes and practiced special routines, such as "encountering" and "criticism and self-criticism" to remove their bad qualities and cultivate the good.

Suppose that some or all these negative qualities are deeply rooted in U.S. citizens and cannot be wrenched out easily or at all. Then the utopian idealists who believed that these traits were unacceptable were caught in an insoluble predicament: they were confronted with their own unacceptable desires, sentiments, and impulses (e.g., lust, selfishness, laziness, and irritability) and they were convinced that these must be removed. This type of struggle often leads to vacillations between periods of self-righteousness and self-blame.

Equipped with self-righteous dogmatism, fired up by romanticism, some radicals attempted to manipulate, deceive, vilify, and slander not only prison administrators, staff, and guards, but other movement members as well. In addition, some applauded or even aided in acts of violence, such as murder. To them, their goals were pure and people who stood in their way were evil, so these acts were justified and necessary.

Opportunists   The prison movement had an unique susceptibility to ex-prisoner opportunists who penetrated many groups, led organizations in the pursuit of the opportunists' personal goals, expended scarce resources to support them and extricate them from personal and legal difficulties, disillusioned and alienated many sincere movement participants, and gen-

118

erally raised the level of internal conflict in the movement. The prison movement's susceptibility was related to two strong sentiments that were widespread among many of its participants. First, many movement people abhorred racism and feared being viewed as racist, especially by fellow participants. Second was the romantic attitude toward prisoners, particularly black prisoners, referred to above. Many of the most active movement members initially believed that prisoners' lives and prison experiences would convert them into talented and dedicated revolutionaries. In the case of some women prison movement participants, their romanticism was enhanced by mixed feelings of love, awe, and worship for some prisoners. For instance, one of the members of the central committee of the Soledad Brothers Defense Committee described her feelings toward the leaders of the Black Panther Party.

> I was in love with Jimmy. He was still mythy to me — and I got off on myths. I was completely fascinated with the Panther elite — the glamor, the bizarreness. It was my Hollywood, I'd never discussed anything with any of them, just watched in total awe. I didn't think I should talk to them or try to know them. They were the vanguard; I was a helper. I figured they were grateful for my help and I knew I loved having them lead me. I loved the way they looked, with their shiny, leather coats, and beautiful shoes (I wore a fatigue jacket and work boots). I was always very polite and obedient, never expecting them to show me any courtesy, but they always showed me respect, which made them just that much more awesome.[34]

The truth is that even at the peak of the prison movement only a very small minority of prisoners were committed to radical political activities. Most white prisoners, in fact, remained conservative. Probably the majority of nonwhite prisoners paid lip service to radical or revolutionary ideals, but avoided involvement in radical activities. However, it was not just the dedicated revolutionaries who joined the movement. Many opportunists and many more politically ambivalent individuals gravitated to the prisoner support groups.

[34] Betsy Carr, "Afterword," in James Carr, *Bad: The Autobiography of James Carr* (New York: Herman Grof, 1975), p. 209.

119

Contrary to many radicals' initial romantic beliefs, the prison experience and the life of deprivation before prison render a few individuals highly unscrupulous, self-serving, mean, crafty, and somewhat fearless. These same life experiences cause many more to be cynical and ambivalent. Many of the latter have participated in various deviant social worlds that justify or even glorify individualist, exploitative, and illegal courses of action, such as drug addiction, theft, pimping, and hustling. Usually, these seasoned "cons" are not totally committed to these deviant social worlds, but understand them and see them as life alternatives, especially in the absence of other, more rewarding conventional lifestyles.

When the political movements of the 1960s and then the prison movement loomed up, they appeared to prisoners inside the walls to be much larger, exciting, and lucrative than they were in actuality and to be, therefore, appealing alternative lifestyles. The prison movement sprouted in a wasteland and was picked by many prisoners as one of the rare, potentially rewarding options open to them.

On release the few committed convict revolutionaries, such as Eldridge Cleaver, tended to move quickly beyond the prison movement to larger political wars. Most of the ambivalent ex-prisoners tried the movement, were disappointed, and moved on, very often back to deviant activities (not necessarily because they preferred deviant to conventional lifestyles, but because there were no satisfying conventional ones available to them). Many opportunists, however, found the movement especially suited to their talents and needs. It offered them access to "movement chicks," fame, some financial support, a front for illegal activities, and a defense — that of police harassment because of their political activities — when they were arrested.

A few skilled opportunists were able to rise to positions of leadership in existing organizations or to gather a following and establish their own by playing on the susceptibilties of the participants who were not ex-cons, the vast majority of whom were white. The opportunists exploited their ex-convict status and their race (if they were nonwhite) and cleverly employed deceit and threats of violence. Once in a position of leadership, they were difficult to neutralize or expel. If they were black, it was more difficult. The other members were continually deceived by the opportunists' duplicity or intimidated by fear of being physically harmed or labeled racist. The opportunists splintered or destroyed many groups, led others in directions harmful to the goals of the movement, and drove away many sincere movement participants.

The Prisoners' Union coped with many opportunists who came to our meetings, sometimes continued to work with us while they looked for self-serving possibilities, and usually left when it became clear that there were little money and not much fame or other advantages. But one exemplary opportunist stayed on and came close to destroying our organization. He loudly presented himself at the second organizing meeting by challenging the legitimacy of the interim board of directors, which had been chosen at the first, small meeting. Because of his reputation as a bully and informer in prison, he was disliked by most of the ex-prisoners present, but his aggressive display in the style of the "hog" (a tough convict) won him election to the first board of directors as the minister of prisons. For the next year, he participated in the planning and public activities of the union, always presenting himself as a true convict who was looking out for the interests of prisoners. He was extremely aggressive and threatening to the other organizers, and three board members left the union because of his intimidation. All the while, he continued a full "street life": pimping, hustling, and dealing drugs.

After tolerating his behavior for more than a year, those of us in the San Francisco office unsuccessfully attempted to eject him from the union. When we failed, we organized a new corporation with a new board of directors, but the same philosophy and goals. He continued to lead the original union, but, for all intents and purposes, it continued as a mechanism for supplying him with financial support, entrée into movement events, a front for illegal activities, and a defense when he was arrested. Between 1970 and 1974, he was arrested at least four times for felonies, but never convicted. On one occasion, he was returned to prison for parole violation, which precipitated demonstrations by prison movement groups. He was released after a few months. On two occasions, persons arrested with him were sent to prison for felonies. On two others, the main witnesses changed their testimony in his favor. In one of these cases, he had persuaded one of the very radical and violent groups to help him intimidate the witness. He was shot while sitting in his automobile with a young, female schoolteacher from a small town north of San Francisco.

Our efforts were damaged considerably because of his attempts to alienate other groups from us. He widely claimed that we ejected him because he was black and we were racists, that we were misusing funds, and that we had turned him in to the police, all of which were untrue and very damaging accusations among ex-prisoners and movement groups. Whether or not they believed his accusations, many groups would not cooperate with us for many years.

CONCLUDING REMARKS

When the external supports for the organizations were withdrawn, these internal weaknesses intensified and fractionalized the movement. At present, the public cannot be bothered with prisoners. The courts are shamelessly taking back some of the rights extended to prisoners at the height of the movement, and various state and federal legislatures are juggling punitive and rational sentiments in adopting less indeterminate sentence laws. (This motion will be discussed in chapter 8.) Meanwhile, prison administrators are recovering from the relief that they experienced when it became clear that the movement was rather puny after all. Now they are starting to notice the wreckage that was left after the movement subsided. This wreckage, they should recognize, was produced more by their overreaction and by other conflicts within the staff than by the movement itself. To understand the present situation, we must examine the reaction carefully.

5
Reaction

The administrative reaction surpassed the prison movement in impact and consequences. An underlying conflict that had been festering within many prison administrations ever since their serious experimentation with rehabilitation added force to the reaction. In some prisons the older "custody" faction had been relegated to secondary importance, and in all treatment-oriented state systems it had its power and prestige reduced by the ascendant "treatment" faction. The old guard never stopped struggling to maintain its integrity and hold on to power. When the prison movement swung things back into its direction, this group returned to full power with renewed strength and considerable vengeance. To understand its return to power and the consequences of this return, we must first understand the two factions and their struggle.

The Custody Faction   No matter what other goals prisons have attempted to achieve from time to time — reform prisoners or earn money with convict labor, for example — two tasks have always been their primary responsibility: preventing escapes and maintaining internal order. The guard force — the captains, lieutenants, sergeants, and line officers — have been charged with these as their first and almost exclusive duties. Combining their class and ethnic orientations with their experiences on the job, these guards have generated a special approach to prison work, the custody orientation. It rests upon three basic tenets: (1) the primary purposes of prisons are to punish prisoners and protect society; (2) prisoners cannot be trusted; and (3) in order to maintain control over prisoners, strict discipline must be maintained. Guards openly defend these tenets as the most important aspects of their work. For instance, Louis "Red" Nelson — an old-school administrator — addressed the prisoners after replacing the treatment-oriented warden following the near race riot at San Quentin in 1967; he reminded them that they were in prison primarily to be punished. Members of the guard faction have consistently articulated the theme that prisoners cannot be trusted. S. K. Weinberg, in his study of the prison community before World War II, recorded the following statements: "The officials, especially the guards, regard the convicts as criminals after all, 'as people who can't and shouldn't be trusted,' and as 'degenerates who must be put in their place at all times.' " [1] Donald Cressey, who wrote about the conflict between the "custodial-punitive" and the treatment orientations emphasized the discipline aspect of the custody orientations:

> Orders are to be obeyed simply because they are given by a prison employee, and rules are to be followed simply because one is a prisoner. Disobeying rules or orders is "insubordination" and is tantamount to seeking freedom illegally, for such action disturbs the routine and "discipline" of the organization. [2]

Most custodial factions share other attitudes that they do not admit so openly, but are very relevant in understanding their reaction to the movement. The most important is racial prejudice. This should not surprise us, because they are mainly white Americans and racial prejudice has been a widespread, if not dominant, attitude in the United States. But guards are more racially prejudiced than the average citizen, partly because they come from a highly racist segment of the society. James B. Jacobs and Norma Meacham Crotty describe the social characteristics of guards:

---

[1] "Aspects of the Prison's Social Structure," *American Journal of Sociology,* Mar. 1942, p. 719.

[2] "Prison Organizations," in J. March, ed., *Handbook of Organizations* (New York: Rand McNally, 1965), p. 10.

Because most prisons are located in remote rural areas, the guards tend to be drawn from the ranks of the unemployed and marginally employed in small towns and farm areas. A study in Illinois found that 41 percent of the respondents were unemployed at the time they became guards. The great majority of all prison guards are white males; in 1968, only 10 percent of line corrections officers were nonwhite. In that year, the average age of a correctional officer was about forty, and only 10 percent of the guards had educational credits beyond high school. Only 54 percent of the guards in Illinois had a high school diploma; eleven guards in the entire state had four-year college degrees.[3]

In other words, guards have been largely white, rural, relatively less educated and unemployable males who took a job at a prison because they could not find more desirable, better-paying work elsewhere. This set of characteristics delimits one of the most prejudiced categories in the United States.

Guards' racism takes three forms. First, they do not like, and in fact often hate, nonwhites. A guard who had denied to the Attica Commission that there was racism at Attica explained why prisoners practiced voluntary segregation in the mess hall: "How would you like to sit between two coloreds while you were eating?"[4] Moreover, most white guards believe that nonwhites are inferior. Another officer explained to the Attica Commission that black and Spanish-speaking prisoners had the undesirable jobs in the prison, because they were "better suited for these jobs," and another stated that "it is hard to find coloreds who can do good clerical work."[5] (In truth, 17 percent of the black prisoners, as compared with 28 percent of the white, had finished high school.[6]) Finally, the guard force, with a rural background and poor education, misunderstand the perspectives or subcultures of most prisoners, particularly of nonwhite, urban prisoners. They not only completely fail to comprehend the categories and meanings of the

[3] *Guard Unions and the Future of Prisons* (Ithaca, N.Y.: Institute of Public Employment, Cornell University, 1968), p. 2.

[4] *Attica: The Official Report of the New York State Special Commission on Attica* (New York: Praeger, 1972), p. 81.

[5] Ibid., p. 81.

[6] Ibid., p. 490.

various subcultures that abound among prisoners, but also attribute false motives and values to prisoners.[7]

Another attitude that most guards share because of their class and ethnic background is conservatism. Like their richer, somewhat more prestigious cousins, the city policemen, guards tend to support politicians like Barry Goldwater, George Wallace, and Ronald Reagan; to hate communism; to believe that traitors to America, particularly radical Jews, blacks, and hippies, are destroying the country; and to be intolerant of homosexuals, drug use, and deviant practices.

The nature of guards' work tends to underscore these tenets and prejudices and to render guards more hostile and inhumane toward prisoners. In an experiment at Stanford University, a mock jail was constructed and a group of volunteers from Palo Alto were randomly divided into guards and prisoners. With the sole instruction to "maintain the reasonable degree of order within the prison necessary for its effective functioning," the guards began to treat prisoners in a "hostile, affrontive, and dehumanizing" manner, so much so that the experiment had to be aborted after six days because of the stress experienced by the prisoners.[8] The experimenters argue that the tendency to develop inhumanity is inherent in the guards' position. I tend to agree with this conclusion, but I am not sure that this is what this particular experiment revealed. The volunteers were all naive about prisons and knew that this was an experiment. They seemed to be attempting to imitate their distorted images of the guard and prisoner. The guards, for instance, wore the mirror sunglasses seen on a guard in a popular movie, *Cool Hand Luke,* that had been released two years earlier. The experiment may have created a very unique dynamic or been more like a hazing, in which young men attempt to make it difficult for pledges, but are not

[7] For four years, I worked as the clerk for the kitchen sergeants or as a waiter in the officers' dining room and was the unobtrusive, sole prisoner audience to many conversations between guards. I was repeatedly amazed at their misinterpretations of prisoners' values, beliefs, and motives.

[8] Craig Haney, Curtis Banks, and Philip Zimbardo, "Interpersonal Dynamics in a Simulated Prison," *International Journal of Criminology and Penology,* 1973, pp. 69–97

guided by well-established routines. (Hazings result in very cruel punishments, even deaths.)

Whether or not simulated guards' work creates inhumanity, there are aspects of actual guards' work that do so. It must be remembered that prisoners are held in real deprivation for long periods of time. Also, there is a long tradition among prisoners of hating bulls, screws, or hacks. Even in the era of the Big House, when prisoners tended to achieve an accommodation with guards, prisoners did try to express their hostility, often subtly, and to manipulate guards to their own advantage. In particular, they very often intimidated or attempted to corrupt new and younger guards who were often unsure of themselves and sometimes tried to make a good impression on prisoners. Malcolm Braly, in his novel about San Quentin, has captured a typical experience of new guards.

> Then Preston heard a sound he dreaded. In one of the cells just across from him an inmate hidden in the darkness was pushing his breath through his teeth to make a noise like air leaking from a punctured inner tube, bubbling through the spit. Preston knew what to expect.
>
> "See the sweet little bull?" an anonymous voice asked in a tone that combined both amusement and obscenity.
>
> Preston jerked his eyes away. He felt his face growing hot. Pay no attention to them, his watch lieutenant had told him; if they see they're getting to you they'll never let you up.
>
> "Pussy on the gun rail," another voice called.
>
> "Hey, sucker, don't rank my action," the first voice continued with mock seriousness. "I saw her first. Didn't I, baby? Slip over here on the tier and I'll give it to you through the bars." [9]

Another aspect of guards' work that promotes negative attitudes toward prisoners and also stems from the prisoners' state of deprivation is that guards must commingle constantly with other humans, some of whom they know well and like, who live in obviously reduced circumstances and are unhappy in them. This poses a moral dilemma for the guards. They must have an explanation and justification for the disparity between

[9] *On the Yard* (Boston: Little, Brown, 1967), p. 52.

the prisoners' circumstances and their own and a rationale for refusing to respond to the prisoners' frequent supplications for special favors or contraband. Their solution has been to embrace the readily available theory that prisoners deserve their fate.[10]

One last aspect of guards' work rounds out the orientation. Their primary tasks are extremely difficult, and there are no proven strategies for accomplishing them. A few prisoners will continue to devise new methods of escape and engage in new forms of conflict and disruption. A demonstration of the difficulty and the absence of expertise in these areas is the failure of Warden Red Nelson, an ex-captain with a reputation of being tough, but fair. When he was appointed warden of San Quentin after the 1967 near riot, the associate warden told me, "now most of the nonsense will stop just because Nelson's warden." San Quentin under Nelson, in spite of his long experience and the support of the guard force, experienced the bloodiest era in modern prison history.

When prisons are reproached for escapes, riots, and other forms of disorder among prisoners, the guard force receives the brunt of the criticism. On the other hand, they are not rewarded for any accomplishments, not even prevention of escapes and maintenance of order. (The prison receives no attention when things are running smoothly.) Rewards for rehabilitative progress, if it is claimed, go to the treatment branch. The guards are only criticized or ignored.

The strategy and the values that have resulted from this bind parallel those in the military, which the prison guard force resembles in many ways. They all revolve around the theme of playing it safe by never letting responsibility fall on oneself:

[10] Not only guards embrace this theory. When Federal District Judge George Harris questioned Soledad Prison's chief physician and psychiatrist to discover how they could tolerate the horrible conditions that existed in the prison's solitary confinement, they offered him theories of unworthiness. The medical officer defined an "incorrigible": "one that the psychiatrists have given up on, we have given up on and everybody else has and there is not much hope for him." The psychiatrists talked about "destructive code" followers and "the expert group of miseries of mankind" (Ming S. Yee, *The Melancholy History of Soledad Prison* [Harper's Magazine Press, 1973], Op. Cit., pp. 19–21).

"Cover your ass." There are two main techniques of accomplishing this. First, never innovate. Follow standard procedures. If something criticizable occurs and standard procedures ("the book") were followed, the individual cannot be blamed. Second, never make a decision without getting approval from above. The collective effect of this approach is the norm of maintaining existing practices and a resultant strong tendency to meet any change with individual discomfort and resistance.

THE TREATMENT ORIENTATION

The treatment orientation must be divided into two phases, early and late. The early orientation was built around the concept of the criminal as an emotionally disturbed or maladjusted individual, and it was a system of individualized responses to his sicknesses. Donald Cressey, in his contrast of the custody and treatment orientations, described the ideal of early treatment employees:

> The assumption in the treatment prison is that, to the fullest extent possible, each role in the organization must be integrated in a system directed at a single goal, rehabilitation of inmates according to their individual needs for treatment. The conception is likely to be that of a "stream of action" in which clients or patients, like raw materials, pass through the prison and have various rehabilitation operations performed on them, each according to his needs. The security and housekeeping activities are, at most, a "framework" in which these operations take place.[11]

In actuality, the early treatment orientation almost invariably had to develop within existing prison operations, which had been dominated by the custody approach. So, except for a few atypical experiments — usually in very small institutions, perhaps minimum security camps — treatment staff had to share power with custody; this meant that they had to make important concessions when real or imagined matters of custody were involved. It also meant that they developed an ability to live with this dilution of their philosophy and approaches and to continue to operate as if treatment were possible and most im-

[11] "Prison Organizations," p. 14.

portant, although actually custody had influenced or dominated the decision making. For example, the classification committees referred to earlier typically included both custody and treatment people. Custody staff prevailed in many decisions, because they could raise the specter of escape or violence. Treatment staff acquiesced in these instances, because they shared a concern for avoiding these outcomes or they were aware that the top administration would side with custody on disputes involving these dangers. When they gave in, treatment staff often constructed a therapeutic rationale for the decision. They participated in this hypocrisy, because they were trying to keep up the appearances of a humane, individualized treatment routine in order to maximize participation on the part of the prisoners. They understood that faith in treatment routines was their cornerstone.

It has been my impression that the type of staff person who filled the treatment ranks tended to be the less intelligent, less creative, and less ambitious college graduates with B.A.'s in the social sciences or social welfare. The prison received many highly intelligent, creative, and ambitious individuals, but the low pay, ongoing conflict with custody, and general sluggishness of a prison bureaucracy tended to drive the more talented away. It also stifled the ambitions of the many who remained.

In the late 1960s the early treatment orientation fell into disrepute. The treatment arm did not give up, however. They fashioned a new version of treatment, which was more consistent with the new conceptions of the individual that followed the civil rights movement. In another study I referred to this new approach as an "active" conception, as opposed to the earlier "passive" one:

> The "passive" conception of rehabilitation has become unacceptable to many humanitarian, well-meaning social scientists and penologists. They have been unwilling to abandon the dream of practicing rehabilitation successfully even though, for many reasons, moral and scientific, it is suspect. What has occurred is that a new form of rehabilitation has appeared. It will be referred to here as the "active" version of rehabilitation. In it, the intent is to improve the quality of the

130

clients' lives and the society by reshaping those to be rehabilitated into more effective, self-sufficient, self-actualized,
socially aware, and socially involved individuals. Many correctional programs have been introduced in the last few years
which operate with some version of this active conception
of rehabilitation.[12]

In the new treatment era a small number of more adventurous individuals joined the prison treatment enterprise,
and some of the existing treatment staff were inspired to strike
out in more assertive and innovative directions. The new mood
of the country, generated by the civil rights and other political
movements and by the government's apparent endorsement of
radical political change through the "war on poverty" and the
Office of Economic Opportunity, had reached the prison staff.[13]

Most of these new treatment people were also college
graduates who had participated in or at least brushed against
civil rights and war protest activities in their college years.
Most of them were ignorant about prisons, but convinced that
prisons were bad and most prison personnel were reactionary,
intolerant, and mean.[14]

THE STRUGGLE BETWEEN CUSTODY AND TREATMENT

In the first era of treatment, about 1950 to 1965, the conflict
between custody and treatment was contained. Custody staff
resented the treatment staff, who received most of the accolades
and the top jobs in states where rehabilitation was emphasized,
such as California, New York, and New Jersey. They also resented the deflation of their values about handling prisoners.
In addition, custody- and treatment-oriented staff constantly
disagreed in the day-to-day running of the prison. Custody
people wanted strict rules backed up by punitive measures;

---

[12] John Irwin, "The Trouble with Rehabilitation," *Criminal Justice and Behavior,* June 1974, p. 140.

[13] OEO funded several prison college education programs that
were based on the active conception. See ibid.

[14] These conclusions were reached from interviews with program
staff in college education programs.

treatment people wanted individualized, discretionary decision making tailored to the particular instance and the individual. Custody people wanted a hierarchy of command and prestige, with distance between prisoners and guards being strictly maintained; treatment people wanted a spread of responsibility, more equal distribution of respect, and close interaction with prisoners. A formal accommodation was achieved by establishing two administrative branches, one in charge of custody matters and the other of treatment matters. The top administrators, the wardens or superintendents, tried to relegate particular tasks and decisions to one branch or the other. When this could not be done neatly, which was typical of major decisions, they skillfully negotiated compromise between the two branches. Usually, they leaned toward custody and helped fabricate treatment justifications for doing so. Successful administrators in this era were persons who understood that the prison must appear to be mainly rehabilitative, but above all must fulfill its custody functions.

In the last phase of the treatment era, the active phase, the conflict increased and custody smoldered. The new activist mood made the treatment people more assertive, defiant, and intolerant of custody. There was much more close and sincere interaction between prisoners and the new treatment activists. Many of them were hip — that is, moral liberals. They smoked marijuana (or were not against others' doing so) and were more tolerant of deviance in general. They made an effort to understand, even imitate, some of the patterns of prisoner groups and appeared to treat prisoners as equals. This further irritated the old guard. The earlier treatment staff had at least believed that prisoners were less than whole, or sick, and they maintained a paternalistic relationship toward them. Now, in the new approach, prisoners were simply other human beings who, because of social and political arrangements, committed certain crimes for which they were caught and severely punished. Many new active treatment staff respected and liked prisoners more than guards. This was intolerable to the old guards, whose members were engaged in an intense moral struggle with prisoners in which they had strong needs to feel superior.

In some prisons the conflict between the two groups intensified, and accommodation was difficult. The new treatment people were willing to take chances, and they fought the old guard over every decision with an unwillingness to compromise. When new programs were introduced by new treatment staff, the old guard bided their time until they could sabotage them and, if they could, catch some of the treatment staff in improprieties or crimes, such as delivering messages, smuggling contraband, or covering up rule or law violations for prisoners.[15] This was a likely occurrence, because the new treatment people were naive about the rules and pitfalls in the prison.

THE PRISON MOVEMENT AND THE OLD GUARD

The prison movement was like a blast of pure oxygen on a smoldering fire. Most of the movement activities and the new consciousness among politicized prisoners threatened and infuriated the custody force. Guards' work, though poorly paid, demeaned, and monotonous, had been safe. Suddenly, it became dangerous. In addition, the activists' vituperative condemnations of guards and the prison staff enraged the custody force. The radical movement spokespersons eloquently articulated a world view in which the prisoners were elevated not to equality, but to superiority, and the prison staff, particularly guards, were relegated to the lowest level of humanity. Many, perhaps most, of the prisoners who delivered these vilifications were blacks, the very group whom the prejudiced white guards hated most and considered to be the most inferior. Two passages from

[15] The OEO-funded Newgate college program at Ashland, Kentucky, provided a good example of this sequence. The original staff of the program fits the active description. They struggled with the custody staff over many issues, such as classification of particular prisoners to the program and special rules and privileges for persons in the program. But some of the staff persons were naive about prisons, and their discovered improprieties and laxity eventually enabled the custody branch to bring the program under custody's control. The custody-oriented staff applied pressure through the U.S. Bureau of Prison's central office. For a description of the history of the program, see Marjorie J. Seashore et al., *Prisoner Education: Project Newgate and Other College Programs* (New York: Praeger, 1976). Another study of an eventual takeover by custody of a program administered by active treatment staff is contained in Elliott Studt, Sheldon L. Messinger, and Thomas P. Wilson, *C-Unit: Search for Community in Prison* (New York: Russell Sage Foundation, 1968).

George Jackson's letters exemplify the derogatory characterization of guards that was delivered by leading prisoner and non-prisoner activists and accepted by hundreds, perhaps thousands, of prison movement followers:

> The great majority of Soledad pigs are southern migrants who do not want to work in the fields and farms of the area, who couldn't sell cars or insurance, and who couldn't tolerate the discipline of the army. And, of course, prisons attract sadists.
>
> Pigs come here to feed on the garbage heap for two reasons really, the first half because they can do no other work, frustrated men soon to develop sadistic mannerisms; and the second half, sadists out front, suffering under the restraints placed upon them by an equally sadistic, vindictive society. The sadist knows that to practice his religion upon the society at large will bring down upon his head their sadistic reaction.[16]

The condemnations were not restricted to the radical activists. Radical and even liberal criminologists, civil rights–minded citizens, and sections of the media accepted and circulated a highly derogatory conception of guards and prison administrations. At least, this is the way in which many guards and prison administrators perceived it. The deputy commissioner of the New York Department of Corrections revealed this sensitivity when the coroner reported that all hostages at Attica were killed by police fire; he told a reporter: "Go on, make us the murderers and the other guys Sunday school teachers." [17]

In addition, the prison movement was the source of more routine irritations to guards and other staff members. Formerly, the prison had been left alone. The only regular outsiders coming to the prison were visitors, prisoners' family members or friends who had gone through the discretionary screening process and become eligible to visit the prisoners on visiting days under the close scrutiny of guards. These individuals were almost as uninfluential as the prisoners themselves and could

---

[16] *Soledad Brother* (New York: Bantam Books, 1970), pp. 23, 164.
[17] *Attica,* p. 460.

134

be pushed around — searched (even "skin searched") or denied a visit — at the whim of the prison staff. Less frequently, an academician studying the prison or prisoners, someone's lawyer, or a representative of a do-gooder reform group like the American Friends Service Committee dropped by. These persons tended not to be openly critical of the prison. If they were, they were simply barred from the prison. After the beginning of the prison movement, the prisons were besieged by new types: radical lawyers, politicians, reporters, and pesty political activists. The new class of visitors had much more influence than former visitors. Consequently, the isolated and exclusive domain of the prison worker was regularly entered by potentially critical and more resourceful outsiders. This was a decided irritant to the prison employees who had grown accustomed to privacy and autonomy in carrying out their work.

The lawyers did more than visit and criticize.[18] They litigated and inspired, supported, and even tutored the local pest: the jailhouse lawyer or writ writer, a prisoner who spends a great deal of time researching his and other prisoners' cases and files petitions to the court. The result of the lawyers' and the writ writers' litigations were the changes in the prisoners' legal status described in chapter 4. The courts' new interventions unsettled and infuriated the entire prison staff in two different ways. First, they implied that prison administrators and guards could not be trusted with the discretion and autonomy that they formerly enjoyed. This was a severe blow to their self-respect. Second, and more concretely, the staff, particularly the guard force, believed that the decisions handcuffed them in carrying out the necessary measures to maintain order in prison. Custody has traditionally made many decisions that result in increases in punishment of particular individuals. The decision to place an inmate in segregation, sometimes indefinitely, is a leading example. Guards have always had the power to do this without being required to establish guilt for a particular crime or rule violation. Strong suspicion of acts committed or planned by prisoners was enough. Custody has

[18] James Jacobs documented this significant increase in lawyers' visitations to Stateville between 1968 and 1974 (*Stateville* [Chicago: University of Chicago Press, 1977]), pp. 119–20.

argued that legal proof in prison is almost impossible to obtain, and they must use informal information-gathering methods to prevent violence, escapes, and other intolerable activities. The court decisions threatened this type of operation, which custody has contended is absolutely essential in running a prison.

As a matter of fact, the court decisions did not drastically alter custody's mode of operation. Jacobs observed:

> Where decisions have been implemented, their impact has often been blunted. For example, contrary to the opinion of prison administrators that the courts have destroyed discipline, there is strong evidence at Stateville and elsewhere that the court decisions affecting prison discipline have had little effect on the inmates serving isolation and segregation time.[19]

The prison administrators and custody forces found methods to evade or ignore the spirit, if not the letter, of the law. However, the decisions did result in more work and some increase in accountability, and these irritated administrators and guards, who have enjoyed autonomy and a slow-paced work routine.

Finally, some of the new visitors, particularly movement activists, were suspected of improper and illegal interaction with prisoners and of highly disruptive and illegal acts: planning strikes and demonstrations, smuggling weapons, and aiding in escapes. Some of the persons drawn to the prison during the prison movement did intentionally violate prison rules and laws in their contacts with prisoners. It appears that in at least two events in California — the escape of Ron Beaty from Chino and the attempted escape of George Jackson from San Quentin — outside activists helped plan and execute incidents that resulted in the homicides of guards. But many guards and prison administrators tended to see conspiracies everywhere, and their reaction to this type of threat was disproportionate.

The Shape of the Reaction The activities described above greatly strengthened the power of the custody arm. The real and imagined conspiracies, the actual acts of violence, and the constant condemnation of prison employees not only enraged and activated the custody faction, but also drove many

[19] Ibid., p. 114.

136

members of the treatment operation over into the custody camp. Custody, long muffled, began to lampoon treatment philosophy and to reassert their punitive penal approach. The following statement, delivered by James Gaffney, an old-timer in prison work, to the wardens convened at an annual meeting of the Wardens' Association of America (October 7, 1970), reveals both custody's bitterness toward rehabilitation and the resurgence of punitive philosophy. According to one observer, who submitted the statement to the *Freeworld Times,* Gaffney's talk "brought the entire room to its feet in ringing applause at the close."

In the words of Minnie Pearl, "How-dy! I'm so proud to be here." Proud to sit again with compadres of long-standing who were charter members of an old group known as the "Wrecking Crew." In times past, we were able on occasions to stymie the encroachments of our adversaries, the "Longhairs" of that day. It is sad now that more wrecking wasn't undertaken and done. . . .

For more than three decades, I supervised several federal penal establishments. And built some on barren terrain. Being right down in the arena where the action was, I did acquire some insight into the mentalities, behavior patterns and lying and conniving shenanigans of convicts. They are deeply ingrained with attitudes of "to-hell-with-you-bub." And, in my judgment, they cannot be cleaned and made upright by being sponged with soft soap.

That said, I'd suggest experimenting for [a] spell with running the more crusty ones through daily showers of firm disciplining and then scrubbing the harder-to-clean lot with a potent solution of old-time administrative grit. I've a strong feeling that treatments of this sort would soon brighten their outlook and calm the merry trouble makers.

Some thirty years ago, the so-called "Longhairs" of that period came into complete control of all prison operations and dubbed it "Modern Penology — Enlightened Penology." The thing covered every facet of crime and imprisonment and adherents, many with scant fitness, ranged far and wide shouting "hallelujah" and "praise be!"

As a part of this all-inclusive cure-all came the prophecy that it would, if given broad and full-blown application, eradicate crime and its causes, reclaim the wrong-doers, empty the pens and hasten the day when police forces could be skeletonized. Well, sir, the backfiring of this venture is frequently and factually reported in crime and prison population statistics to the painful realities hoisted upon everyone concerned.

The "panacea" is laced through and through with pamperings and appeasements. Costs are out of the question for most prison systems. Paper work is mountainous. Custody and discipline are given "B" ratings in importance. Jobholders, boards, and committees abound. Prisoners clutter passageways days on end, slouching and gabbing while waiting turns to be oriented, classified, mollified and generally demoralized by interviews, previewers, and reviewers.

Among these mind probers, assigned the duties of compiling voluminous files of asserted chaff, there are not many face cards in the deck. Elsewhere, prisoners sprawl and spew gutter-talk in plushed-up cubicles set aside for the likes of group discussions, group therapy, inmate council meetings, et cetera, et cetera. No one seems to have been assigned to anything. Remember that most jobs around the place are spoken of as demeaning.

With the foregoing, the panacea prescribes venturesome programs of treatment nonsense in the name of rehabilitation. There's just too much of this afoot to cite one by one. So, let's settle for one lu-lu that comes to mind.

Some years back, we federals took off on lending public monies to prisoners being released on their worthless signatures. Wow! We really got burned before we could turn that potato loose. Blisters that have not healed yet. The federal system and California — California having been the beneficiary of unstinted federal guidance — or years ago — plunged into the "panacea" up to their ears.

New Mexico — federalized by request from away back — tags along in a sort of pauper fashion. But, she's geared and prancing to dive in head first if the dinero can be come by. Others have tested the temperature and decided just to wade around a bit.

With all this rehabilitation to-do, the nation has been blessed with far more recidivists than with reclaimed wrongdoers. And don't you forget it. The older of us wonder, I suspect, about the absence of all the earlier jargon of skeletonizing police forces. I imagine that the continuing criminal capers of rehabilitated cons, parolees, and probationers laid that to rest.

Equating, we can see some parallel in results accruing from some spotty application of the "panacea-doctrine" and Ben Spock's book on how not to bring up children. Old Benji — for money alone — penned theories of spare the rod that run counter to the teachings of Christ and all sages since the beginning of time. He has spawned more than two generations of hair, hate, hussies, and harassers. Yes, and right now he's dabbling in filth and brotherhooding with hordes of filthy and un-American rabble. He's at home among them.

Truthfully, I'm gravely concerned with the permissiveness and crime around us and the way in which neither is being handled. Somebody must come along and soon and make it safe once more to walk a street, visit a park, see a show, and answer a doorbell after sundown. You are at liberty to barge forth on any of these today at your own peril. Let's marshal our voting forces and clean the mess up — starting today! (Mr. Gaffney is a retired warden of the Saint Cloud Reformatory in Minnesota).[20]

The public, whose sympathy for prisoners had been replaced by fear of crime and hostility toward criminals, generally supported or ignored this reassertion of punitive penal philosophy. Many staunch treatment advocates, particularly older ones who had already been disturbed by the active orientation toward treatment, were repulsed by the movement activities and shifted their allegiance to the custody faction. For example, while attending a large session at the 1972 annual meeting of the American Correctional Association, I heard Austin Mac-Cormick, a respected prison reformer, react to Gloria Steinem's and Kate Millett's criticism of prisons and support of radical changes; he indicated angrily that he had been moved to the punitive side by the criticisms and actions of radicals. Many top administrators who had been straddling the fence for years, juggling custody and treatment forces, leaped over to the custody side. Walter Dunbar, who rose up to the top of the California Department of Corrections during its most intense ex-

[20] *Freeworld Times,* February 1972, p. 5.

perimentation in treatment and who ended up in New York as deputy commissioner when the Attica riot occurred, denied that he had witnessed brutality in his inspection of Attica with Senator Dunne of New York, although the senator testified that he and Dunbar saw "corrections officers on either side of the corridor swinging their clubs and striking men who were running through there." [21] Dunbar also released the false story of the prisoners murdering and castrating hostages. The Attica Commission wrote the following description of Dunbar's actions after the riot:

> Later in the day, Dunbar reported to the press and to legislators, whom he conducted on a brief tour, accounts of the hostages' deaths and mutilation, all of which proved untrue. He pointed out to the legislators the naked inmate lying on the table with the football under his chin as the castrater of a hostage. According to two legislators on the tour, Assemblyman Eve and Congressman Badillo, Dunbar told them the "castration had been filmed from a helicopter, as well as observed through a rifle's telescopic sights." Around 5:00 P.M. on Monday, Dunbar guided the press around the prison and recounted to them the untrue "fact" that some hostages had been killed before the attack, in addition to repeating the "fact" that hostages died from slashed throats. After that tour, Dunbar was quoted in the *New York Times* as having given an account of the death of "Mad Bomber" Sam Melville, which was untrue in almost every detail. [22]

Apparently, the defiance and violence at Attica was more than Dunbar could bear. After years of ambivalence, he finally made up his mind: the punitive approach was right and prisoners could not be trusted. Many other treatment staff, up and down the administration, were doing the same. Some of the top administrators who refused to move over to the custody side or at least to lean in that direction were attacked by the press, criticized by conservative legislators, and often removed from their offices. In 1973, John Boone, the top administrator of the Massachusetts Department of Corrections, was criticized and then fired after he refused to back the officers who walked out

[21] *Attica,* p. 443.
[22] Ibid., p. 446.

of Walpole Prison and who wanted to use force and punitive measures to control the prisoners who had run the prison for eleven weeks in the guards' absence.

The custodial faction moved back into power with a revised ideology. To their old punitive philosophy, in which prisoners were worthless and untrustworthy, they added new categories for the prisoners and outsiders who were criticizing prisons and guards and participating in the prison movement activities. The outsiders were dirty, hairy, hippie freaks or seditious, traitorous communists, and the prisoners who sided with them were a new type of vicious psychopathic opportunist. In California, Associate Superintendent of Camps L. H. Fudge wrote the following in a widely circulated departmental memo:

> I have just finished reading the pocket book *Soledad Brother* by George Jackson. This book provides remarkable insight into the personality makeup of a highly dangerous sociopath who sees himself not as a criminal but as a Revolutionary dedicated to the violent destruction of existing society. This type individual is not uncommon in several of our institutions, namely Folsom, San Quentin, and Soledad. Because of his potential and the growing numbers, it is imperative that we in Corrections know as much as we can about his personality makeup and are able to correctly identify his kind.
>
> I recommend that *Soledad Brother* be placed on the "must" reading list of every employee in the Department of Corrections. I plan to purchase copies and issue them with a cover letter to the staff of each conservation camp in Northern California. This is one of the most self-revealing and insightful books I have ever read concerning a criminal personality.[23]

The criticisms delivered by prisoners like George Jackson and his supporters were explained by this newly embellished punitive philosophy in a manner that returned the custodial people to a position of superiority and respect, justified punitive actions against prison movement activists, and did not suggest any changes that were not consistent with punitive principles. Equipped with a new punitive ideology, back in power,

[23] State of California, Department of Corrections, memorandum, November 4, 1970.

the custodial faction proceeded to remove the new threats to their position of power and dignity.

Unofficial Action   Small groups of guards, probably without any official or informal instruction or encouragement from the top administration, committed many acts of brutality against individual prisoners who were defiant or involved in political activities. The evidence is strong that guards beat the prisoners charged with crimes related to George Jackson's escape attempt. According to the testimony of a Marin County attorney, guards repeatedly beat Hugo Pinell, who was charged with other San Quentin Six defendants and also had been convicted of assault and homicide of a guard.

> On September 6, 1971, Mr. Pinell was viciously attacked which resulted in lacerations requiring six sutures. He had a fractured tooth on his left side, which we have as evidence. He sustained either a fractured jaw or a badly bruised jaw, so much he could hardly talk. . . . On September 22, he was again assaulted. . . . On October 5, upon his return from Superior Court in Marin County, he was again assaulted. . . . The situation has gotten so bad, our client is fearful of even leaving his cell while in San Quentin. . . . I will state for the record that I am a registered Republican from conservative background. This is such a shocking thing for me that I can't believe it exists.[24]

In some of these retaliatory attacks on prisoners, deaths have occurred. In a suit against the prison system the family of Fred Billingslea, an emotionally disturbed and politically active black prisoner, has charged that four San Quentin guards gassed and then killed Billingslea.[25]

These brutal acts of retaliation against militant, particularly black militant, prisoners are probably the result of spontaneous bursts of hostility and prejudice on the part of a group of guards and are not planned or condoned by prison administrators. But prison administrators, almost without exception,

[24] *The San Quentin Six* (San Francisco: San Quentin Six Defense Committee), p. 12.
[25] This suit was settled outside of court with the family receiving $30,000.

142

have refused to investigate these cases vigorously or to take action against guards guilty of these acts. In fact, they have often joined in the effort to cover them up. The Attica Commission, noting this stance by the New York Department of Corrections, commented about this propensity among all law enforcement agencies: "The Division of State Police, like many established institutions, has developed a tradition in which members find security, take pride, and defend one another vigorously." [26]

In some instances, brutal and deadly retaliation was more open and much larger in scale. The action against black prisoners at the Indiana Reformatory in 1969 was such an incident.

> In 1969, black prisoners at the Indiana Reformatory petitioned to end such practices as placing prisoners in the hole without a hearing, forcing prisoners to stand barefoot on a painted line for four hours as punishment for "silent insolence," using guards who had cited prisoners for rule violations as judges hearing their own complaints, and the use by guards of derogatory racial epithets such as "boy," "black boy," and "nigger." When the petition brought no results, the black prisoners staged a sit-in in the recreation area and while they were sitting quietly, the guards opened fire. Two inmates were killed, forty-six were wounded. The protestors who escaped injury were placed in segregation and denied visitors, reading matter, or writing material. [27]

However, the most brutal and murderous retaliation occurred in the retaking of Attica. The prisoners had controlled part of the prison for four days (September 9–13, 1971) and held forty-three hostages. Many acts by prisoners had antagonized the guards and police who retook the prison. In the initial moments of the uprising some prisoners beat a guard; he died three days later. After several days of negotiating with a team of observers picked by the prisoners, the prisoners rejected a list of twenty-eight points that had been accepted by the com-

[26] *Attica,* p. 336.
[27] American Friends Service Committee, *Struggle for Justice* (New York: Hill and Wang 1971), p. 6.

missioner of corrections. They refused to accept it because total amnesty was not included, and the death of the guard meant possible murder indictments for some prisoners. After this rejection, several prisoners escorted eight hostages into full view of the guards and police on the walls, held knives to their throats, and warned that they would slit the hostages' throats if the guards and police tried to move in. Soon after this (9:46 A.M., September 13), a combined force of state troopers, national guardsmen, and the prison's guard force started taking back the prison. They killed ten hostages and twenty-nine prisoners in that operation and then beat and mistreated prisoners for several days.

Before the assault, the guards, state troopers, and many of the townspeople had become extremely hostile toward the prisoners and the outside observers. Tom Wicker, a *New York Times* columnist and one of the observers, wrote:

> The emphasis on guns and clubs during the crisis was incredible; it had to be seen to be believed. . . . these guns, moreover, were in the hands of men who left no doubt they wanted to use them. Correction Commissioner Oswald's long delay of the assault and his effort to negotiate were met with anger and impatience by the prison staff; the observers who were trying to prevent bloodshed saw hostility at every turn. A guard bringing them a box of food said as he put it down, "If I'd know it was for you, I wouldn't have brought it." [28]

According to Herman Badillo and Milton Haynes, an observer "reported that a woman in a restaurant not far from the prison refused service to a newspaperman, a state senator, and a state assemblyman on the observer's team, and told them: 'I hope they kill all of you'." [29] The Attica Commission wrote that "by the end of Saturday night, many troopers and correction officers were tired, restless, frustrated, and increasingly angry." [30]

The Attica Commission concluded that the retaking pro-

[28] Quoted in Herman Badillo and Milton Haynes, *A Bill of Rights: Attica and the American Prison System* (New York: Outerbridge and Lazard, 1972), p. 75.
[29] Ibid.
[30] *Attica*, p. 310.

ceeded without an adequate plan to prevent unnecessary violence and that a shooting spree resulted in which "anyone identifiable as an inmate who moved or remained standing on the catwalks once the shooting began was likely to draw fire" and there "was clearly indiscriminate firing into congested areas by men who did not value the inmates' lives. Indeed, several witnesses told the Commission they heard troopers bragging later in the day about their exploits on the morning of the assault." The commission further claimed that there

> was no justification for the many instances of shooting into tents, trenches, and barricades without looking. The 21 deaths and more than 50 wounded in D yard cannot all be explained by the incident involving Lieutenant Christian or other hostile acts. Even where there was some provocation, such as in the assault on Lieutenant Christian, the repeated discharge of "00" buckshot pellets into D yard ranges far exceeding the weapons' intended use unquestionably wounded, and perhaps killed, many inmates who were not engaged in any acts of hostility or resistance whatever.

After the prison had been secured, there occurred a series of brutal acts that lasted for days.

> In fact, correction officers, and to a lesser extent state troopers and sheriffs' deputies, engaged in frequent and systematic acts of retribution against inmates. National Guardsmen and other outside observers, as well as a few troopers and correction officers, confirmed the almost universal inmate descriptions of widespread beatings, proddings, kickings, and verbal abuse of the vilest nature.
>
> Physical reprisals, accompanied by racial and sexual epithets, began as inmates were herded out of D yard to be stripped and searched, continued as inmates were run through a gauntlet to cells in A block, and did not subside even after they were locked naked three to a cell. Reprisals were especially severe in HBZ, where the suspected leaders of the uprising were taken. There were even some incidents of reprisals on the following days. Eight days after September 13, doctors assigned to make a physical inventory reported bruises, lacerations, abrasions, and broken bones among 45 percent of the inmates who had been in D yard.

The commission concluded: "An uprising in which inmates had demanded above all that they be treated as human beings thus ended with their being treated inhumanly." [31]

In some states, particularly California, the fear of subversion from the radicals and revolutionaries led to the development of clandestine, counterintelligence operations. In the early 1960s, the California Department of Corrections had established a "special services" group that investigated internal activities. When the prison movement gained force, this branch began investigating movement individuals and groups. During Ronald Reagon's tenure as governor, special services officers and a network of guards who were engaged in clandestine activities reported directly to his office, stepping around the head of the department of corrections. Some of their activities were similar to those of Nixon's "plumbers."

For instance, on December 16, 1971, the vice president of the California Correctional Officers' Association, another correctional officer, and a member of the state's attorney general's office transported an inmate, Tony Pewitt, from the maximum-security unit at Chino to Frank Rundel's home. Rundel had been the head psychiatrist at Soledad and was removed when he refused to turn over his file on a prisoner who was charged with killing an employee. Rundel was suspected by some officers and staff of being part of the communist conspiracy that was trying to undermine the prison and was responsible for the death of several guards. One officer told Pewitt: "I believe that Rundel is involved with the Communist Party and so is Procunier [the director of the department]. I believe that Rundel led these people to kill McCarthy and Conant [Soledad staffers] and I want you to get the evidence." [32] Pewitt, while engaging Rundel in a casual conversation, showed him the transmitters inside his clothes and informed him in writing that "Moe" Comacho of the California Correctional Officers' Association and a person from the attorney general's office were in a car down the street. From a pay phone Rundel phoned an attorney and then private detectives, one of whom

[31] Ibid., pp. 380, 402, 338, 339.
[32] Don Jelinek, "The Soledad Frame-Up," *San Francisco Bay Guardian,* June 22, 1972, p. 4.

came to his house and gathered evidence of the attempted entrapment.

The activities of the counterintelligence network within the department were similar, though on a much smaller scale, to those of the CIA and the FBI in their fight against the "communist conspiracy." They tapped phones, paid informers, and infiltrated prison movement organizations.

Open Policies and Action Against the Prison Movement These unofficial acts of retaliation and the clandestine activities were clearly unethical, illegal, and horrendous, but not as consequential as the open actions of many prison administrations. The new coalition of old guards, apostate treatment staff, and pragmatic administrators leaning toward custody set out systematically to repress all activities that they believed were political. They had concluded that the prison political movement was the biggest threat that prisons had ever faced. Of course, the new form of defiance and violence against prison staff threatened them directly and profoundly. But the pending revolution threatened them in a deeper, more diffuse, ill-defined manner. It challenged their values, not only on penal matters, but on life in general. And it threatened their careers and their general economic and social stability.

They responded by screening all prisoner organizations that had emerged in recent years and abolished most of them, particularly groups organized on ethnic or racial lines and suspected of being involved in political activities. Warden Nelson at San Quentin wrote the following memo to his associate wardens on March 22, 1971, announcing the new policy:

> We are reading in the public press and hearing via television and radio that the best breeding and/or recruiting ground for neo-revolutionaries is in the prison system.
>
> I am being told that our new educational systems must encompass preparing the men for community activity, whatever that means, upon release.
>
> I am witnessing the deterioration of our ethnic organizations, which were once dedicated to the educational improvements of our men inside San Quentin, to para-military organizations with revolutionary overtones. It appears to me that by pursuing this path, the organizations are destined to

147

undo all the good they may have done, and may result in harm, in the form of added time coming to all men confined within our walls. For if the prisons of California become known as "Schools for Violent Revolution," the Adult Authority would be remiss in this duty to not keep the inmates longer.

I do not believe that as the administrator of this institution it is proper for me to utilize State facilities or State monies for the purpose of providing facilities or time for the propagation of revolutionary acts or material. In fact, I believe it to be the exact opposite of my duty.

I have been told that if I deny organizations the right to use para-military methods of operation, they will go underground. This is an alternative that they may choose. The alternative they might better choose is to revert to the purposes established in their constitution and to adhere strictly to them. None of the organizations were set up as "political" organizations. Their motivation of minorities to enter our educational programs is commendable but their purpose is not in itself to educate, nor are they an educational entity within the prison; if they were, they would be required to operate with our structured educational department.

I intend to draw the line at revolutionary education. I do so with the full knowledge that criticism will be heaped on my head but I believe I have a deeper and more abiding responsibility to the State of California than I do to the small handful of individuals who are dedicated to the overthrow of our present system of government.

No one can shake the hand of a man who has his fist clenched over his head.[33]

Prisoners belonging to SATE (Self-Advancement Through Education, a black self-help group) had made critical statements about the prison on a San Francisco educational television station shortly before this memo. After it, the leadership of several ethnic groups were transferred from San Quentin to Folsom. During the next two years the California prison system carefully policed the prisoner organizations. All groups sus-

[33] Erik Olin Wright, *The Politics of Punishment* (New York: Harper Row, 1973), pp. 96–97.

148

pected of political activities were banned. Individuals suspected of political activities were transferred, segregated, or paroled. The Adult Authority began questioning prisoners appearing before them about the prisoners' political activities and conveyed the impression that involvement in political organizations would result in longer sentences. Erik Olin Wright, who was observing Adult Authority hearings in this period, reports on the following appearances:

In February, 1971, I observed one day's sitting of the Adult Authority at San Quentin. One of the prisoners who appeared before them was a young black who had openly proclaimed that he was a member of the Black Panther Party. He had spent three years at San Quentin for second-degree burglary, and during that time had had only a few minor disciplinary infractions for such things as "abusive language to an officer" or "refusing to obey an order." When he sat down before the Adult Authority, the first questions he was asked was: "Tell me, why are you a Panther? What do you see in them?" He replied: "All black people in America are really Panthers because all black people in America are oppressed." There followed a long discussion about the meaning of "oppression" and the legitimacy of the Panthers' response to that oppression. One of the Adult Authority members admitted that "there has been a certain amount of injustice against Negroes over the years, but things have gotten much better recently, and I just don't see how you can say that you are oppressed. This is a democracy and if you have grievances, there are non-violent ways that you can solve them." The prisoner replied, "It may be a democracy for you, but it isn't for blacks, and particularly it isn't for me. George Washington broke the laws of King George because he thought that they were oppressive. And he broke them violently. We are just doing the same thing. This country is more oppressive against us than England ever was against George Washington. Washington just didn't want to pay a tax on tea; we want to live like human beings." The discussion continued, and one of the Adult Authority members asked the prisoner, "Well, even if there are still some injustices against Negroes, do you think that it is justified to steal like you did?" The prisoner replied, "Everyone here steals, everyone. This country is built on stealing. A shop owner steals when he raises his prices so that the people in the ghetto can't afford to buy enough to eat. That is stealing as much as burglary." After about twenty minutes of heated political discourse (nothing else was discussed), the hearing ended. The prisoner was denied a parole.

Later in the day, in another parole hearing, an inmate appeared who had been actively involved with the Minutemen before he was sent to prison five years before. He was asked by one of the Adult Authority members: "Are you still a Weatherman?" "Weatherman?" replied the inmate. "There weren't any Weathermen when I was on the outside. You mean 'Minuteman' — they're all the same thing anyway." Later in the interview, the prisoner was asked, "What do you now feel about Minutemen, Weathermen, Nazis, Panthers, and those kinds of groups?" The inmate tactfully replied, "Well, like you said, they are really all the same. They may have different rhetoric, but there is no real difference in their organizations. They are all on ego trips." The prisoner was recommended for a parole.[34]

These repressive efforts were duplicated in many states. Leo Carroll described the attempts of the administration of a Rhode Island prison to stop a suspected planned insurrection:

> Late in the evening of November 18, 1971, eleven prisoners were transferred from ACI to various federal and state prisons across the country. Without prior notice, they were taken from their cells, stripped to the underwear, handcuffed and shackled, placed in state police cars, and driven immediately to their destinations. Five of those transferred were black; six were white. The blacks transferred included the President and Vice-President of the Afro-American Society, the Executive Advisor to the President, and one of the directors of the organization. The whites transferred were an assortment of types having only one characteristic in common — they were all regarded as troublemakers by the prison administration. Only two, however, could be regarded as leaders.[35]

[34] Ibid., pp. 98–99.
[35] *Hacks, Blacks, and Cons* (Lexington, Mass.: Lexington Books, 1974), p. 198.

150

CONCLUDING REMARKS

The forces described in chapter 4 stifled the outside prisoner movement activities. The repression of political activities by prison administrators stopped its momentum among prisoners. However, the authorities stopped more than the random attacks on guards and other prison employees and the subversive activities perpetrated by some political activists. Most prisoners and groups involved in political activities were not threatening violence or subverting the prison. Most were working in an open fashion toward the cessation of blatantly cruel, unfair, and racist practices in the prison and toward the establishment of a humane and equitable system of incarceration. At times, their actions in pursuing these goals appeared to administrators to be unnecessarily defiant and threatening and their recommendations excessive. But neither the tactics nor the goals were very outlandish, considering the style of protest and the new perspectives that had emerged in the late 1960s in the outside society. A careful reading of the lists the Folsom manifesto, the twenty-eight points agreed on at Attica, and other lists of prison demands confirms the protesting prisoners' reasonableness, insight, and sophistication.[36]

The repression of these efforts was unnecessary, but, more importantly, it was very detrimental in an unanticipated manner. During this period of rapid changes in the prisoner population and prisoner relationships, in which the old informal systems of order were demolished, the administrators stopped the development of alternative group structures that could have prevented the rise of hoodlum gangs involved in rackets, formed on racial lines, and engaged in extreme forms of prisoner-to-prisoner violence. During the prison movement many of the most respected and resourceful prisoners were involved in political organizations. The direction of these organizations was toward a formal accommodation between different racial groups. Prisoners of all ethnic groups participated and respected the work of the political organizations. They were a source of identification, activities, and hope for them. If permitted to develop, this incipient movement might

[36] See Appendix A for these lists.

151

have been the basis for a new prisoner social order. It would have been more formal and it would have been bothersome to the administration, because, in order for it to succeed, it would have had to have some real power. However, in its intense and vengeful retaliation, the administrations stopped this development, and violent cliques and gangs emerged as the dominant force in many prisons.

6
Community
Corrections
THE EXPERTS' SOLUTION

Prisoners, outside prison movement activists, and prison employees were not the only persons interested in the events and conditions in prisons. After 1970, large sections of the general public, many influential individuals, and other interest groups, along with the mass media and government officials, agreed that prisons were a serious social problem. These parties increasingly pressured the government, particularly the federal government, to begin solving the problem. The government, as it usually does when the public demands action on a social problem, called on "experts" to conduct an official analysis of the situation. Working in a variety of government-sponsored forums, experts on prisons and corrections devised a solution — community corrections — which, though it did not solve the problem, altered many aspects of the operation of the criminal justice system as a whole and directly and indirectly changed prisons. To understand the failure of community corrections and the changes that it produced, we must first consider the limits within which all experts called on by the government work, and then we must trace the development, analyze the implementation, and examine the public reaction to community corrections.

The experts called to work in one or another official structure (a Presidential Commission or Task Force, for example) on a solution to a pressing social problem are expected to construct a solution that is politically feasible, will solve as many aspects of the problem as possible, and will reduce organized public dissatisfaction. To be politically feasible, a solution may not extend outside implicit limits or what Robert R. Alford, in his summary of important studies of political decision making, refers to as "the narrow agenda of alternatives determined by constraints of political and economic structure and culture."[1] What this means is that government problem-solving assemblies will avoid solutions that necessitate changes in such things as basic economic relationships (private ownership or profit structures), solutions that take power away from some groups and transfer it to others, and solutions that contradict deeply rooted moral values (such as family solidarity).[2]

The experts are called from the field and from the universities. The field experts, persons who work in governments or private agencies attached to the areas experiencing the problems, usually have reputations as innovators. In addition to their practical experience, many of them have conducted research and published material on the problem area. But what is most important is that their experiences in the field have taught them to work within the limits imposed by political feasibility and to approach solutions to problems always with these limits in mind.

In general, academics produce solutions that extend beyond the limits of political feasibility, but many persons from universities are able to work in the government assemblies and accept the limits because they function either as "accommodators" or pragmatists. Accommodators are sympathetic to government concerns and highly sensitive to the issue of political feasibility. Representatives of this type are willing to squeeze existing academic theories into the space created by the agenda

[1] *Bureaucracy and Participation* (Chicago: Rand McNally, 1969), p. 194.

[2] The possibility always exists that an official assembly will wander outside the agenda of alternatives. Some of the experts may not understand or may refuse to accept the limits. This was more likely in the late 1960s, when the large political movements pushed different actors into the formerly exclusive decision-making circles and more conservative individuals were moved toward radical perspectives by the mood of the times. Also, problem-solving assemblies have a dynamic of their own, and sometimes they get carried away. When they recommend solutions with features that protrude outside the limits, more conservative functionaries who follow up the assemblies' efforts trim them off.

154

of acceptable alternatives or even to create new ideas that fit within these limits. Their purpose in doing so is to lend the solutions academic respectability and not to develop theoretically consistent solutions. They accept the limits of political feasibility, because they believe it to be the only means of converting academic ideas into policy. Often, they justify the compromises that they must make with arguments like these: Conditions will be improved by the implementation of even diluted academic ideas; It is better that persons with a fuller understanding of the issues devise a solution; or It is possible through astute use of academic understandings to move the limits somewhat.[3]

After 1970 the situation in prisons in the United States loomed as a full-blown serious social problem of national scope, and the government convened a group of experts to develop a solution. Actually, the prison problem was seen as one aspect of a broader crisis in our criminal justice system, and the Law Enforcement Assistance Agency sponsored the National Advisory Commission on Criminal Justice Standards and Goals to examine the broader issue. The Task Force on Corrections within the commission tackled the subproblem of prisons and devised a politically feasible solution to reduce the uproar over prisons.

THE TASK FORCE SOLUTION

The task force offered "community corrections" and its affiliate, "diversion," which had already been designed and tested by

---

[3] There are two additional types who actively analyze the problem areas, but they do not contribute to the politically feasible solution. One is the *academic critic,* who persists in analyzing the problem too broadly, pointing out that effective solutions will require changes that are outside the agenda of alternatives (for example, redistribution of wealth or large shifts in social values), and criticizing the politically feasible solutions as ineffectual or counterproductive. The other is the *academic vacillator,* who seeks respect from the less corruptible academic types and from government functionaries who not only call experts, but also control the distribution of many of the financial awards and prestige bestowed on academicians. The vacillator cleverly wavers between criticism and accommodation, always avoiding the final dirty work of devising a politically feasible solution or delivering harsh criticism. He usually escapes these pitfalls by invoking one of the safe defenses inherent in the posture of a value-free science: "our knowledge or under-

Californians, the nation's leading correctional experts. Californians had begun working on the concept of community corrections in the early 1960s when a group of prison administrators and researchers (including Richard McGee, Milton Burdman, Douglas Grant, John Conrad, and Margaritta Warren) were extending the philosophy of treatment along several courses. At this time they were confronted with growing evidence that the first stage of the state's experimentation with treatment had not reduced recidivism. They speculated that identifying the individual's deficiencies or problems and then offering treatment in the conventional prison, even a model conventional prison like Soledad, was too weak, and they began planning more intense and complex treatment modalities, such as the I Level treatment strategy, which separates prisoners according to measured immaturity levels and offers special treatment for each level.[4] Some experts concluded that they must reduce the profoundly deleterious impact of the traditional prison, and they planned to convert the prison into a "therapeutic community" or completely to avoid the prison experience by immediate or early diversion of prisoners to probation, parole, or new forms of community treatment. California had already increased the number of felons on parole and built treatment as well as surveillance into the parole routine.

The planners anticipated that the public, believing that crime would increase, would resist community corrections. To dissipate this resistance, the California correctional planners set up an experiment, the California Community Treatment Experiment, in which wards of the Youth Authority who were to be sent to the youth prisons were randomly divided into control and experimental groups. Those in the experimental

---

standing of the area is incomplete," "we have no adequate theories in the area," or "more research is needed before action should be taken." These two types do not exhaust the possibilities. There remains the pure academician, who avoids policy issues and pursues pure, obective, abstract understandings. To this type, policy always implies value assertion and science must be value-free.

[4] For a description of this approach, see M. Q. Warren, "Implications of a Typology of Delinquents for Measures of Behavior Changes: A Plea for Complexity," *California Youth Authority Quarterly,* Fall 1965, pp. 6–13.

group were released immediately to parole supervision, and the controls were sent to youth prisons and released after serving a normal sentence. The follow-up study of differential recidivism revealed that those released immediately were less likely to be returned to prison.[5] With this questionable evidence of no increase in criminal activity, these community corrections advocates persuaded the California legislature to embark on a large probation subsidy program, in which the state paid counties to place convicted felons on probation instead of sending them to the state's prisons.

At this juncture (about 1965), crime emerged as a major social problem and the president of the United State appointed the President's Commission on Law Enforcement and Administration of Justice to study it. Although this commission predated the prison's being identified as a special problem, it included a committee on corrections in its organization. Corrections was related to the crime problem, according to professional and popular wisdom, because a significant part of society's crime is caused by previously arrested persons who return to crime when released from prison. The Task Force on Corrections' mandate was to analyze the failure of rehabilitation.

California dominated this task force. Eight of the sixty-three consultants listed in the *Task Force Report* were employees of the California Department of Corrections or Youth Authority, and seven more were California academicians who had worked closely with that department in planning the new treatment strategies. In contrast, there were only five consultants from the massive federal prison and four from all other state prison systems. A group of seven full-time consultants spent the summer of 1966 preparing working drafts for the task force. Two of the seven were from the California Department of Corrections, and another two were California academi-

---

[5] See Ted B. Palmer, "California's Community Treatment Program for Delinquent Adolescents," *Journal of Research in Crime and Delinquency,* January 1971, pp. 74–92. Paul Lerman has disputed the results and argued that superior performance of the experimental group was due to more permissive decisions of the parole agents who were encouraged to make the experiments look better ("Evaluating the Outcomes of Institutions for Delinquents," *Social Work,* July 1968, pp. 55–64).

cians. This group, according to the preface of the *Task Force Report,* was influenced by *Alternatives to Incarceration,* a publication by LaMar T. Empey, a California rehabilitation expert.

At the time of the president's crime commission, the prison problem was viewed mainly as the failure of "fortress" prisons, which militated against the new systems of rehabilitation, particularly community corrections. In the introductory overview the report states:

> There are today about 400 institutions for adult felons in this country, ranging from some of the oldest and largest prisons in the world to forestry camps for 30 or 40 trusted inmates. Some are grossly understaffed and underequipped— conspicuous products of public indifference. Overcrowding and idleness are the salient features of some; brutality and corruption of a few others. . . .
>
> There are still many large maximum-security prisons operating in the United States today. The directory of the American Correctional Association showed a 1965 average population of over 2,000 inmates in 21 prisons. Four of these had well over 4,000 inmates each: San Quentin in California; the Illinois State Prison complex at Joliet and Stateville; the Michigan State Prison at Jackson; and the Ohio State Penitentiary at Columbus.[6]

The report argues that a major problem with these fortresses is that they are remote from urban communities:

> Although most inmates of American correctional institutions come from metropolitan areas, the institutions themselves often are located away from urban areas and even primary transportation routes. . . . Remoteness interferes with efforts to reintegrate inmates into their communities and makes it hard to recruit correctional staff, particularly professionals.[7]

In addition, it emphasized that fortress prisons were very expensive: "more than 40 percent of all spending for operating

[6] The President's Commission on Law Enforcement and Administration of Justice, *Task Force Report: Corrections* (Washington, D.C.: U.S. Government Printing Office, 1967), p. 4.
[7] Ibid., p. 6.

corrections in 1965" went to operate institutions, and the bulk of the money went "to feed, clothe, and guard prisoners."[8]

The task force recommended more rehabilitation, including the other two modes being experimented on by the Californians: differential treatment strategies for different types of offenders and therapeutic communities. However, they leaned heavily toward community correction.

> In several senses, corrections today may stand at the threshold of a new era, promising resolution of a significant number of the problems that have vexed it throughout its development. At the very least, it is developing the theory and practical groundwork for a new approach to rehabilitation of the most important group of offenders—those predominantly young and lower-class who are not committed to crime as a way of life and do not pose serious dangers to the community.
>
> . . .
>
> The general underlying premise for the new directions in corrections is that crime and delinquency are symptoms of failures and disorganization of the community as well as of individual offenders. In particular, these failures are seen as depriving offenders of contact with the institutions that are basically responsible for assuring development of law-abiding conduct: sound family life, good schools, employment, recreational opportunities and desirable companions, to name only some of the more direct influences. The substitution of deleterious habits, standards, and associates for these strengthening influences contributes to crime and delinquency.
>
> The task of corrections, therefore, includes building or rebuilding solid ties between offenders and community, integrating or reintegrating the offender into community life—restoring family ties, obtaining employment and education, securing in the larger sense a place for the offender in the routine functioning of society. This requires not only efforts directed toward changing the individual offender, which has been almost the exclusive focus of rehabilitation, but also mobilization and change of the community and its institutions. And these efforts must be undertaken without

[8] Ibid.

giving up the important control and deterrent role of corrections, particularly as applied to dangerous offenders.[9]

To implement community corrections, the task force recommended new small institutions in urban settings.

> This would be architecturally and methodologically the
> antithesis of the traditional fortress-like prison, physically
> and psychologically isolated from the larger society and
> serving primarily as a place of banishment. It would be small
> and fairly informal in structure. Located in or near the
> population center from which its inmates came, it would
> permit flexible use of community resources, both in the
> institution and for inmates to work or study or spend short
> periods of time at home.[10]

In addition, it recommended that parole services be strengthened, that the entire criminal justice system be given more cohesion and rationality, including better coordination between
the parts and clearer overall objectives, and that prisoners be
more carefully differentiated for both treatment and control
purposes.

THE NEW CRIMINOLOGY

After this presentation of their new schemes to the nation, the
Californians went to work on a large-scale demonstration
project — the Model Community Correctional Program — in
San Joaquin County, California.[11] However, their progress
toward implementation of the new era was interrupted by the
explosion of the prison problem and the prison movement and
by radical shifts in many new and old experts' thinking about
prisons. Between 1967 and the assembly of the next commission in 1971, many people's perceptions and definitions of
crime, criminal justice, and the prison changed.

In the preceding chapters we have examined changes in

9 Ibid.
10 Ibid., p. 11.
11 See Institute for Study of Crime and Delinquency Society,
California, *Model Community Correctional Program: Summary Report,*
(1969). This institute was a private corporation with a governing body
composed mainly of top administrators of California Department of
Corrections.

the perspectives of prisoners and other participants in the prison movement. More directly relevant to any government problem-solving ventures was the proliferation of "critical" criminologists. Two new attitudes toward crime and its treatment form the frame of their new analysis. One is the belief that crime is more than a problem of the lower classes. New research indicated that crime is much more evenly spread out through the social class system, and that the upper classes commit the most serious crimes, at least monetarily.[12] The second attitude is that rehabilitation programs do not and probably never will reduce recidivism.

In the late 1960s, information about the failure of rehabilitation programs to reduce recidivism began circulating among criminologists. Early in that decade Gene Kassebaum and David A. Ward had studied prisoners released from California's most recently built treatment-oriented prison. They discovered that whether or not prisoners had participated in group counseling or in different types of group counseling made no difference in their likelihood to return to prison. By the end of the 1960s, their findings, which were eventually published in 1971, were familiar to most criminologists interested in recidivism and rehabilitation.[13] Leslie T. Wilkins of the School of Criminology at the University of California, Berkeley, reviewed several treatment efforts and recidivism and in a 1969 publication shed doubt on the effectiveness of rehabilitation programs.[14] Then three social researchers conducted a survey of treatment programs for the city of New York and, after reviewing several hundred published reports of treatment efforts, concluded that treatment has not worked. For several years the city tried to bury their report, but one of the three researchers,

[12] Several studies in the 1960s revealed that the majority of Americans had committed crimes for which some people are regularly jailed or imprisoned. Two surveys that reported this were sponsored by the president's crime commission; see *The Challenge of Crime in a Free Society: A Report of the President's Commission on Law Enforcement and the Administration of Justice,* (Washington, D.C.: U.S. Government Printing Office, 1967).

[13] See Gene Kassebaum, David A. Ward, and Daniel M. Wilner, *Prison Treatment and Parole Survival* (New York: John Wiley, 1971).

[14] Leslie T. Wilkins, *Evaluation of Penal Measures* (Berkeley and Los Angeles: University of California Press, 1969).

Robert Martinson, stubbornly persisted in publicizing the information.[15] By 1970 the opinion of critical criminologists was that nothing that correctional program planners could do would significantly alter rates of recidivism.

These criminologists, along with other individuals with more critical views on criminal justice than the earlier experts, became active in the public debate on the prison issue. The critical criminologists attended many of the conferences sponsored by the prison movement groups; and, in return, many lawyers, ex-convicts, and citizen activists who demonstrated knowledge and wisdom on prison issues were invited to participate in the activities sponsored or controlled by the academicians — university classes, symposiums, conferences, and, finally, task forces and commissions. When the National Advisory Commission on Criminal Justice Standards and Goals convened in 1971, its Task Force on Corrections could not ignore critical perspectives that were being developed in these private and university circles.

The new critical perspectives generated within this academic section of the prison movement divide into two main categories: the justice perspective and the radical perspective. The former is epitomized by *Struggle for Justice,* written by a working party for the American Friends Service Committee.[16] The Friends, a Quaker social action organization, felt deep responsibility for the prisons (since Quakers had been prominent in planning the first prisons in the United States) and had been active in prison issues for decades. Their working party on prisons included a law professor who had been imprisoned twice as a conscientious objector in World War II and later became a highly respected scholar and critic of the criminal justice system; two other ex-convicts (including myself); five persons active in the civil rights and war protest movements; and seven persons with long affiliations with the Friends and

---

[15] After several years of announcing the group's findings, Martinson published a summary: "What Works? Questions and Answers about Prison Reform," *Public Interest,* Spring 1974. Then the full report was published in 1975: Douglas Lipton, Robert Martinson, and Judith Willes, *The Effectiveness of Correctional Treatment* (New York: Praeger, 1975).

[16] *Struggle for Justice* (New York: Hill and Wang, 1971).

experience with prisons. The party was an excellent representative sample of the advocates of justice.

In an introduction to the analysis of the prison problem, we (the working party) recognized that it and the broader problems in the criminal justice system are rooted deeply into social injustice:

> These chronic deficiencies of the criminal justice system assume alarming proportions at a time of escalating challenge to the legitimacy of the American power structure. Intractable racism, a stratifying culture of poverty, and a growing despair in the ability of American society to change and to respond to crisis require decisive change.[17]

Moving from the basic and intractable problems of social injustice to our analysis of criminal justice, we went around the "cruel fortress prisons" and the lack of community integration and identified discrimination as the most critical issue in the criminal justice system. The system, we argued, selects the rich and influential for preferred treatment and the poor and uninfluential for harsh punishment. This systematically unfair selection begins long before arrests, prosecution, and sentencing. It begins in the construction of criminal law.

> The selection of candidates for prosecution reflects inequality in the larger society not only because of bias on the part of police or prosecutors but because the substantive content of the law affects those who are not social equals in quite different ways. A wealthy industrialist has little difficulty in having his opinions on political questions heard at the highest levels of government; he doesn't need to demonstrate or sit in to be sure that his ideas will receive consideration. Lobbyists for all kinds of special interest groups frequent the corridors of legislative office buildings and the chambers of judges. The wealth and votes they command carry weight and help shape the content of the law. But who speaks for the unemployed, the welfare mother, the habitual drunkard, the inmate, the drug addict, the recidivist? Laws forbidding armed robbery and burglary have very different impact for a millionaire and for an unemployed twenty-year old black male in a ghetto where the unemployment rate is

[17] Ibid., p. 9.

25 percent and a Governor Reagan is crusading against "welfare fraud." [18]

We concluded that the rehabilitative ideal or the "individualized treatment model," which purports to select out persons on the basis of requirements for treatment and future dangerousness, actually supplies the criminal justice decision makers — police, prosecutors, judges, prison administrators, parole boards, and parole officers — with the discretion to accomplish this unfair selection and other publicly inadmissible purposes, such as restraint of categories of people who threaten more powerful parties in the society. In addition to progress toward general social justice, we recommended several specific changes in the criminal justice system. Briefly stated, these recommendations were:

1. Change the criminal law so that it prohibits acts that constitute actual harm instead of controlling classes of people or expressing moral sensibilities.
2. Punish this larger group of offenders for short periods in a humane system of incarceration.
3. Offer to all offenders as well as all free persons who seek it, help as they, the seekers, define it.

This summary does not address the difficult conceptual issues raised in our recommendations. A fuller discussion of these is contained in *Struggle for Justice* and several books that followed and were inspired by it.[19] Here, the point is that a new class of critics offered solutions to the prison problems that fell outside the limits of political feasibility. The solutions hinge on reduction of discretion throughout the criminal justice system, but many unstated purposes of the system require wide margins of discretion in the hands of police, prosecutors, prison administrators, parole boards, and parole officers.

The radical faction of the academic critics focused on the class struggle in a capitalist society. They argued that crime is

[18] Ibid., p. 15.
[19] See especially Andrew von Hirsch, *Doing Justice* (New York: Hill and Wang, 1976); David Fogel, *We Are the Living Proof* (Cincinnati: W. H. Anderson, 1975); and Norval Morris, *The Future of Imprisonment* (Chicago: University of Chicago Press, 1974).

164

mainly or entirely an artifact of capitalism in the United States. For example, Erik Olin Wright, who became part of the Berkeley network of radical critics of the prison, wrote in his collection of papers by himself and the more radical commentators:

> The following discussion will examine how patterns of crime in America emerge out of the social forces which confront people in the society. Social structure influences the pattern of crime in three essential ways: by creating *problems*, especially economic problems; by creating a particular pattern of *options* available to individuals for solving those problems and by creating constraints which influence the *decision* to adopt a particular option for solving problems.[20]

By assuming that crime is only a property of unjust economic arrangements, the radicals were able to skip over the issues of improving the criminal justice system. It is seen simply as an oppressive mechanism operated by the more powerful classes to keep lower classes under control. The thrust of their analysis is on the promotion of a continual struggle that will advance revolutionary change. Their general attitude in regard to the particular issues in the prison and criminal justice is that these will dissolve as we approach broader revolutionary goals. Whatever residual deviation remains can be handled humanely and informally in peer communities, much as it was being done (according to radicals) in China.

Although they were able to ignore the radical criticism, the National Advisory Commission on Criminal Justice Standards and Goals could not completely ignore the advocates of justice. The antiestablishment mood was too powerful, and government-sponsored groups were obliged to include representatives from various social segments — minority groups, the working class, and ex-offenders, for example. So the new Task Force on Corrections was composed of a mixture of the traditional type of experts and a sprinkling of more critical, new participants in government commissions.

In accomplishing its mandate, that is, devising a politically

[20] Wright, *The Politics of Punishment* (New York: Harper & Row, 1973), p. 6.

feasible solution to the prison problem, the task force skirted around the edges of the broader criticism contained in *Struggle for Justice.* Like the earlier crime commission, it stressed the crippling effect of imprisonment.

> The failure of major institutions to reduce crime is incontestable. Recidivism rates are notoriously high. Institutions do succeed in punishing but they do not deter. They protect the community but that protection is only temporary. They relieve the community of responsibility by removing the offender but they make successful reintegration into the community unlikely. They change the committed offender but the change is more likely to be negative than positive.[21]

In the spirit of the times, the task force was highly sensitive to prisoners' rights.

> Until recently, an offender, as a matter of law, was deemed to have forfeited virtually all rights upon conviction and to have retained only such rights as were expressly granted to him by statute or correctional authority. The belief was common that virtually anything could be done with an offender in the name of "correction," or in some instances "punishment," short of extreme physical abuse. He was protected only by the restraint and responsibility of correctional administrations and their staff. Whatever comforts, services, or privileges the offender received were a matter of grace—in the law's view, a privilege to be granted or withheld by the state. Inhumane conditions and practices were permitted to develop and continue in many systems.[22]

It even ventured a few paces into the area of discrimination, but not far enough to travel outside the limits of political feasibility. What it did was argue that injustice in discretionary decision making was restricted to postconviction decisions.

> The United States has a strong and abiding attachment to the rule of law with a rich inheritance of government of law rather than men. This high regard for the rule of law has been applied extensively in the criminal justice system up to

[21] *Corrections,* National Advisory Commission on Criminal Justice Standards and Goals (Washington, D.C.: U.S. Government Printing Office, 1973), p. 1.
[22] Ibid., p. 18.

the point of conviction. But beyond conviction, until recently, largely unsupervised and arbitrary discretion held sway. This was true of sentencing, for which criteria were absent and from which appeals were both rare and difficult. It was true of the discretion exercised by the institutional administrator concerning prison conditions and disciplinary sanctions.[23]

By restricting its focus to the misuse of discretionary powers in decision making after conviction, the task force passed over most of the difficult issues of injustice: the discriminatory selection inherent in substantive law and that practiced by police, prosecutors, and judges. In effect, they avoided the basic criticism leveled by the advocates of justice — that the criminal justice system tended to select out less influential and poorer lawbreakers (who were not necessarily the most dangerous or harmful), detain them arbitrarily in jails, and punish them too harshly. Then the task force smuggled in the solution that traditional rehabilitation experts had been offering for a decade, community corrections. The task force described it in a manner suggesting that it solves the problems of both discriminatory selection and the severe punishment and damage inherent in imprisonment.

> Many arguments for correctional programs that deal with offenders in the community—probation, parole and others—meet the test of common sense on their own merits. Such arguments are greatly strengthened by the failing record of the prisons, reformatories, and the like. The mega-institution, holding more than a thousand adult inmates, has been built in larger number and variety in this country than anywhere else in the world. Large institutions for young offenders have also proliferated here. In such surroundings, inmates become faceless people living out routine and meaningless lives. And where institutions are racially skewed and filled with a disproportionate number of ill-educated and vocationally inept persons, they magnify tensions already existing in our society.[24]

[23] Ibid., p. 8.
[24] Ibid., p. 1.

167

They implied that turning away from "mega-institutions" to correctional programs in the community will erase the problems of institutions which are "racially skewed and filled with a disproportionate number of ill-educated and vocationally inept persons." What they actually offered was a tradeoff. In return for keeping discretionary decision making, they promised to divert almost everyone to less punitive, community correctional systems.

In addition to community corrections, the task force did recommend expansion of prisoners' rights and limitations on discretion in correctional decision making. These, as it turned out (this was not apparent when the task force completed its work), were outside the area of political feasibility and were ignored by policy makers in planning and implementing programs. What took hold was community corrections and diversion.

Selling Community Corrections In the early 1970s the proponents of community corrections stepped up their promotion of the new penology. Persons from many different sections of the growing public segment interested in prison reform, even from most factions of the prison movement, became supporters of the community corrections solution. For example, a coalition of liberal prison abolitionists wrote in their pamphlet entitled *The Price of Punishment:*

> Almost all of the men and women now in prison would be better off (and so would the rest of society) if they were allowed to stay outside on the street and offered one or more of the following options:
> Community probation service
> Guaranteed employment at a living wage
> Free education or vocational training
> Assistance in obtaining decent housing, medical care or related services
> Free mental health services or similar counseling for alcoholics, drug abusers, gamblers and persons with similar problems.[25]

[25] Prison Research Project, *The Price of Punishment* (Cambridge: Urban Planning, 1974), pp. 59–60.

168

They, too, failed to address the problem of misuse of discretionary power when they admitted:

> There are a handful of people now in prison who are truly dangerous and must be confined. But even these people should not be cut off from all outside contact, locked up in cages, and treated like animals. They could be confined in small group homes instead of in fortresses like Walpole, Concord, or Bridgewater.[26]

But these reformers missed one simple fact: If one is *confined* somewhere, it is not a home, but a prison.

Even the more radical critics found the notion of community corrections consistent with their ideas about crime and its treatment in the future socialist society. Erik Olin Wright comments on punishment in the future:

> *Whenever possible, punishment is not alienated from the community.* In the same way that there would be collective responsibility for an offense, there would be collective responsibility for punishment. A hierarchy of punishment would still exist but the lower levels of the hierarchy would be firmly rooted in community control. For a wide variety of relatively minor offenses, some type of "criticism/self-criticism" in a socialist society would be the basic technique of dealing with the offense. For more serious offenses, the central sanction would be some form of community surveillance. Such surveillance would differ from "probation" or a "suspended sentence" in that members of the community would actively participate in the social control of the offender rather than having the control handled by a probation bureaucracy. Similarly, if short-term incarceration facilities were necessary, they would be locally controlled and integrated into the general community.[27]

The proponents of community corrections had their hopes raised high when Jerome Miller swiftly and unexpectedly closed all the youth prisons (the "industrial schools") in Massachusetts. Miller, after appointment as director of Youth Services in 1970,

[26] Ibid., p. 62.
[27] Wright, *The Politics of Punishment,* p. 341.

experimented with various methods of reducing the prison populations in an incremental fashion and encountered considerable resistance within his own agency and from other quarters. Then in 1972, after conducting a publicity campaign for "community treatment," he transferred all but thirty-five or forty of the juvenile prisoners to community locations, mainly halfway houses, that private individuals and groups quickly prepared.[28] By the time the legislature (which was in recess when Miller emptied the prisons), other government agencies, and members of his own agency could respond, the shift had been accomplished. Miller left Massachusetts, but other supporters of his ideas have been able to hold the line and not reopen the youth prisons. Miller's accomplishment seemed to demonstrate what is possible in the prison field, both youth and adult, and the community corrections advocates were inspired by it. They failed to consider, however, that Miller caught the public and the state government by complete surprise and that, from then on, other states would be ready. (As a matter of fact, Miller has tried with no success to duplicate his action in Illinois and Pennsylvania, where he has occupied high administrative posts in the correctional bureaucracies.) Moreover, what is possible in the field of juvenile justice is not necessarily possible in the adult field. The fact that the public tolerated juvenile offenders' being diverted from prison does not mean that they will accept the same policies for adults, whom they perceive very differently. As it has turned out, Miller instilled false hope.

Describing Community Corrections By and large, the community corrections planners' dreams have materialized in furloughs from prison, work release from prisons, probation, parole, and halfway houses. The more ambitious plan for a community institution that would be located in an urban center, "would be small and fairly informal in structure," and "would permit flexible use of community resources, both in the institution and for inmates to work or study or spend short periods of time at home" usually smashed against an unanticipated

[28] Many of the locations were temporary. For example, some youths were temporarily housed in dormitories at the University of Massachusetts in Amherst.

barrier: local community resistance. The case history of Eagle River Correctional Facility is a telling example of the original dream's failure. In the late 1960s and early 1970s, Alaska, with its new wealth from the North Slope oil development and a relatively liberal attitude toward crime and punishment, planned a new model prison. They hired some of the most prestigious correctional experts — such as LaMar Empey from the University of Southern California and Charles Adams, an innovative correctional administrator from Vermont — and the nation's leading innovative prison architects — Helmut, Orbata, and Kassebaum. The latter had spent several years studying the new corrections. In their program description of Eagle River, they wrote:

> the community integration approach views the offender as the product of a hazardous social environment and stresses the role of social institutions, communities and neighborhoods as powerful forces opposing the perpetuation of crime and delinquency. The implication is that correctional programs are to be defined in terms of services such as more fully developed remedial programs of education and vocational training, employment counselling, and job placement assistance.[29]

This mixture of experts designed a humane, pleasant institution that would serve as a minimum-security unit for about eighty prisoners, from which they could be released for work or school in the community and to which individuals and organizations from the community could be drawn. The comfortable physical plant, which opened in 1975, incorporated the latest design features in innovative prison architecture. The prisoners resided in two modules, each of which had a recreation room and four separate clusters of ten rooms. Each cluster had its own sitting room, showers, toilets, and washroom. The institution had a spacious dining room, which adjoined a sitting area; a library; a full-sized gym; and a large shop area. From the outside, with its rough redwood siding, large glass windows, and unobtrusive fence, the prison looked like a small, modern college building. On the inside, except for some solid metal

[29] *A Research Design to Evaluate the Correctional Center* (San Francisco: Marshal Kaplan, Gans, and Kahn, 1976), p. 5.

doors between areas, it looked like a college dormitory. There were carpets on the floors; the furniture was modern, heavy oak; and the rooms resembled small, college dorm rooms.

The prison never achieved community corrections status. When faced with resistance from some parties in Anchorage and with downtown property prices, the state correctional planners fixed the actual location of the new prison to be thirteen miles from the center of Anchorage on property already owned by the state (this policy of prison site selection often prevails). Then as the hand-picked Eagle River staff began establishing work- and study-release programs, certain individuals in the Anchorage community, particularly one of the more popular and controversial television news broadcasters, precipitated an intense community reaction toward Eagle River and the other jails in Anchorage, all of which were operated by the state's Division of Corrections. The ostensible target of the criticism was poor security, which the critics implied endangered the Anchorage community. They focused on several escapes, particularly two in which the individual escapees committed violent acts, a rape and a murder, immediately after the escapes.

It became clear to me while visiting and studying Eagle River during this period that lying just below the surface of this criticism and very frequently jutting through the surface was the actual source of Anchorage's ire: Eagle River was too pleasant. The charges that the media commentators were making about the escapes and the security risks of Eagle River were distorted. The two escapes that received most of the attention had not been from Eagle River proper. One downtown jail prisoner had escaped while being taken to a dentist. The other prisoner was being held in a special maximum-security section of Eagle River, which was as secure as any prison maximum-security unit. (A careless guard had let a convicted murderer being temporarily held at Eagle River's special maximum-security section stay unwatched in a small fenced-in yard next to the unit. The prisoner climbed over the fence, in spite of a strand of barbed wire at the top.) The few escapes that occurred from Eagle River in its first months of operation did not result in any violence, and, in fact, most of the escapees were caught coming back to the prison intoxicated. Many of the reports subtly attempted to obscure these facts. The following passage from the *Anchorage Daily News* failed to clarify the escape picture and conveyed the impression that prisoners frequently escaped from Eagle River and committed dangerous acts.

> The suspect in the shooting of the policeman was one of 28 inmates who in the past 15 months, have been listed as escapees by the state Department of Corrections.
>
> Twenty-six of the inmates were listed as having escaped from the custody of the three institutions in the Anchorage area.
>
> Seven of the escapees left state custody while on work release from the Anchorage Correctional Center at Third Avenue downtown. Another six were on work release from the Eagle River Correctional Center. Three men escaped from medium or maximum security settings—one each from the Third Avenue and Eagle River facilities and one from the Correctional Center Annex at Sixth Avenue and C Street.
>
> An additional six men escaped from the Eagle River facility by climbing a wire fence. Three inmates walked away from drug or alcohol minimum security treatment facilities where they were housed. And one—the man charged with the policeman's death—eluded a corrections officer while at a doctor's office.[30]

The newspaper and television reports regularly sprinkled information about the luxury of Eagle River in their discussion of the poor security. During one week I observed the newscaster who launched the attack allude to Eagle River's excessive comfort several times. One night, after interviewing Eagle River's high school teacher, a young, attractive female, he joked about "how hard the prisoners have it with pretty women like this working at Eagle River." A letter to the *Anchorage Times* during this period reveals the sentiments of many citizens toward Eagle River:

> We have urgent need for a maximum security prison with armed guards with no telephone privileges, with no parking

[30] Sally W. Jones, "Is Alaska Coddling Criminals?" *Anchorage Daily News*, September 9, 1975, p. 1.

lot for prisoners' vehicles (yes, inmates should be called "prisoners," not "clients"); no visiting lounge where inmates may mingle freely with visitors, no locked rooms to which the inmates carry the keys. In short, we need at least one punitive institution because rehabilitation can't hope to succeed without punishment. The prospect of a paid vacation to a plush resort is no deterrent to crime.[31]

Anchorage's criticism precipitated a local grand jury and a government's task force investigation, the resignation of Charles Adams, and a complete reshuffling of Eagle River's top administration. In the fall of 1976 a temporary superintendent with a reputation for toughness was brought in, and all release programs were stopped. The community corrections aspect of Eagle River withered; in fact, Eagle River withered. When I visited the prison in January 1977, months after the shake-up, Eagle River had a prisoner population of about fifty, half of its capacity. There were no release programs and very few other programs. There were mandatory daily group sessions, a craft program, and a few elementary and high school classes. The morale of the staff and prisoners was extremely low. The community corrections dream had been shattered by a harsh reality that the original planners of community corrections ignored. This reality may be stated in the proposition recognized many decades ago: In general, the public will not allow convicted felons to live at a level of luxury or privilege above the lowest classes in the society.[32] The proposition seems fair; in fact, its inherent fairness is its basis. Rational planning of prison policies should be consistent with it. When the public has believed that this rule was violated, reactions similar to those in Alaska have resulted in the abandonment of programs and practices that increased the comfort, privilege, and mobility of prisoners.

Appraising Community Corrections   In the last decade

---

[31] *Anchorage Times,* July 26, 1975.

[32] This proposition was brought to my attention by Caleb Foote, who suggested that its violation was partly instrumental in the abandonment of transportation as a major form of punishment in English in the nineteenth century.

there has been massive experimentation with variations of community corrections and diversion, and now there is enough information to begin evaluating the effectiveness and the impact of the programs. But first, we should examine the flawed logic of the new penology. The idea that community corrections promotes the reintegration of the offender into the community distorts or stretches conceptions of community. The notion of a community is a holdover from rural or folk societies, and it is not exactly clear what it refers to in a modern city. One of the essential meanings of the concept is a supportive network of people living in a geographical area who know, come into contact with, and provide services for each other. There may be some locations in modern cities that approximate this, but most do not. Moreover, many of those that do are not the type of supportive networks that planners of community corrections have in mind. In an analysis of the idea of community corrections, David Greenberg points out that offenders may have been well integrated into an *undesirable* community:

> The emphasis on community disorganization and the need to make provisions for reintegration may obscure the degree to which some offenders prior to arrest were quite well integrated into the social life of their communities, but in a criminal mode — to which they may desire to return in order to obtain financial rewards, status, and excitement.[33]

Greenberg points out that correctional planners have no resources or techniques to improve "bad" communities.

> The National Advisory Commission's *Report on Corrections* . . . ignores the extent to which high levels of unemployment and structural features of the labor market may hinder the ex-offender from "pursuing a lawful style of living in the community." If it is true that lack of contact with good schools and adequate housing contributes to criminality and there are no good schools or adequate housing in the community, how can a community corrections center remedy this?

[33] "Problems in Community Corrections," *Issues in Criminology,* Spring 1975, p. 5.

175

It is in no position to improve the schools or bring slum apartments into conformity with housing codes.[34]

It does not necessarily follow that community corrections is a less expensive correctional strategy. This would be certain only if the program were limited to probation or parole, which is not what the planners have in mind. Erecting treatment centers in downtown areas and providing schooling, job training, surveillance, food, and clothing can be more costly than traditional forms of punishment.

Likewise, community corrections may be as inhumane as imprisonment. The programs, as they have been conceived, are definitely coercive. The combination of close surveillance in the community and the enlarged possibilities for engaging in unacceptable and illegal acts places the client in a situation of temptation, strain, and increased legal jeopardy, all of which may add up to increased inhumanity.

In the actual implementation of most community corrections programs, many of the anticipated benefits failed to occur, and some undesirable, unexpected consequences have resulted. When the correctional agencies have tried to locate community facilities (such as halfway houses) in many neighborhoods, the local residents have vigorously protested and successfully resisted the attempts. Often, therefore, the centers or houses have been located in deteriorating "interstitial" or slum neighborhoods, where there is little or no organized opposition. These are hardly the communities into which the planners intended the offenders be reintegrated.

Most of the programs have added very little to the traditional probation and parole routines. Halfway houses, in which offenders must remain for some hours of the day or week and from which they depart to seek jobs, work, or attend school, are the most frequent programs other than probation and parole. These have had very few job-training or placement and education components. The few more ambitious programs have proven to be extremely expensive, and their superiority in reducing recidivism is questionable.

Many of the programs have very high rates of absconding

[34] Ibid., p. 5.

(as high as 25 percent), indicating that many offenders experience the community corrections as punitive.[35] Note that absconding is a crime and will invariably increase the length and severity of punishment when the absconder is caught. Evidently, many persons in community treatment institutions, although they willingly accept them as an alternative to jail or prison, discover that the mixture of heavy surveillance, difficulties of living in a shabby, crowded halfway house in a slum area, and temptations that abound in the neighborhood constitutes a subtle, but harsh, form of punishment.

Moreover, community corrections often fails to reduce and sometimes aggravates other forms of punishment. Paul Lerman reports that the community treatment program in California resulted in the creation of a new discretionary detention procedure in which the parolees in the program were locked up for short lengths of time on the discretion of the parole agent. Then this detention routine, which had the effect of increasing the amount of lockup of parolees, was extended to all categories of Youth Authority parolees.[36] Many states, in the rush to implement the new correctional mode, relabeled old downtown city or county jails as community treatment centers and held convicted felons there, even though they are more unpleasant and punitive than prisons. In practice, community corrections has fallen far short of being a significant step in the direction of humane treatment of offenders.

It is now apparent that community corrections and diversion have failed and probably will continue to fail to reduce prison populations. There are some exceptions, but state prison populations have generally risen. Instead of dipping into the small percentage of defendants who were sent to prison, the community corrections and other diversion programs receive those who were formerly filtered out of the system through dismissal, reduction of charge, and probation. Moreover, the system now draws into its net many persons who formerly were

[35] See LaMar T. Empey, "Juvenile Justice Reform," in Lloyd E. Ohlin, ed., *Prisoners in America* (Englewood Cliffs, N.J.: Prentice-Hall, 1973), p. 45.

[36] *Community Treatment and Social Control* (Chicago: University of Chicago Press, 1975), chap. 4.

diverted informally. A study of prearrest diversion of juveniles in southern California revealed that police were referring to diversion programs those juveniles whom they formerly released with a warning.[37] Before there were diversion programs, the police released the youth, because they believed that the acts were too petty. But now that there are nonpunitive alternatives available, the police decide to use them. In fact, many city and county police departments have made it mandatory that policemen use the diversion programs in the cases in which informal diversion was practiced. The final result is that those who were diverted through informal channels, dismissal, and probation are now diverted, but often go to programs with more surveillance; and the felons who went to prison still go to prison.

Instead of ameliorating the problem in prison, community corrections has aggravated them. The approach failed to remove the category of defendant who was always sent to prison, and so prison populations held steady and then in 1972 surpassed the former high level reached in 1961.[38] Since then, they have been soaring to new heights.[39] The decline up to 1968 can be attributed partly to the early experimentation with expanded probation programs, but is probably due more to general decreases in sentences.

The subsequent increase in prison populations, as well as the swing back toward punitive penal practices, can be partially blamed on the heavy promotion, if not the practice, of community corrections. In presenting the concept to the public, the proponents greatly exaggerated the nonpunitiveness and eventual scope of the program. The impression was conveyed that most convicted felons were to be diverted to programs that offered extensive services. In doing this, the promoters ignored

[37] See Malcolm Klein, "Issues in Police Diversion of Juvenile Offenders," in Robert M. Carter and Malcolm Klein, eds., *Back on the Street: The Diversion of Juvenile Offenders* (Englewood Cliffs, N.J.: Prentice-Hall, 1975), pp. 73–104.

[38] See U.S. Census Bureau, *Statistical History of the United States from Colonial Times to the Present: Statistical Abstract of the United States, 1970, 1972* (Washington, D.C.: U.S. Government Printing Office).

[39] Prison populations reached 278,141 in 1977, as compared with less than 200,000 in 1967 and 1968 (U.S. Department of Justice).

retribution, a function of the criminal justice system that at the time was unfashionable among the experts. The public had indicated strong support for rehabilitation in the mid-1960s, but then it believed that punishment, perhaps too much punishment, was occurring. When the advocates of the new penal philosophy stressed that immediately releasing offenders to probation, parole, and various community treatment institutions would not increase crime and would be a more effective and humane system of rehabilitation, they failed to consider that some large portion of the public wants offenders to be punished. They kept from the public the reality that most of those who were not diverted before would not be diverted under the new penology (an outcome that the planners were not aware of) and that the diversion programs are punitive. The public began supporting, often insisting on, more punitive sentencing policies. A swing toward longer, mandated sentences (which will be discussed in chapter 8) was precipitated in part by the reactions to community corrections. So not only did community corrections fail to reduce prison populations, but it also played a part in new sentencing policies that increased prison populations.

Prison administrators, on a punitive tack after their reaction to the prison movement, have used the community corrections programs as a rationale for more secure and punitive prison policies. They have argued that the good prisoners are being skimmed off before prison and that they are receiving only the dangerous criminals. The fact that there has been no reduction in the number of commitments has not deterred them from drawing this conclusion. Now prison systems, such as New York and California, have been seeking new funds from the state to build new maximum-security prisons to hold the concentration of dangerous prisoners left to them, as more and more diversion programs are employed.

This politically feasible solution to the prison problem, community corrections, failed because it did not extend to the practices and relationships located outside the agenda of alternatives. One set of these, such as racism and poverty, are characteristics of the society over which a correctional system has little influence. However, discretion employed to discriminate between more and less influential persons is within the purview of the criminal justice system, and the experts ducked it because it was politically unfeasible to attempt to remove it. In not addressing discretion, the experts passed up a much more promising solution: short, uniform sentences for all persons guilty of a certain crime. This would reduce prison populations and the debilitating impact of imprisonment, as well as other problems. But this apparently rational and fair solution is politically unfeasible.

7
The Contemporary Prison

The reverberations from the 1960s left most men's prisons fragmented, tense, and often extremely violent. The old social order, with its cohesion and monotonous tranquility, did not and perhaps will never reappear. The prisoners are divided by extreme differences, distrust, and hatred. Nonwhites, especially blacks, Chicanos, and Puerto Ricans, have risen in numbers and prominence. A multitude of criminal types — dope fiends, pimps, bikers, street gang members, and very few old-time thieves — assert themselves and compete for power and respect.

Nevertheless, chaos and a complete war of all against all have not resulted. They never do. When human social organizations splinter and friction between the parts increases, people still struggle to maintain old or create new collective structures that supply them with basic social needs, particularly protection from threats of violence. Complex social forms and a high degree of order still exist among prisoners, even in the most violent and fragmented prisons, like San Quentin, but it is a "segmented order" similar to that which Gerald Suttles discovered in the Addams slum area in Chicago.[1]

This particular slum had features like many contemporary prisons. Several different, relatively poor, working-class and lower-class segments — Italians, Mexicans, Puerto Ricans, and blacks — shared the neighborhood and were generally prejudiced and hostile toward each other. In addition, this slum,

---

[1] Gerald Suttles, *The Social Order of the Slum* (Chicago: University of Chicago Press, 1968).

like most slums, contained many persons who lacked the commitment to public morality that ordinarily promotes a high degree of safety among strangers. In this situation of distrust, people living in the Addams area employed two main strategies for increasing their safety, voluntary segregation and personalized realtionships. In Suttles's words:

> First, social relations can be restricted to permit only the safest. Families can withdraw to their households where they see only close relatives. Age grading along with sex and ethnic segregation are maneuvers that will avoid at least the most unfair and likely forms of conflict and exploitation. Remaining in close proximity to the household cuts down on the range of anonymity and reduces the number of social relations.
>
> Second, slum residents can assuage at least some of their apprehensions by a close inquiry into each other's personal character and past history. Communication, then, should be of an intimate character and aimed toward producing "personal" rather than formal relations. In turn, social relations will represent a sort of private "compact" where particularistic loyalties replace impersonal standards of worth.[2]

So it is in prison today. Races, particularly black and white, are divided and hate each other. In general, prisoners distrust most other prisoners whom they do not know well. The strategies for coping with this are similar to those employed in the Addams area. There are virtually no sex strata [3] and much less age stratification in the prison, but increasingly prisoners restrict their interaction to small friendship groups and other small social units (gangs, for example) formed with members of their own race. Other than race, prisoners retreat into small orbits based on social characteristics such as (1) criminal orientation, (2) shared preprison experiences (coming from the same town or neighborhood or having been in other prisons together), (3) shared prison interests, and (4) forced proximity in cell assignment or work.

[2] Ibid., p. 8.
[3] The prison-identified homosexuals — the queens, punks, and kids — do constitute a very small, separate stratum.

RACIAL DIVISIONS

The hate and distrust between white and black prisoners constitute the most powerful source of divisions. After being forestalled by the moves toward unity during the prison movement, the conditions and trends discussed in chapter 3 were reestablished. Black prisoners continued to increase in numbers and assertiveness. Whites, led by the more prejudiced and violent, increasingly reacted. Hate, tension, and hostilities between the two races escalated. An Illinois black prisoner describes the posture of black prisoners toward whites.

> In the prison, the black dudes have a little masculinity game they play. It has no name, really, but I call it whup or fuck a white boy — especially the white gangsters or syndicate men, the bad juice boys, the hit men, etc. The black dudes go out of their way to make faggots out of them. And to lose a fight to a white dude is one of the worst things that can happen to a black dude. And I know that, by and far, the white cats are faggots. They will drop their pants and bend over and touch their toes and get had before they will fight. So, knowing this, what kind of men did this make us? They told us where, how, when to shit, eat, sleep.[4]

White prisoners, whether or not they were racially hostile before prison, tend to become so after experiencing prison racial frictions. Edward Bunker, who served several terms in California prisons and writes insightfully about contemporary prison processes and relationships, described a middle-class white prisoner's entrance into racial hatred:

> After 10:30, the noise dropped a decibel or two, and from the morass of sound Ron began to recognize certain voices by timbre and catch snatches of conversation. Above him, perhaps on the second tier, he picked up a gumboed black voice saying he'd like to kill all white babies, while his listener agreed it was the best way to handle the beasts — before they grew up. A year earlier, Ron would have felt compassion for anyone so consumed by hate and whenever whites casually used "nigger" he was irked. Now he felt tentacles of hate

[4] Billy "Hands" Robinson, "Love: A Hard Legged Triangle," *Black Scholar,* September 1971, p. 29.

spreading through himself — and half an hour later, he smiled when a batch of voices began chanting: "Sieg Heil! Sieg Heil! Sieg Heil!" [5]

Whites hate and, when they are not organized to resist, fear black prisoners. Carroll quoted a white prisoner in the Rhode Island prison that he studied:

> They think they're superior and they push us around all the time. Like in the dining hall. If I was late and trying to catch up with a buddy and cut in front of one of them, I'd probably get piped. But they cut in front of white men all the time and nothing happens. . . . It's the same in the wings. The tier I'm on used to be all white. Now it's 50–50 and it ain't safe for a white to walk along it. If he does, he better walk quick and keep his eyes open. [6]

The divisions and hatreds extend into the guard force and even into the administrations. Leo Carroll and Erik Olin Wright documented bias against black prisoners in administrative decisions, particularly disciplinary proceedings. [7] Black prisoners have consistently testified that white guards verbally and physically abuse them and discriminate against them. [8] Some radical commentators have suggested that guards and administrators have political motivations in their expression of racial hatred. This may be true, in some very indirect fashion. But the discrimination against blacks by white staff has a more immediate source: hatred for black prisoners. In expressing their hate, they sometimes give license to racist prisoners. Edward Bunker describes the situation in San Quentin:

> But he knew that some of the license given tough white and Chicano convicts by certain other guards was because of the

[5] *Animal Factory* (New York: Viking Press, 1977), p. 92. This novel, in which Bunker employs his extensive direct experience and excellent sociological imagination, is used here as a source of data for San Quentin.

[6] Leo Carroll, *Hacks, Blacks, and Cons* (Lexington, Mass.: Lexington Books, 1974), p. 147.

[7] Ibid., chap. 6; Erik Olin Wright, *The Politics of Punishment* (New York: Harper & Row, 1973), p. 114.

[8] *Attica: The Official Report of the New York State Special Commission on Attica* (New York: Praeger, 1972) has the most convincing reports on such testimony.

racial conflict. Blacks had killed several guards in the three tough prisons during the past two years and guards who had once been mild bigots were now outright racists. Certain of them would frisk a white or Chicano convict, feel a shiv and pass the man by. It was an unholy alliance, alien to all of Earl's values.[9]

White and black prisoners do not mix in informal prisoner groups, and many form groups for the purpose of expressing racial hatred and protecting their friends from the other race. A wife of a San Quentin prisoner described her husband's drift toward organized racial hatred: "He didn't used to be prejudiced but now he hates blacks. He and some other white friends formed an American National Socialists group which I guess is a nazi group because they hate blacks so much." [10]

Like the Addams area, the public spaces are divided by the different racial groups, particularly white and black prisoners. Leo Carroll charted the patterns of segregation in a Rhode Island prison, shown in figures 7.1–7.3. And Edward Bunker described the patterns in San Quentin:

> The blacks, however, congregated along the north cellhouse wall, an area nicknamed "Nairobi." A decade of race wars had made it impossible to relax without a territorial imperative.
>
> . . . Blacks turned into one row, while whites and Chicanos turned into another. When their row filled before that of the blacks, they started another. Official segregation had ended a decade earlier; the regulations now said that convicts could enter any of three rows but nobody crossed lines and nobody wanted to. Racism was a mass obsession that infected everyone and there was continual race war. So, the mess hall had a row of blacks, followed by two or three rows of whites and Chicanos, then another row of blacks.[11]

Other minority groups, such as Chicanos, Puerto Ricans, Chinese, American Indians, and French Canadians, relate to whites and blacks in a more complex fashion. For instance, Chicanos in California prisons are more hostile toward black

[9] *Animal Factory,* p. 42.
[10] Interview, San Francisco, January 1978.
[11] *Animal Factory,* p. 20.

than toward white prisoners. White prisoners generally fear, distrust, and dislike Chicanos, because Chicanos speak Spanish or Calo and are believed to have a tendency to attack other prisoners with relatively less provocation than members of other groups. However, most white prisoners respect them for their toughness and do not threaten or derogate other white prisoners who befriend, hand around, or identify with Chicanos. Many white and Chicano prisoners have associated with each other in the "streets" and other joints and still maintain close friendship ties, even in the racially divided prison mileu. Puerto Rican, American Indian, French Canadian, and other racial or ethnic minorities have similar, ambivalent positions in the complex racial matrix.

VIOLENT CLIQUES AND GANGS

In many men's prisons today, groups of prisoners regularly rob and attack other prisoners and retaliate when members of their clique or gang have been threatened or attacked. This has intensified the fear and widened the gap between prisoners, par-

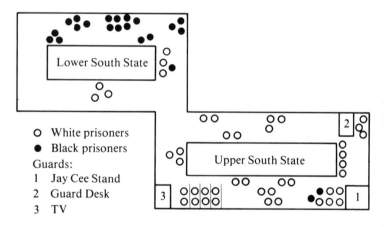

FIGURE 7.1. Racial Segregation in Informal Groupings in South State Wing

Source: Reprinted by permission of the publisher, from Leo Carroll, *Hacks, Blacks, and Cons: Race Relations in a Maximum Security Prison* (Lexington, Mass.: Lexington Books, D.C. Heath and Company, Copyright © 1974, D.C. Heath and Company), p. 162.

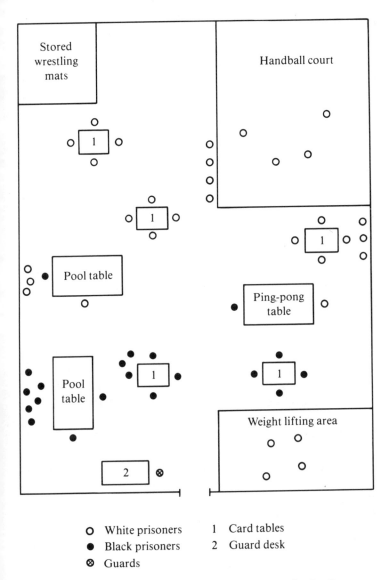

O	White prisoners	1 Card tables
●	Black prisoners	2 Guard desk
⊗	Guards	

FIGURE 7.2. Racial Segregation of Prisoners in the Gym

Source: Reprinted by permission of the publisher, from Leo Carroll, *Hacks, Blacks, and Cons: Race Relations in a Maximum Security Prison* (Lexington, Mass.: Lexington Books, D.C. Heath and Company, Copyright © 1974, D.C. Heath and Company), p. 169.

187

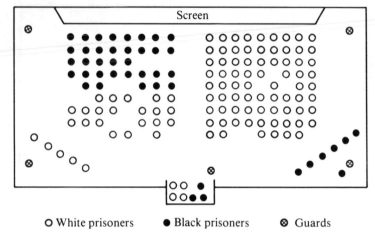

O White prisoners ● Black prisoners ⊗ Guards

FIGURE 7.3. Racial Segregation of Prisoners at the Movies

Source: Reprinted by permission of the publisher, from Leo Carroll, *Hacks, Blacks, and Cons: Race Relations in a Maximum Security Prison* (Lexington, Mass.: Lexington Books, D.C. Heath and Company, Copyright © 1974, D.C. Heath and Company), p. 160.

ticularly between prisoners of different races. Presently these groups — which range from racially hostile cliques of reform school graduates, friends from the streets, biker club members, or tough convicts to large, relatively organized gangs — dominate several prisons.

Prisons have always contained violence-prone individuals, who were kept in check by the elders and the code enforced by the elders. In the 1950s and 1960s, small cliques of young hoodlums, such as the lowriders described earlier, hung around the yard and other public places together, talked shit (loudly bragged), played the prison dozens, occasionally insulted, threatened, attacked, and robbed unprotected weaker prisoners, and squabbled with other lowrider groups, particularly those of other races. Billy "Hands" Robinson, a prison writer, characterized a group of these youngsters in an Illinois prison:

> There were four other dudes in the hole cell they put him in when he first got there, all of them young, what Tank called gang-bangers. He didn't like or understand the youngsters

but the joint was full of them now and he couldn't avoid them. They were like a herd of animals, he thought. They wolf-packed people and were nothing as individuals.[12]

Most of these early lowriders were young juvenile prison graduates and fuck-ups (unskilled, lower- and working-class criminals) who had low respect among older, "solid" criminals and regular convicts. But they were a constant threat to the other prisoners who were trying to maintain peace. For most of the 1950s and 1960s, other prisoners disparaged, ignored, and avoided the lowriders, whose activities were kept in check by the general consensus against them and the belief (accepted by the lowriders and most other prisoners) that if the lowriders went too far, the older prison regulars would use force, including assassination, to control them.[13]

Lowriders steadily increased in numbers. In the states with large cities whose ghettos bulged during the 1950s and 1960s and whose youth prison systems expanded to accommodate the increase in youth crime, the adult prisons began to receive growing numbers of tough youth prison graduates and criminally unskilled, more openly aggressive young urban toughs. They could no longer be controlled. They entered the growing racial melee and stepped up their attacks and robberies on other prisoners. When there were no successful countermoves against them, they took over the convict world and particularly one of its most important activities: the sub rosa economic enterprises.[14]

In different states the young hoodlums arrived at the adult prisons with different backgrounds and consequently formed different types of groups in the prison. In California the take-over began in 1967 in San Quentin when a tightly knit clique

[12] "Love: A Hard Legged Triangle," p. 39.
[13] This was usually the case, but Richard McCleery reported that a group of young reform school graduates, allied with older, violent prisoners, took over the prison in Hawaii during a period of disorganization by a changeover in administration and the introduction of rehabilitation ("The Governmental Process and Informal Social Control," in Donald Cressey, ed., *The Prison* [New York: Holt, Rinehart and Winston, 1961] p. 177).
[14] Virgil Williams and Mary Fish use this label in the best study to appear on prisoner economic systems: *Convicts, Codes and Contraband* (Cambridge: Ballinger Publishing, 1974).

of young Chicanos, who had known each other on the streets of Los Angeles and in other prisons, began to take drugs forcefully from other prisoners (mostly Chicano). The clique gained a reputation for toughness and the label of "the Mexican Mafia." Other aspiring young Chicano hoodlums became interested in affiliating with the Mafia, and, according to rumor, the Mafia members insisted that initiates murder another prisoner. This rumor and the actual attacks aroused and consolidated a large number of "independent" Chicanos, who planned to eliminate the Mafia members. On the planned day, the other Chicanos pursued known Mafia members through San Quentin, attempting to assassinate them. Several dozen prisoners were seriously wounded and one was killed in this day-long battle, but the Mafia held its ground, won many of the knife fights, and was not eliminated. After this unsuccessful attempt, some of the formerly independent Chicanos, particularly from Texas and the small towns in California who had been in conflict with Los Angeles Chicanos for decades, formed a countergroup: La Nuestra Familia. In the ensuing years, the conflict between the two Chicano gangs increased and spread to other prisons and even to the outside, where the gangs have tried to penetrate outside drug trafficking.[15] The attacks and counterattacks between members of the two gangs became so frequent that the prison administrators attempted to segregate the gangs, designating two prisons, San Quentin and Folsom, for the Mafia and two, Soledad and Tracy, for La Nuestra Familia. When Chicanos enter the California prison system, they are asked their gang affiliation; if they are to be sent to any of those four prisons (which are the medium- to maximum-security prisons), they are sent to one dominated by their gang.

The Chicano gangs' escalation of robbery, assault, and murder also consolidated and expanded black and white low-

[15] The policy agencies in California have argued and produced some evidence that activities of the prison gangs have splashed out of the prisons. The gangs are believed to struggle with each other, with factions within the gangs, and against other drug dealers. Many outside assassinations have been blamed on the gangs. "Pierce [a police lieutenant] said authorities believe a feud between two gangs, the Mexican Mafia and La Nuestra Familia, to be responsible for a recent chain of crimes in the area" (*San Francisco Chronicle*, March 7, 1977, p. 20).

rider groups, some of which had already been involved in similar violent and rapacious activities, but on a smaller scale. Two gangs, the Aryan Brotherhood and the Black Guerilla Family, rose in prominence and violent activities. Eventually, the Aryan Brotherhood formed an alliance with the Mafia and the Black Guerilla Family with La Nuestra Familia, and a very hostile and tentative stalemate prevailed. However, peace has not returned. Other racist cliques among the black and white prisoners occasionally attack other prisoners; the Chicano gangs still fight each other; and there seem to be factions within the Chicano gangs themselves. Although the California prisons have passed their peak of violence, the violence and fear are still intense.

In Illinois, black Chicago street gangs — the Blackstone Rangers (changed later to Black P Stone Nation), the Devil's Disciples, and the Vice Lords — and a Latin street gang named the Latin Kings spread into Stateville and finally took over the convict world. According to James Jacobs:

> When the gangs emerged at Stateville in 1969, they placed the old con power structure in physical and financial jeopardy. For the first time, those convicts with good jobs were not necessarily protected in their dealings, legitimate or illegitimate. Seeing strength in numbers, the gang members attempted to take what they wanted by force. They seemed unconcerned about doing fifteen days in the hole (the limit imposed by the courts). When they went to the hole, they were thrown in a cell with five or six fellow gang members. For the first time in history, the old cons who "knew how to do time" found their lives disrupted and in danger. Gang members moved in to take over the "rackets." One informant described an instance where a half dozen "gang bangers" simultanously put knives to his throat. Rather than cut the gangs in, many of the dealers went out of business.[16]

By 1974 the aggressive black and Latin gangs had precipitated counterorganizations among white prisoners who, in their reduced numbers, had been extremely vulnerable to assault, robbery, rape, and murder by the other gangs.[17]

[16] *Stateville* (Chicago: University of Chicago Press, 1977), pp. 157–58.
[17] Ibid., p. 159.

191

The activities of these violent groups who, in the pursuit of loot, sex, respect, or revenge, will attack any outsider have completely unraveled any remnants of the old codes of honor and tip networks that formerly helped to maintain order. In a limited, closed space, such as a prison, threats of attacks like those posed by these groups cannot be ignored. Prisoners must be ready to protect themselves or get out of the way. Those who have chosen to continue to circulate in public, with few exceptions, have formed or joined a clique or gang for their own protection. Consequently, violence-oriented groups dominate many, if not most, large men's prisons.

THE NEW CONVICT IDENTITY

The escalation of violence and the takeover of the violent cliques and gangs have produced a new prison hero. Actually, the prison-oriented leader has been undergoing changes for decades. In our earlier study, Donald Cressey and I separated the prison world into two systems, one with the ideal type, the "right guy," who was oriented primarily to the prison.[18] In my later study of California prisons, conducted in a period when the right guy was disappearing, the "convict" identity was a blend of various vestigial criminal and prison identities.

> This [the convict perspective] is the perspective of the elite of the convict world—the "regular." A "regular" (or, as he has been variously called, "people," "folks," "solid," a "right guy," or "all right") possesses many of the traits of the thief's culture. He can be counted on when needed by other regulars. He is also not a "hoosier"; that is, he has some finesse, is capable, is levelheaded, has "guts" and "timing." [19]

The upsurge of rapacious and murderous groups has all but eliminated the right guy and drastically altered the identity of the convict, the remaining hero of the prison world. Most of all, toughness has pushed out most other attributes, particularly the norms of tolerance, mutual aid, and loyalty to a large number of other regulars. Earlier, toughness was reemphasized

[18] "Thieves, Convicts, and the Inmate Culture," *Social Problems,* Fall 1963, pp. 145–148.
[19] John Irwin, *The Felon* (Englewood Cliffs, N.J.: Prentice-Hall, 1970), p. 83.

as a reaction to the soft, cooperative "inmate" identity fostered by the rehabilitative ideal. Ted Davidson, who studied San Quentin at a time when more and more prisoners were denouncing rehabilitation and reasserting an opposition identity, described the return of the old type of prisoner, the convict who was much more antagonistic to the administration.

> A general disillusionment began to grow among most prisoners. More and more prisoners recognized that their own illegal and rule-breaking activities were more important to them than the staff's rehabilitation activities. Although even convicts superficially played the game and programmed, the basic opposition between staff and prisoners became apparent to more prisoners. With growing numbers of convicts, the opposition became fierce and an intense unity once more prevailed against the staff as enemy. The convicts who had earlier faded into insignificance reappeared and multiplied.[20]

As described in chapter 5, the stiff and divisive administrative opposition weakened convict unity, and then the attacks of violent racial groups obliterated it. When the lowrider or "gang-banger" cliques turned on the remaining convict leaders (many had been removed from the prison mainline because of their political activities) and the elders were not able to drive the lowriders back into a position of subordination or otherwise to control them, the ancient regime fell and with it the old convict identity.

Toughness in the new hero in the violent men's prisons means, first, being able to take care of oneself in the prison world, where people will attack others with little or no provocation. Second, it means having the guts to take from the weak. Leo Carroll describes the view of manhood shared by a clique of young "wise guys" who were one of the most powerful groups in the prison that he studied and who preyed on other unorganized prisoners:

> Prison, in their eyes, is the ultimate test of manhood. A man in prison is able to secure what he wants and protect what he had: "In here, a man gets what he can," "nobody can

20 R. Theodore Davidson, *Chicano Prisoners: The Key to San Quentin* (New York: Holt, Rinehart and Winston, 1974), p. 47.

force a man to do something he don't want to," are key elements of their belief system. Any prisoner who does not meet these standards is not a man, "has no respect for himself," and is therefore not entitled to respect from others.[21]

Loyalty to other prisoners has shrunk to loyalty to one's clique or gang. In Illinois, James Jacobs found that

> gang members simply see nothing wrong with "ripping off" independents. The fact that they occupy adjoining cells does not seem to offer a basis for solidarity.
>
> While at one time inmates may have endorsed the principle of "doing your own time," the gangs endorsed the morality of "doing gang time." [22]

In addition to threats of robbery, assaults, and murder, the threat of being raped and physically forced into the role of the insertee (punk or kid) has increased in the violent prison: " 'Fuck it. It's none of my business. If a sucker is weak, he's got to fall around here. I came when I was eighteen and nobody turned me out. I didn't even smile for two years.' " [23]

Prison homosexuality has always created identity problems for prisoners. Long before today's gang era, many prisoners, particularly those with youth prison experiences, regularly or occasionally engaged in homosexual acts as insertors with queens, kids, or punks, though not without some cost to their own masculine definitions. There has been a cynical accusation repeated frequently in prison informal banter that prisoners who engaged in homosexual life too long finally learn to prefer it and, in fact, become full, practicing homosexuals, both insertees and insertors: "It was a jocular credo that after one year behind walls, it was permissible to kiss a kid or a queen. After five years, it was okay to jerk them off to 'get 'em hot.' After ten years, 'making tortillas' or 'flip-flopping' was acceptable and after twenty years anything was fine." [24] The constant game of prison dozens among friends and acquaintances, in which imputation of homosexuality is the dominant

[21] *Hacks, Blacks, and Cons,* p. 69.
[22] *Stateville,* p. 157.
[23] Bunker, *Animal Factory,* p. 32.
[24] Ibid., p. 86.

194

theme, reflects and promotes self-doubt about masculinity. Presently, the threat of force has been added to the slower process of drifting into homosexuality, and fear about manhood and compensatory aggressive displays of manhood have increased drastically.

Today the respected public prison figure — the convict or hog — stands ready to kill to protect himself, maintains strong loyalties to some small group of other convicts (invariably of his own race), and will rob and attack or at least tolerate his friends' robbing and attacking other weak independents or their foes. He openly and stubbornly opposes the administration, even if this results in harsh punishment. Finally, he is extremely assertive of his masculine sexuality, even though he may occasionally make use of the prison homosexuals or, less often, enter into more permanent sexual alliance with a kid.

Convicts and Other Prisoners Today prisoners who embrace versions of this ideal and live according to it with varying degrees of exactitude dominate the indigenous life of the large violent prisons. They control the contraband distribution systems, prison politics, the public areas of the prison, and any pan-prison activities, such as demonstrations and prisoner representative organizations. To circulate in this world, the convict world, one must act like a convict and, with a few exceptions, have some type of affiliation with a powerful racial clique or gang.

This affiliation may take various shapes. Most of the large racial gangs have a small core of leaders and their close friends, who constitute a tightly knit clique that spends many hours together. Moving out from this core, a larger group of recognized members are regularly called on by the core when the gang needs something done, such as assistance in an attack or display of force. Very often these fringe members are young aspiring initiates who want to be part of the inner core. Then, if the gangs are large, like the Mexican Mafia or the Black P Stone Nation, many more, sometimes hundreds of prisoners, claim an affiliation and are available when a massive display of force is needed.

Most prisoners who circulate in the convict world fall into one of the three categories. However, some highly respected

195

convicts have very loose friendship ties with one or more of the gangs and circulate somewhat independently with immunity from gang attack. Bunker's Earl Copen is one of these figures:

> So, although Earl was at home, it was in the way that the jungle animal is at home — cautiously. He had no enemies here who posed a threat, at least none that he knew, though some might have been threats if he didn't have the affection of the most influential members of the most powerful white gang and friendship with the leaders of the most powerful Chicano gang.[25]

A few very tough independents circulate freely, because they have withstood so many assaults from which they emerged victorious. Nevertheless, they still have to be careful with the more powerful gang members, because nobody can survive the attacks of a large group committed to murder.

In some large prisons a few prisoners who refrain from violent and sub rosa economic activities and devote themselves to form organizations and coalitions in order to pursue prisoners' rights and other political goals are tolerated by the gangs and other violent and rapacious prisoners. Occasionally, these organizers are able to create coalitions among warring gangs on particular issues. They have immunity only as long as they stay away from the other activities of the convict world and avoid disputes with the convict leaders.

Finally, other independents circulate freely, because they are viewed as unthreatening to the power of the convict leaders and they supply the convict world with some service. This includes characters and dings, who supply humor, and less desirable homosexuals. Younger, more desired homosexuals, however, must have affiliations with powerful individuals or groups.

In some of the large, more violent prisons, certain groups of prisoners, such as the Muslims and the cliques of "syndicate" men and their friends, are prominent in indigenous prison worlds even though they do not follow the aggressive and rapacious patterns of the gangs. Other prisoners believe that these groups will protect their members and retaliate against attacks; consequently, the other prisoners fear and respect

[25] Ibid., p. 25.

196

them.[26] These groups often become involved in a prison's informal political and economic activities and sometimes assume leadership in periods of disorder. When these groups are present and prominent, they are a stabilizing force that prevents the complete takeover by the violent cliques and gangs.

Withdrawal In the Addams area, many of the residents coped by withdrawing to their households and restricting their interaction to close relatives. In violent prisons, the majority of the prisoners follow a similar course. The are no households or families, but increasingly prisoners are shying away from public settings and avoiding the activities of the convict world. Although they occasionally buy from the racketeers, place bets with gamblers, trade commodities with other unaffiliated prisoners, or sell contraband on a very small scale, they stay away from the rackets and any large-scale economic enterprises. They dissociate themselves from the violent cliques and gangs, spend as little time as possible in the yard and other public places where gangs hang out, and avoid gang members, even though they may have been friends with some of them in earlier years. They stick to a few friends whom they meet in the cell blocks, at work, through shared interests, in other prisons, or on the outside (home boys). With their friends they eat, work, attend meetings of the various clubs and formal organizations that have abounded in the prison, and participate in leisure time activities together. Collectively, they have withdrawn from the convict world. In a series of articles based on lengthy interviews of a prisoner in Green Haven, a New York medium-security prison, Susan Sheehan includes the prisoner's diary of five days. It demonstrates his and his friends' almost complete avoidance of the convict world. One of these days (slightly abridged) proceeds as follows:

> Tuesday, August 10, 1976
>
> 6:30 A.M. Bell rings very loud and long. A certain C.O. (correction officer, or guard) does this (rings bell long) whenever he comes on duty, and I and many other inmates here would like to hit him with a shoe, as he seems to do this on purpose!

26 See Carroll, *Hacks, Blacks, and Cons,* pp. 64–68.

God — I hate to get up, I feel so tired!! Serves me right for staying up doing glass painting till 1:55 this morning. But — get up I must and do so. Wash up, shave and get dressed in my work clothes which is green regulation issued pants and shirt and work shoes. Put on water to be boiled for my coffee. Have coffee and 2 do-nuts. Smoke a cigarette and listen to news, via earphones.

7:15 A.M. Doors open up. I immediately rush off to the mess hall entrance area on the West Side entrance, being I'm one of the first inmates up — no one is near that area at this time of the morning. Terry, a friend of mine (inmate) who works in the kitchen, is there awaiting me. He hands me a large cardboard box which contains 20 dozen eggs (fresh ones), about 20 pounds of raw bacon, about 20 pounds of macaroni, 20 to 30 oranges, 2 large cans orange juice and one large can of olive oil for cooking. I immediately rush back to my cell, to avoid the other inmates about due to start going to the mess hall for their breakfast.

Hide all said food items in my cell and my friend Andy's cell. Andy is just at this time up and washing. We joke together about our sudden good windfall from our friend.

7:40 A.M. Andy and I proceed to go to work, the parole clothing department located at the basement of the Administration Building. Terry stops us to ask us to please get him some shorts, 2 white shirts and black socks. We tell him that we'll give it to him next morning. We reach the check point gate of the Administration Building, get pat frisked and we sign the logbook at the desk to verify at what time we arrived to work. Also, left our institutional passes at this check point with the C.O. assigned there, as must be done.

We arrive at the basement parole area where we work. C.O.s Stevens and Barton are both there already. Stevens works the 7:20 to 3:20 shift. C.O. Barton does not usually arrive this early because he works extra early over-time as he has been assigned to drive one of the inmates to an outside hospital for a medical appointment.

The coffee pot is ready as C.O. Stevens always plugs in this pot early as he arrives about 20 minutes to 7, each morning. So Andy, I and Stevens all have coffee and cake. C.O. Barton is busy with the checking of papers for the inmate he is due to take to the hospital so he doesn't join us. We have the radio playing and listening to the local news broadcast. Meanwhile, there are 4 men going home on parole this morning and they just arrived and are getting dressed. Andy and I both help and make certain that all these 4 inmates going home, have all their clothes and personal property packages they may own. They have cups of coffee and relax in casual and happy conversation about the steaks, drinks and women they'll soon enjoy out there, etc.

Andy and I, both at times, have been asked by many persons — does seeing men talk like this and seeing them go home each day bother us? We don't see it that way as Andy and I, feel very glad to see as many as possible leave any prison as prison represents "hell," in all respects!!

8:05 A.M. We have an extra relief C.O. to stay with us, as C.O.s Stevens and Barton are out on assignments. Said relief C.O.'s name is Officer Dover (works in officers' mess from 10 A.M. onward), who is one of the best natured officers in all respects that I have ever come across. Good sense of humor, always smiling and happy go lucky. Very well mannered, fair and easy to relate with. Should be made a warden.

Andy and I, go to our kitchen room at our basement job area and have another cup of coffee and do-nuts. We relax and talk about general topics on the outside.

8:30 A.M. Another 3 inmates that work with us now arrive to work also. They are Danny, Benno, and Ned.

This morning — we have to take a full inventory of all the stock garments we have and record each item in our general inventory stock so we will know what to order, we are short of. After Danny, Ned, and Benno all have their coffee and buns, all 5 of us get ready to do the inventory.

8:50 A.M. Andy and I, start counting the jackets, slacks, socks, handkerchiefs, belts, shoes and shirts. Danny and Ned start to count the ties, topcoats and the other apparel that the men wear to go out on furloughs, death visits and to courts.

10:35 A.M. We all are caught up on our inventory and go to have coffee again and relax. During all this time of inventory taking, Benno sat at the desk to answer all phone calls of general inquiry and also made up lists for calling men the next day — that have to be fitted out with civilian clothes for their due release dates soon.

11:05 A.M. Benno starts to prepare the foods that he will cook for our lunch as we are not going to go to the mess hall as there is only franks for lunch. Benno is making steaks, fried onions, French fried potatoes, sauce gravy and sweet green peas for our lunch meal. Benno is an exceptional cook! When he cooks, we all leave the kitchen to be out of his way and also, not to distract him then. One or more of us are available to help him — if he calls us, but most times he does it all by himself.

Of course, he cooks — so all others of us do the cleaning up and wash the pots and dishes.

11:40 A.M. We are just about ready to start eating. We all are in conversation about how good Benno cooked the steaks, the high price of food outside, etc. The radio is playing a late song hit and we all are enjoying the food and are in a good mood.

1:15 P.M. We all now sit around the desks and are in conversation about many topics. The parole board's unjust decisions, rehabilitation, politics, and prison mismanagement, etc.

2:55 P.M. All of us leave our job area in basement, get pat frisked again at check out gate, pick up our passes and proceed to our cells in C block, all except Ned as he locks in J block.

3:05 P.M. I arrive at my cell, change clothes, wash up and go to the wash room on my gallery's end, to wash out and hang up the clothes I left there to soak yesterday.

3:25 P.M. Returned to cell, put water on for my thermos bottle to make my coffee. Layed down, smoked a cigar and relaxed listening to some soft music via earphones.

4:10 P.M. Got up, made cup of coffee, had a ham and Swiss cheese sandwich. Cleaned up table, brushed teeth and started to get all the necessary materials ready to do my glass painting. Worked on glass painting until lock in.

5:05 P.M. Bell rings — lock-in time. Doors close and 2 C.Os. walk by and check the doors and count as they walk past my cell. I continue on working on the glass pictures.

5:25 P.M. C.O. stops at my cell and hands me 8 letters (personal), 2 more business letters and 1 magazine on real estate. C.O. continues handing out mail to other cells.

Read 3 of these letters which come from the Philippines. One from my sweetheart, one from her sister and the 3rd from her mother. Finish reading all mail and lay down to catch the prison phone bulletin announcements on prison news.

5:55 P.M. Get up, wash up, brush teeth and get all my papers and materials ready for my Jaycees meeting due tonight at the school class building at J block, from 6 to 8:30 P.M.

6:00 P.M. Doors open up. I proceed to block door exit where many other men are waiting to go to different night classes and program classes. The block C.O. checks each one of us out on his master sheet.

I arrive at my Jaycee class room and start writing out on the black board the agenda for tonight's meeting. An outside male Jaycee coordinator arrives and our Jaycee meeting starts. We discuss various project possibilities. One project involves bringing boys from the high school within a few miles of Green Haven to the prison to see what it is like so that they will never want to commit crimes and will never wind up in prison. We also form committees for each project. Meeting ends at 8:25 P.M. and all of us leave to return to our blocks.

8:35 P.M. Returned to cell. Wash and make cup of coffee and smoke 2 cigarettes. Start to work again on my glass pictures and continue until 10 P.M. I stop to eat a salami and cheese with lettuce and tomato sandwich. Smoke 2 cigarettes and relax on my bed.

I start to think of my sweetheart in the Philippines. What's she doing, etc.? That's rather silly 'cause since it is a 12 hour difference in time from N.Y. City, it goes without saying it has to be about 10 A.M. there so of course, she can't be sleeping.

10:55 P.M. The bell rings and that means it's time to lock in for the night. Doors close and the 2 C.O.s again check the doors and take the count. I continue on working on the glass pictures. I feel very tired tonight so I stop working on these pictures at 11:40 P.M. I clean up all paint brushes, table and put away to a safe area, the glass paintings to dry during the night. Have a fast cup of coffee, then wash up, brush teeth and get undressed.

11:55 P.M. Put on only small night lamp, put on phones to catch midnight news. Light up cigarette and listen to the news on phones. Music (Western songs) comes on by some local Poughkeepsie disc jockey and I listen to it until 12:30 A.M.

12:35 A.M. I put out light, pull phone plug and go to sleep.[27]

[27] Susan Sheehan, "Annals of Crime," *New Yorker,* October 31, 1977, pp. 48–55.

The convicts disrespect those who withdraw, but usually ignore them: "If a dude wants to run and hide, that's all right." [28] They even disrespect formerly high-status prisoners, such as older thieves, who previously received respect even if they avoided prison public life. Prisoners who withdraw occasionally have to display deference or acquiesce subtly in accidental public confrontations with convicts, but they face minimal danger of assault and robbery. This is much less true for young and effeminate prisoners, who will be pursued by aggressive, homosexually oriented convicts, perhaps threatened or raped, even if they attempt to stay to themselves and to avoid the convict world. Segregation may be their only safe niche.

The strategy of withdrawal has been encouraged and facilitated by prison administrations, which have always feared and hindered prisoner unity. The history of American prisons, in a sense, is a history of shifting techniques of separating prisoners.[29] The original Pennsylvania prisons completely isolated prisoners. The Auburn system, which prevailed in the initial era of imprisonment in the United States because of cheap costs, employed the "silence system" to reduce interaction between prisoners and to forestall unity. More recently, the system of individualized treatment, emphasizing individual psychological adjustment, was a mechanism of psychological separation. In the last decade, convinced that large populations of prisoners are unmanageable, prison administrators have recommended, planned, and built smaller institutions for the primary purpose of separating prisoners into smaller populations. In the large prisons that are still used (not by choice, but by economic necessity) some states have split the prison into small units and have formally separated the prisoner population within the large prison. In many prisons these separate units (usually cell blocks with some additional staff and restrictions on access) vary in levels of privilege, some being designated "honor" units that offer many more privileges, more mobility for the residents, and less access for nonresidents.

[28] Interview, San Francisco, September 1977.
[29] Donald Cressey made this point years ago in his criminology lecture.

202

Since the late 1960s, prison administrations have contravened the movements toward prisoner-organized unity by allowing, even encouraging many small apolitical organizations. In a study of college education in several prisons in the United States, we discovered that this strategy was being successfully employed by the warden of the federal prison at Lompoc.·

> The Warden, in attempting to recognize and control the growing organizational propensities of convicts, allowed convict "clubs." To form a club, a group of convicts had to find a sponsor from the staff and produce a constitution and by-laws to be approved by the administration. They were given a cubicle in the activities wing and the privilege of holding weekly meetings. Approved persons from the outside community (but no more than 15 at a time) could attend every other meeting. The organizations and clubs recognized by the prison included: The Hawaii's Sons, Auto Club, Cultural Forum, Nordic-Celtic, 7 Steps, Jaycees, Alcoholics Anonymous, Pathfinder, Afro-American Society, Gavel Club, Tribe of Five Feathers, and Operation Success.[30]

Prisoners who withdraw have certain channels provided by the administration to help them and make prison less onerous: if they maintain a clean disciplinary record, they can eventually move to an honor block or unit which houses a preponderance of persons who are withdrawing like themselves, which affords many more privileges, and to which access is restricted. In addition, they may fill in their leisure hours with formal organizational activities located in closed rooms away from the yard and other settings of the convict world.

More recently, in some prisons the administrations are combining the unit structure, segregation, and behavior modification into a system of hierarchial segregation that encourages withdrawal and conformity and greatly reduces contact between prisoners. For instance, San Quentin presently has the following units:

> *SHU* (segregated housing unit). Small maximum-security unit for prisoners charged with serious violence in prison.

[30] Marjorie J. Seashore et al., *Prisoner Education: Project New Gate and other College Programs* (New York: Praeger, 1976), p. 306.

Prisoners locked in single cells continually except for four hours of exercise per day in a special yard. Two meals served in cells. Visits through glass with telephone. Prisoners in unit for six months or longer.

Max B. large unit (500) for "troublesome" or high-escape-risk prisoners. Prisoners locked in cells continually except for four hours of exercise per day in special yard. Face-to-face visits in special section of visiting room.

East Block. Large cell block (1,000) for mainline population. Prisoners released to yard or work after breakfast. Locked back in cells after evening meal. Must be out of cell block or in cells during day. No extra decorations or furniture in cells. Regular face-to-face visits.

PCU (protective custody unit). Small unit for nonviolent prisoners who need protection. Single cells. Special yard. Special canteen. Freedom to circulate in unit during day.

Alpine. Small unit for some workers (for example, kitchen crew) who must be released at odd hours and during lock-downs. Freedom of movement in unit. Normal privileges.

West Block Honor Unit. Medium-sized unit (500) for prisoners who have clean disciplinary records for eighteen months. Electrical outlets in cells (which means prisoners may have televisions, stereos, and other appliances in cells). Special furniture allowed in cells. Special decorations of cells allowed. Locked in cells at 10:00 P.M. Freedom of movement in cell block. Special canteen and yard.

Citizens' Row. Special honor unit within West Block for prisoners who have served seven or eight years and have clean disciplinary records for three years. Same privileges as the rest of the honor unit with the addition of not being locked in until midnight and never locked down during disturbances.

This stratification system has succeeded in facilitating withdrawal, but has not eliminated violence in the prison. It has merely concentrated it in the lower levels of the hierarchy. Also, it has produced some added undesirable consequences. Individuals housed in the maximum-security (and more punitive) units become increasingly embittered and inured to violence. Many of them believe that they have been placed and are held there arbitrarily. (Often this is the case, because suspicions and prejudices operate in the classification to various units.) Intense hate between prisoners and guards builds up in the maximum-security units. Different clique and gang members, different races, and guards and prisoners verbally assault each other. Often guards on duty in the units, having grown especially hostile toward particular prisoners, depart from the formal routine and arbitrarily restrict the privileges of certain prisoners (for example, not releasing them for their allowed short exercise period).

All this precipitates regular violent and destructive incidents. San Quentin continues to experience incident after incident in its most secure and punitive units. In February 1978, for several days the prisoners in Max B fought among themselves during exercise periods and defied or even attacked guards who were trying to control them, even though they were risking injury, death, and long extensions of their segregation and prison sentences. More recently, in April 1979, a group of prisoners in the same unit continued to damage their cells for three days. They were protesting not having received their "issue" (toilet paper, tobacco, and the like), showers, or exercise periods for five weeks. They broke their toilets, tore out the electric lights in their cells, burned their mattresses, and pulled the plumbing from the walls. Finally, a large squad of guards (the "goon squad") brought them under control. A guard told Stephanie Riegel, a legal aide who had been informed of the incident by one of the prisoners involved, that "this type of destruction in that section is fairly routine."

Race and Withdrawal The strategy of withdrawal is more open and appealing to white prisoners. In general, independent black prisoners are not as threatened by gangs. Blacks have more solidarity, and the black gangs tolerate the independents, most of whom are pursuing a more present-oriented expressive mode in prison:

> Them white dudes be always looking ahead to the end of that ten or twenty-five and crying and complaining. I don't know any "brothers" that even know how much time they got left. Take me. I don't think about my time. I know I'm getting short, but if you was to ask me how many days I got left, I couldn't tell ya. I count the years, ya know, but not the days.

> All the "brothers" take their time day by day and involve themselves with the "brothers" here.[31]

Unless several black gangs become very organized and hostile to each other (as in Stateville), unaffiliated blacks participate much more in the convict world and hang around much more in public places, such as the big yard.

With few exceptions, Chicanos in the large California prisons — Soledad, San Quentin, Folsom, and Tracy — must have at least a loose affiliation with one of the Chicano gangs. The gangs force this. However, many have token affiiliations and actually withdraw and largely avoid the trouble and gang activity that abound in the convict world. However, they may occasionally be called on for some collective action; and if they ignore the gangs' call, they might be attacked.

PRISONERS' ECONOMICS

Although prisoners have always combatted their state of material deprivation and persistently operated sub rosa economic systems, recently the economic activity has become much more complex and extensive and interlaced with the clique and gang activity. By and large, when the violent cliques and gangs dominate the prison, they control most of the large-scale sub rosa economic systems. Moreover, these economic activities are both the source of a great deal of conflict and the only pervasive mode of interaction between hostile groups.

Virtually all prisoners enter into the prison sub rosa economy. They do so primarily to increase their luxury and pleasure. The prison supplies relatively undesirable food, plain clothing, and a small, austere domicile. All other material, except for inferior-grade tobacco for "roll your owns," must be purchased through the canteen, sent from outside, obtained through the sub rosa economic channels, or forsaken. Susan Sheehan described the legitimate commodity sources:

> There are many things not provided by the state that most prisoners regard as even more necessary than people on the outside do — for example, talcum powder and deodorant, because of the prisoner's more limited bathing facilities.

[31] Carroll, *Hacks, Blacks, and Cons,* p. 105.

Store-bought cigarettes, instant coffee, immersion coils for heating water and between-meal snacks — especially for the fifteen-hour period between supper and breakfast — also seem necessary and help to fill the empty spaces of prison life.

There are two ways an inmate can legitimately obtain such items at Green Haven. He can get them in the two monthly packages that a prisoner in New York State may receive from people on his approved visiting list, or he can go to the commissary every two weeks and buy up to forty-five dollars' worth of groceries, toiletries and miscellaneous items, if he can afford to. . . . The wife of one of George Malinow's friends, who knows how much it costs the state's taxpayers each year to keep her husband in prison, figured that it also cost her $2,000 a year to make his life more agreeable there.[32]

In the past two decades, the items that prisoners may purchase or receive through legitimate channels have greatly increased. In addition to the items that Sheehan mentioned, prisoners in many prisons receive or purchase televisions, stereos, typewriters, musical instruments, books, and street clothing. However, to acquire all these items legitimately, prisoners must have had money before coming to prison, earn money through a prison-pay job or sales of handcrafted items, or be sent money or commodities from friends and relatives. Most prisoners do not earn or have access to enough money to reach the level of material comfort possible through legitimate means and must turn to the sub rosa markets to increase their standard of living.

Moreover, prisoners desire a vast array of items, many of which are taken for granted on the outside, that are contraband in prison. Williams and Fish comment on the "exaggerated importance" of some items in prison:

Truncated supply results in prison demand for goods and services inconsequential or even bizarre to the free world denizen. Goods and services that would not be consumed at all outside prison can attain exaggerated importance inside the prison simply because the inmates are denied the use of things that constitute a normal part of their living standard outside.

For example, the offender who engages in some relaxation

32 "Annals of Crime," p. 46.

and escapism on the outside by becoming pleasantly intoxicated on aged bourbon may be horrified and disgusted at the thought of getting drunk by sniffing glue.[33]

A better example of "bizarre" prison substitutes for unavailable ordinary commodities is nutmeg, a contraband narcotic in prison that is used whenever it is available.

Prison contraband goes beyond the ordinary street items and includes many types of drugs, prison-brewed alcohol, and weapons. Together, the legitimate items and contraband have significantly raised the standard of living of many prisoners. Affluent prisoners eat more and better food, which they purchase through the canteen and sub rosa market, occasionally or regularly consume drugs and alcohol, smoke good tobacco products, wear more comfortable and fashionable clothing, cell where and with whom they choose, enjoy expensive appliances in their cells, attend extra prison activities (especially movies), have abundant books, or art and craft materials, and even buy prison sex.

With the increase in commodities, which are distributed unevenly in the prisoner population, prisoners form more pronounced status hierarchies. Generally, those who have prison wealth and are successful in the prison economy earn respect from other prisoners, particularly from those who are more oriented toward the prison.

In the more affluent contemporary prison, some prisoners accumulate money for use after release. Prisoners who work at the very small number of better-paying jobs (twenty cents or so an hour) and live frugally can save a few hundred dollars before release. Some prisoners save more money through the sales of handcrafted items, such as leather belts, purses, and wallets, jewelry, lamps, and paintings, which are sold in stores administered by the prison officials. The prison administration of Thomaston, Maine, has encouraged this activity to the extent that after a five-hour workday on state industries, the industrial area and the machinery are turned over to prisoner craftsmen. Prisoners "own" patents on their products, which are registered in a prison patent office; hire other prisoners for piecework; sell

[33] *Convicts, Codes and Contraband,* p. 50.

their products in a state-run store on a highway near the prison; and, in 1972, earned a per capita average of about $1,500 a year.[34]

The result of all these legitimate economic activities is that a small minority of prisoners leave prison with a few hundred dollars. In recent years another group, perhaps not as large, have accumulated cash while in prison through the sub rosa economic system and leave with a contraband "stash" of bills, which they must smuggle out of prison on their person or through a friend. This is possible now because of the heightened sub rosa economic activity and the increase of cash in prison. The prison sub rosa economic system has taken on vastly different and enlarged dimensions.

Prison Money Cigarettes are the standard prison currency. Williams and Fish tell us why.

> There appear to be considerable advantages to the use of "cigarette money"; cigarettes are not contraband items and are not subject to seizure by guards, nor can the inmate be punished for being found with them in his possession. Trade is facilitated because of the rather stable, well-known standard of value; all brands of cigarettes within the prison have the same monetary value per package or carton and this value is known to everyone.[35]

Prisoners think and talk in terms of cartons and packs in the same way that outsiders think and talk in dollars and cents. Many times I have heard recently released prisoners jokingly inquire of their companions or the clerks how many cartons an item costs. Prisoners who do not smoke keep cartons of cigarettes to use for trading purposes.

Other stable, nonperishable items sold in the prison canteens, such as jars of instant coffee and packages or cartons of Bugler tobacco, are similar to Canadian dollars in the outside economy; they are almost as negotiable as cigarettes, and their value is almost as well known.

Paper bills, particularly twenty-dollar bills, are more

---

[34] This figure and the information on the economic routine were given me by the assistant warden in conversations in 1972.
[35] *Convicts, Codes and Contraband*, p. 55.

common and required in certain types of transactions. Their disadvantage is that they are contraband and, therefore, have to be smuggled in; possessing them is very risky. However, they are necessary for most smuggling operations, because cash is required to purchase outside commodities. (Outside drug dealers and persons who "pack" contraband into prison must be paid in cash.) Often friends and relatives produce the actual cash for smuggling activities, but the new affluence in prison makes it possible for some prisoners to accumulate paper money and enter the rackets without outside financial backing.

The Commodities: Prison Contraband The contraband available in prison starts with ordinary prison supplies and services, such as food, clothing, drugs from the prison hospital, cell changes, movie unlocks, and now even conjugal visits.[36] They become contraband when they are distributed illegitimately for profit. Another type is prison-manufactured contraband, such as pruno or raisin jack, tailored clothing, stingers, and shivs. Outside consumer products that have been sent into the prison legitimately enter the sub rosa economy when the original owner sells or trades them, which activity is against prison rules. The original owner and the buyer run some risk, because these items are usually recorded as the original recipient's property in his file. However, there is considerable slippage in the recording system, and often prisoners are able to have items removed from or placed on their property list by other prisoners.

Finally, the prisons are being flooded with more smuggled contraband. Heroin and paper bills are the most popular and important, though not necessarily the most common. Other drugs, such as marijuana, speed, barbiturates, nutmeg, and alcohol, are increasingly available. Prisoners place themselves in great risk by possessing these items, but many are willing to

[36] A growing number of prisons allow conjugal visits. Usually the demand exceeds the supply, which is set by the number of locations (trailers, small apartments, or rooms). Often there is a waiting list for visits. Sometimes a visitor cancels, and there is a last-minute substitution. When prisoners administer the lists, there is the possibitity of "selling" these visits, but only to people who are already scheduled for them.

take the risk because the items are very desired and profitable. Their increased availability is a consequence of the increase in money available to prisoners. Guards and other employees smuggle in some of this contraband, but friends and relatives also pass the goods to prisoners during visits or deposit them on the prison grounds; other prisoners who work outside the walls transfer them inside.

The Rackets   The distribution of prison contraband has changed drastically. Formerly, as described in many studies, a few individuals (merchants and politicians) controlled and distributed a large portion of the illegitimate goods and services. Other prisoners demeaned these individuals, but, following the code, tolerated them. Also, the merchants and politicians had considerable power earned through their control of scarce goods and luxuries and their influence with the administration. Other prisoners bought, sold, shared, and traded the remainder of the meager prison commodities on a smaller and less mercenary scale.

When money and contraband, particularly contraband from the outside, became abundant, the gangs emerged and the convict ideal shifted toward toughness and rapaciousness: "racketeers" replaced merchants and politicians. Racketeers operate in groups and rob as well as sell to other prisoners. With their appearance, the individual entrepreneur faded or disappeared. Anyone with a rich stock of valuable commodities and without protection from a group will be threatened and robbed. Edward Bunker describes the "scheming" of Earl Copen's clique and reveals the vulnerability of the unaffiliated entrepreneur:

> When Earl arrived, T. J. uncoiled and squeezed an arm around Earl's shoulders, "Sit down here, boy," he said, "an' help us scheme on gettin' them narcotics."
> "How much has he got?" Earl asked.
> Black Ernie answered, "Half a piece. It come in on a visit a couple days ago and he kept it cool, just selling to some dudes over in the South block." . . .
> "Hunch on down here," Bad Eye said. "We'll run it to you. Ernie brought it to us because it's a white boy. . . . and the

motherfucker didn't throw us our end. We're the mother-fuckers be fightin' when the rugs [black prisoners] start wasting people around here.[37]

Small-scale "traders" or merchants still coexist with the racketeers, but their activities are restricted to distributing prison supplies and gathering a few luxuries for themselves and friends. If they begin to accumulate wealth and remain unaffiliated, they will be threatened, subjected to extortion, robbed, or assaulted. The masses of unaffiliated prisoners sell, share, and trade among themselves and buy from racketeers or small merchants, but they stay out of profit making. They are safe unless they fall into debt by borrowing (at enormous interest rates) or failing to pay gambling bets.

CONCLUDING REMARKS

This is the situation in many — too many — large, men's prisons: not chaos, but a dangerous and tentative order. It is not likely to improve for a while. The sources of conflict are deeply embedded in prisoners' cultural and social orientations. Most male prisoners are drawn from a social layer that shares extremely reduced life options, meager material existence, limited experience with formal, polite, and complex urban social organizations, and traditional suspicions and hostilities toward people different from their own kind. Prisoners, a sample with more extreme forms of these characteristics, are likely to be more hostile toward others with whom they do not share close friendships or cultural backgrounds and less firmly attached to the conventional normative web that holds most citizens together. For decades, the potentially obstreperous and conflictive population was held in a tentative peace by prisoner leaders, a code, and the constant threat of extreme force. When the informal system of peace disintegrated, the formal force was brought in, used (in fact, misused), withstood by the prisoners, and dissipated. For a short period, 1970 to 1973, prisoner organizers pursued the promise of some power for prisoners, mended some of the major rifts that were growing between groups of prisoners, and forestalled further fractionalizing. The

[37] *Animal Factory,* pp. 26–27.

administrations, because they fear prisoner political unity more than any other condition, smashed the incipient organizations and regenerated fractionalization. The parts scattered in familiar paths followed by other splintered populations of oppressed peoples: religious escapism, rapacious racketeering, fascism, and withdrawal.

The administrations are not happy with the results, but continue to apply old formulas to restore order. Mostly, they attempt to divide and segregate the masses and to crush the more obdurate prisoners. In California, for instance, the Department of Corrections has continued to search for gang leaders and other troublemakers, transfer those who are so labeled to the maximum-security prisons, and segregate them there in special units. The growing numbers of segregated prisoners are becoming more vicious and uncontrollable. In recent incidents at San Quentin the prisoners in a segregation unit fought among themselves and defied the guards for several days, even though they were risking injury, death, and extensions in their sentences. When the department has succeeded in identifying gang leaders and removing them, new leaders have sprouted like mushrooms. The prisons remain essentially the same.

The violent, hostile, and rapacious situation will probably continue until all prisoners are held in very small institutions of less than one or two hundred or completely isolated (both at astronomical costs) or until administrations begin to permit and cultivate among prisoners new organizations that can pull them together on issues that are important to them as a class. It seems obvious to me that these issues are the conditions of imprisonment and postprison opportunities. Thus, in order for these organizations to obtain and hold the commitment of a number of leaders and thereby to begin supplanting the violent, rapacious group structures, they will have to have some power in decision making. These organizations, however, are political in nature, and presently this idea is repulsive and frightening to prison administrations and the public.

8
Trends and Possibilities

A SEARCH FOR A NEW IDEOLOGY

Public officials who shape prison policy — prison administrators, guards, legislators, judges, prosecutors — are in a state of confusion. They lack a philosophy that blends their different, often contradictory objectives and enables them to carry out their diverse tasks in unity, with cooperation, and with personal satisfaction. The rehabilitative ideal accomplished this nicely, and that was its main strength. In *Struggle for Justice,* we described the ideals unifying ideological capacity:

> The treatment-oriented correctional routine, with its serious theoretical inconsistencies, was embraced wholeheartedly by most persons involved in the administration of criminal justice, even the punitively oriented. District attorneys, police officers and correctional administrators saw in the rehabilitative ideal criminals they viewed as especially dangerous. . . . Prison administrators also embraced the rehabilitative ideal. . . . However, it wasn't treatment that excited them. It was the prospect of having greater control over their prisons. . . . The rehabilitative system, particularly indeterminate sentencing, offered them a highly effective and less objectionable control method.[1]

Prison administrators still cling to the rehabilitative ideal. A 1975 survey conducted by *Corrections Magazine* revealed that 63 percent of correctional administrators reaffirmed their

[1] American Friends Service Committee, *Struggle for Justice* (New York: Hill and Wang, 1971), pp. 85–86.

faith in rehabilitation's efficacy.[2] They brushed aside the evidence that rehabilitation programs fail to reduce recidivism with a variety of arguments:

> "One has to consider," says Edward Kleckter, corrections director in North Dakota, "that the institution is supposed to be the end-all and correct a whole lifetime of errors, beginning with the family. . . . It's asking a bit much of an institution to completely rehabilitate a person whose history goes back to a long stream of failure."
>
> "If all doctors had to guarantee that every person who came to them had to be permanently cured — never have another cold, never break another bone — you'd put all the physicians out of business."
>
> "Prison administrators agree . . . that many of their critics are looking for a single program that will be effective for everyone. Perhaps the phrase most often repeated in the survey interviews of them was, 'There is no panacea.' They do believe, however, that institutional programs are effective if properly implemented."[3]

Since rehabilitation has been thoroughly criticized, on grounds not only of its ineffectiveness, but also of its violations of civil liberties and its punitiveness, these administrators manifest extreme tenacity. Part of this tenacity stems from their long and sincere commitment to rehabilitation. To abandon it now is admitting that they have been wrong and have wasted their efforts during all these years. Some of the tenacity, however, has other sources. Rehabilitation offered a rationale or a rhetoric for many other, less admissible purposes. One purpose, mentioned earlier, is control of prisoners. Others are purposes that organizations generate as organizations. All top administrators and most employees dislike and take measures to avoid being criticized. In the case of prisons, which hold a potentially explosive prisoner population, the concern to avoid criticism is relatively strong. In addition, administrators of organizations, from an urge either to expand their empire or simply to meet the

---

[2] Michael S. Serrill, "Is Rehabilitation Dead?" *Corrections Magazine,* May–June 1975, p. 5.

[3] Ibid., pp. 7, 24.

demands or desires of their employees, want to increase the size of their organization or, at least, prevent it from shrinking. Finally, prison administrators, like all administrators, enjoy making their own decisions — that is, exercising autonomy. Because the society pushed aside the nasty task of handling felons, prison administrators have enjoyed a relatively large degree of autonomy, and they desire to keep it. The rehabilitative ideal helped further all these purposes. It justified a variety of control techniques and served as a rhetoric to diffuse criticism and justify expansion. Finally, it was the basis for a professional ideology that justified more autonomy.

Prison administrators could retreat to the primary task of keeping prisoners under control, which is what many of the more direct and conservative among them recommend, but this would not satisfy their need to believe that they are doing beneficial work or to accomplish the other covert organizational goals. A new correctional philosophy will be required to accomplish all this.

No new powerful correctional philosophy is in the making. A few theories or models left over from the 1960s, a refurbished ancient theory based on the classical theory of society and of crime and punishment, and an insidious theory of crime rejected many times in the past circulate in the world of prison policy makers. None appear to have a chance of replacing the departing rehabilitative ideal.

Many prison administrators stubbornly support and continue to implement more intensive forms of treatment, particularly variations on intensive group therapy, referred to as "the group method," and on behavior modification. Allen Breed, the director of the California Youth Authority, defends both approaches.

> "I'm convinced that we have early indications that we can help kids," Breed says. He cites as examples two Youth Authority institutions in Stockton, California, one of which adopted a behavior modification token economy program and the other, transactional analysis. In a study by the Youth Authority and the National Institute of Mental Health, it was shown that recidivism rates among the youths committed to both

institutions dropped 10% after the new treatment methods were introduced.[4]

These intensive forms of treatment are extensions of the rehabilitative ideal and are subject to the criticisms that it has received. They certainly will not gain the support required to be established as the new penological philosophy.

There is still strong support for community programs. In a poll by *Corrections Magazine,* 48 percent agreed that "community programs were more effective at rehabilitating offenders than institution programs," and an additional 26 percent agreed that they were more effective for "some offenders." [5] However, community corrections has already met with considerable criticism, and it is receiving much less support than it did in the late 1960s and nothing like the enthusiasm inspired by the rehabilitative ideal in its early years. It will not succeed as the new unifying ideology.

In many states, prison administrators are seeking new funds for smaller prisons. They argue that most of the prisons' shortcomings, inhumanities, and control problems are created or aggravated by the size and age of existing prisons. In addition, some argue that special new institutions will be required to control humanely the growing number of problem prisoners. But this new direction, which has widespread support, is being pursued more on practical than philosophical grounds.

One of the more pernicious penological theories circulating is that of the criminal type. This old notion, which ushered in the age of scientific criminology, has considerable appeal for the more conservative policy makers and, consequently, is regularly recycled. In a recent study entitled *The Criminal Personality,* Yochelson and Samenow, two clinicians who in their many years at St. Elizabeth's Hospital in Washington, D.C., came into contact with persons classified as serious or career criminals, wrote this: "At an early age, the criminal-to-be makes a series of choices that involve going counter to the re-

[4] Ibid., p. 11.
[5] Ibid., p. 5.

217

sponsible forces that prevail in all socio-economic levels." [6] They suggest that criminals become committed to criminal paths in spite of social circumstances, not because of them, and they remain committed in spite of all efforts to help them. The Rand Corporation has recently conducted a study of "intensive" criminals in California and reached similar conclusions. Evidently, the Law Enforcement Assistance Agency (LEAA), which funded the later efforts, is enthusiastically backing the new search for the criminal type.

The resurgence of interest in this old theory is understandable when we consider the appeal of criminal-type theories. If it were true that most serious crime was committed by a relatively small number of people who were permanently different in some identifiable characteristics, then the police, courts, and prisons could locate these persons and keep them under surveillance or isolate them from the community. Society's worries about crime could be solved without having to make any of the difficult adjustments recommended by critical criminologists: redistribution of opportunities, wealth, prestige, and power. However, the alchemists of criminology, dreaming about discovering the criminal type, have been awakened over and over again. The hard reality is that crime is not a property of a few, and humans are flexible (but they change in a somewhat unpredictable manner).

Moreover, the crime that society is most concerned about — street crime — is related more to social circumstances than individuals. For at least a hundred years, the social circumstances in the United States that have produced the highest rate of street crime include being young, male, and poor and living in an inner city area, crowded together with a concentration of other poor people. This set of social circumstances produced high crime rates among Irish, German, Polish, Italian, Jewish, and other European immigrants when they monopolized that social category in the late nineteenth and early twentieth centuries, and today it is producing high rates of crime among blacks, Puerto Ricans, and Chicanos, all of whom have the

[6] Samuel Yochelson and Stanton Samenow, *The Criminal Personality,* 2 vols. (New York: Jason Aronson, 1977), as quoted in Michael Serrill, "Books," *Corrections Magazine,* September 1977, p. 69.

added social circumstance of intense racial discrimination. In recent years, add to this set of social circumstances a significant increase in the relative size of this category and in its aspirations, which were raised by the escalated rhetoric of equality of the 1950s and 1960s. Something akin to "critical mass" was reached, and this new group of young, male, poor, ghetto dwellers surpassed the rates of violent crimes of their predecessors. However, not all occupants of this social category commit violent or any serious crime. These social circumstances are correlates of crime, not personality traits (which is the way that criminal-type theorists treat them). Moreover, even though the crime rate among this group is very high (the highest, if we restrict our focus to street crime), most of the serious crime is committed by people in other social categories. Crime is prevalent all over the social map of the United States, and there are a lot more people in other categories. Also, longitudinal studies of the persons who are in the high-street-crime category and who have been arrested at least once suggest that the vast majority mature out of crime. A follow-up study of all male youth born in Philadelphia in 1945 revealed that at each arrest, no matter how many arrests, the most likely future outcome after release was not to be arrested for any serious offense again. This was true even for those arrested three, four, or five times before.[7]

In the case of the latest two discoveries of the criminal type, the research had such large flaws that it is amazing that the researchers themselves took their ideas seriously. In both cases they reached their conclusions about their subjects' early commitment to crime by talking to them at the *end* of their criminal careers. The obvious problem with this approach is that persons distort their biographies. Most people have a strong tendency not to admit mistakes, particularly important life mistakes. Looking back on a long career of crime and arrests, many individuals will say that they were committed to the criminal life at a very early age. This is more of an attempt

[7] Marvin E. Wolfgang, Robert Figlio, and Thorsten Sellin, *Delinquency in a Birth Cohort* (Chicago: University of Chicago Press, 1972). For a recent excellent discussion of the relationship between crime, poverty, and race, see Charles E. Silberman, *Criminal Violence, Criminal Justice* (New York: Random House, 1978).

to dignify their careers than to describe them accurately. I have maintained close contact with several people over a twenty-year span during which they returned to crime and were reimprisoned several times. In recent years they have talked to me very much like the persons interviewed by the Rand researchers and by Yochelson and Samenow; that is, they now say that they were different from other children or youths and that they were "hope-to-die" thieves. I know differently. I was intimate with them at various stages in their careers, and at many junctures they were very ambivalent about going back to crime. All of them had periods during which they tried very hard to live conventional or semiconventional lives. I also listened to their accounts of their childhoods, and in the earlier versions these were no different than the childhoods of hundreds of prisoners who did not continue in criminal careers. Their later renditions of their lives are reconstructions, fashioned to demonstrate to themselves and others that what they did was somewhat inevitable. It is no trick to locate career criminals at the end of their career. The difficulty — or, I would submit, the impossibility — is to distinguish them from the very large group of people who do not pursue criminal careers, but who measure essentially the same on every knowable characteristic at the beginning.

Even if we assume that the individuals interviewed by these researchers represent a large class of committed criminals, an assumption that is not warranted because their samples were very select groups, it is still foolish to jump to the conclusion that this class accounts for most of the serious crime. This latest attempt to heap the problem of crime on the backs of a few will fail as it has in the past, and penology will have to get along without a criminal-type ideology.

TROUBLE IN THE RANKS

Prison administrators are presently plagued with more than ideological disorganization. Their bureaucracies have factionalized into subgroups that are hostile toward the administration and each other. For years, guards' dissatisfaction has been growing, and they have become increasingly active in countering administrative policies and pursuing their own self-interests.

220

In many prisons, guards are organized into unions that actively seek changes in penological practices in addition to bread-and-butter goals. A study of prison employee unionism, conducted by the American Justice Institute and funded by LEAA reported a series of illegal actions that documents guards' dissatisfaction with administrative policies and their new activism, which in at least half of the fifty states resulted in illegal "sick-outs," "lock-ins," slowdowns, and strikes.[8] In many of these instances, the guards were seeking a reduction in prisoners' rights and privileges and more control over prisoners. A poll by the California State Employees' Association showed that 85 percent of the employees agreed that "inmates had too much power in decisions in administering the institution."[9]

In the future, prison administrators will not be able to decide prison policy unilaterally. Employee activism and collective bargaining, which is steadily corroding the formerly military and authoritarian type of structure, will require that guards and other groups of employees be consulted and that their special interests influence penological policy. It is difficult to make accurate estimates of the long-run outcome of this influence, but at present it clearly suggests a punitive and conservative direction.

The guards and other employees are far from a monolithic group. In addition to the split over treatment and control referred to earlier, new rifts have appeared. A significant one is that between the newer, younger, more urban (often non-white) guards and members of the old school. In 1972, I was at Stateville, in Illinois, with a group evaluating a new guard-training program. In interviews of older captains, lieutenants, and sergeants at Stateville, we quickly discovered that their most intense hostility was toward the new urban guards, not the prisoners. James Jacobs, in his study of Stateville, reports the same shift:

> In the minds of the top guards, the deterioration of the guard force is linked to the massive infusion of minority guards

[8] John M. Wynne, Jr., *"Prison Employee Unionism,"* Project Report of the American Justice Institute, funded by L.E.A.A., 1977, pp. 201–24.

[9] Reported in *San Francisco Chronicle,* June 10, 1977, p. 10.

into the system. It is felt that an increase in narcotics trafficking and in absenteeism is attributable to this group of new recruits. In one captain's opinion, "the new officers from Chicago aren't worth a damn. Some are just in a daze, others don't show up for work and others don't want to work. If they're criticized, they cop an attitude. They don't want to take orders." [10]

In our interviews, the "top guards" complained that the new "Chicago guards" identified with the prisoners more than with the administration. Similar splits based on ethnic or urban-rural differences are dividing guard forces in many states. In California the Correctional Officers' Association has vigorously fought affirmative action hiring and promoting. In addition to this guard organization, which is the largest in the state, there are Mexican-American and black employee associations. Also, there is an organization of correctional counselors. All these different groups are asserting themselves in policy formation. The prison administration is more and more fractionalized, and planning a cohesive penological strategy (even with a powerful unifying philosophy) is less likely to occur.

PRIVATE INFLUENCES

Although most of the large-scale vigorous public interest in the prison has abated, many private groups still work on prison reform, and the major issue that ties most of them together is the prison construction moratorium. These residual, private activists are joined in their moratorium drive by several highly respected professionals in penology, such as William Nagel, director of the Institute of Corrections of the American Foundation, and Milton Rector, director of the National Council on Crime and Delinquency. At a conference in 1977, Nagel argued:

> To insure that we don't saddle future generations of Americans with more prisons and jails than the absolute minimum necessary to quarantine the intractable offenders we must, it seems to me, put our resources and energy elsewhere. Public policy during this decade should seek effective ways to protect

[10] Ibid., p. 184.

the public. A more just society offering opportunity to all its segments will provide some of that protection. The prison, call it by any other name, will not.[11]

The idea binding the different individuals and groups together is that prisons are horrible and counterproductive. This ends their agreement. Many, like Nagel, support the reduction of prison populations by imprisoning only a small group that is variously defined as "intractable" or "dangerous" offenders. Others claim to be in favor of totally abolishing prisons. Together, these groups and individuals have been successful in stopping or delaying prison construction here and there. The moratorium coalition in California has been one of the major forces in delaying the California Department of Corrections' plan to build two or more new prisons. But, in general, the pressures for new space and the argument for replacing deteriorating prisons with new prisons, particularly new small prisons, are overwhelming the moratorium forces, and new prison construction rolls on.

"DETERMINATE SENTENCING"

The theory that is gaining momentum and drastically altering prison policy is not a philosophy of penology, but one of sentencing.

> But there is a movement underway now which has already had a profound impact in some parts of the nation and which promises to turn the entire criminal justice system upside down, for good or bad, before it has run its course. This movement goes by the generic title of "determinate sentencing." It has its origins in the civil rights and prisoners' rights struggles of the late sixties but has since been enthusiastically embraced by both liberals and conservatives, by prison reformers and police chiefs. Determinate sentencing is clearly an idea whose time has come, even though its exact definition heavily depends on the person who is defining it.[12]

[11] William G. Nagel, "On Behalf of a Moratorium on Prison Construction," *Crime and Delinquency,* April 1977, p. 155.
[12] Michael S. Serrill, "Determinate Sentencing," *Corrections Magazine,* September 1977, p. 3.

223

The new sentencing laws passed by several states and the new sentencing policies adopted by prison administrations in others will substantially change the size and character of prison populations and necessitate changes in routine. Although they are referred to as determinate sentencing, they do *not* establish determinate or uniform sentences. Instead, the various statutes passed in California, Maine, Illinois, and Indiana and the policies adopted in Minnesota and Oregon limit or eliminate parole board discretion, but increase judicial discretion. In California the statute establishes four categories of crimes, and each category gives the judge three different sentences: for example, two, three, or four years. The judge can "enhance" the sentence for prior convictions, weapon possession, weapon use, and multiple offenses. Since the enhancements are quite discretionary, the judges operate within very wide margins, sometimes from two to fifteen years, which is far from determinate sentencing. Maine established a maximum sentence that a judge could impose, but no minimum. *Corrections Magazine* summarized Indiana's bill in this fashion:

> Establishes presumptive sentences with substantial range for judicial discretion. Non-capital murder, 40 years, plus 20 for aggravation, minus 10 for mitigation. Class A (e.g.: child molesting, kidnapping, major narcotics) 30 years, plus 30 or minus 10. Class B (rape, robbery with injury, lesser narcotics dealing) 10 years, plus 10 or minus 4. Class C (armed robbery, forgery, drug possession) 5 years plus or minus 3. Class D (simple burglary, credit card deception) 2 years, plus 2 in aggravation, no reduction for mitigation. Non-binding guidelines for judges, prior conviction makes sentence non-probationable: two priors add 30 years to sentence. One-for-one good time. Parole supervision up to one year after release.[13]

In Illinois the judges are expected to set sentences at the median of ranges for crimes of different severity. The different ranges are: one to twenty-five, three to seven, two to five, and one to three. The parole board is abolished, and parole supervision lasts from one to two years. One day of good time is earned for

[13] Ibid., p. 30.

each two days served. The states that have moved toward administrative determinate sentencing have established similar guidelines for the parole boards. In each case that I have examined, the choice within the margin is highly discretionary, the margins are broad, and they can be expanded for mitigating or aggravating circumstances.

In actuality, the indeterminacy that was formerly spread from the police to the parole board is being shifted away from the parole board and piled up in the courts and the district attorney's office. The more invisible indeterminacy in police decision making has not been touched. The prosecutors' and judges' vast margins of discretion have been increased significantly.

Once individuals are sentenced, they have a more definite idea of how much time they will serve. Parole boards, often renamed ("community release board" in California), have some control over good time, which is often half of the sentence; limited power to rearrange the sentence imposed by the judge; and, in some cases, the power of the old parole boards over some categories of prisoners. However, they have much less discretionary power than under the old laws. In the states that have moved toward administrative determinacy, the parole boards are not bound to the guidelines and often move outside them.

Lack of uniformity in sentencing was one of the major criticisms of the indeterminate sentence system, but more uniformity probably will not be achieved under the new sentencing procedures. Judges and prosecutors have wide time margins that they will use in plea bargaining. Persons with essentially the same crimes will arrive at the prisons with very different sentences due to having been sentenced by judges with different estimations of a crime's seriousness and having used different levers in plea bargaining (for example, having made bail or not).

The new sentencing statutes in Maine, Indiana, California, and Illinois will result in an increase in the lengths of sentences for a significant percentage of convicted persons. The laws were designed to establish margins based on existing patterns; but in each case, conservative pressure in the legislatures either moved the margins upward or added enhancements, so that average sentences become extraordinary sentences. Whether or not this trend will be sustained is not certain, and it could even become worse. Several bills to increase the margins are moving through the California legislature.

What went wrong? The criticisms that started the drive to change sentencing laws sprang from the argument that indeterminate sentencing produced longer, disparate, and discriminatory sentences. The end result of the drive in these four states has been new laws with sentences equally as disparate and discriminatory, but even longer. Liberal and civil libertarian groups in cooperation with a few practical legislators and prison administrators had started the motion, but when it appeared that the old laws would tumble, conservative legislators attached themselves to the issue. Making political currency out of the public's fear of street crime and bringing considerable public attention to the bills, these legislators succeeded in cowing uncommitted or ambivalent colleagues. As John Conrad noted, there is "no reliable coolant for the passion of a legislator determined to increase sentences except the common sense of his colleagues and the willingness of a governor to exercise his veto in an unpopular cause."[14] The crime issue was too touchy at the time that the bills were passing through the legislatures, the colleagues revealed more cowardice than common sense, and the governors were not about to buck the punitive tide. The result was that moderate steps toward determinacy and uniformity became large steps toward punitiveness. Discretion that was limited considerably by some of the early drafts of legislation was built back in, and sentences were increased.[15]

In effect, humanitarian activist groups sustained a long drive to abolish indeterminate sentence systems, because they believed that these systems disguised punishment as treatment and punished excessively and discriminatorily. These groups believed that when they were able to convince members of the

[14] John Conrad, "In My Opinion," *Corrections Magazine,* September 1977, p. 0.
[15] Sheldon L. Messinger and Philip D. Johnson traced these developments in California: "California's Determinate Sentence Statute: History and Issues," in *Determinate Sentences: Reform or Regression, Proceedings on Special Conference on Determinate Sentencing* (Washington, D.C.: N.I.L.C.J./L.E.A.A., U.S. Department of Justice, 1978).

legislature and sections of the public that this was the case, the response would be toward fairness and restraint. This was not the case. In the *Outlaw,* the Prisoners' Union characterized the actual response in the following manner:

> We thought that when we exposed rehabilitation as a punitive, arbitrary system legislatures would adopt a rational, uniform sentencing system. We underestimated the strong need many more powerful citizens and organizations have to divert attention to the criminal acts of the poorer people in the society and away from their own unscrupulous, exploitative and illegal acts. They have been drumming up fear of crime in the streets for several years and the result is an almost insane rage against a narrow slice of the whole, very large mass of criminal acts that go on in our society. This was accompanied by a demand for extreme punishment for the felons convicted of crimes which are presently receiving all the attention. What we ended up with here in California, and this seems to be the case in many other states, is the worst of both systems, the old rehabilitative and the new "justice" (or better, punishment) system. We still have all the discretion needed to discriminate between the weak and the powerful and now more punishment is heaped on those selected. Now they call it punishment and feel righteous about it.[16]

What will be the consequences of the changes brought about by the new sentencing policies? It appears certain that prison populations in the states with new sentencing laws will increase. The prison administrations will try to obtain allocations to build new, small, secure prisons.[17] However, smaller prisons are more expensive per prisoner, and the public, as revealed by the property tax revolt, is not in the mood to spend huge sums for new prison construction. Rehabilitation programs will be reduced in number, because they are expensive and legislators are not going to spend money for something with such little support.

Prison budgets will soar, anyway. It is not certain what the

[16] *Outlaw,* Winter 1978, p. 6.

[17] Minnesota is presently building a small, secure, but pleasant-appearing prison for a few hundred long-term prisoners. It may become a model for other states.

reaction to this will be. In the past, conservative legislators and the public have not objected to very large expenditures on police and defense activities. Ronald Reagan, for instance, preached fiscal conservatism and vastly increased the size of the California Highway Patrol during his tenure as governor of California. California has a highway force almost twice as large as any other state's (5,000 compared to New York's 2,500), and even though its crime-fighting functions are not apparent, the public has never objected to this excessive cost. But we are in a new era in which the public may want cutbacks even in prison budgets.

Prison populations will not only grow, but they will change in composition. The four states that have passed determinate sentence bills have all established very long sentences for violent crimes and repeat property offenses. Persons serving time for these crimes — mainly murder, assault, rape, robbery, and burglary — will fill the prisons. This also means that because of the distribution of these crimes in the society and the biased selection of the police and courts, the percentages of nonwhite prisoners will grow.

These prisoners are the most embittered, aggressive, and accustomed to struggling in oppressive situations, such as youth prisons and cities' slums. And these prisoners are not getting along with each other. Different races, territorial cliques (home boys), criminal tips, and gangs hate and distrust each other. The movements toward unity both inside and outside have been crushed. Prison administrations fear unity, which they believe means riot and sedition, and will not tolerate any formal organizations that might be able to bring hostile prisoner factions together, mediate disputes, or coordinate their common interests. The administrations are comfortable only with one type of control approach: classify, separate, and isolate. These methods are highly arbitrary and punitive, and persons punished arbitrarily become more embittered and aggressive. Therefore, isolation has failed to reduce tension and violence in the past and will fail in the future.

The embittered and aggressive prisoners will not strike back in any highly organized fashion, but will continue to operate devious contraband systems, wage war on each other,

228

and (as individuals or in small groups) occasionally and spontaneously assault staff. The administration will try to locate the troublemakers and isolate them, and there will be more classification and segregation. For the present, new troublemakers will sprout from the masses, and many segregated prisoners, having lost hope of being released and struggling to maintain some conception of themselves as active agents, will strike back whenever they see the opportunity.

Eventually, the turmoil inside may subside, but not because of any action by the administration. In the most violent, clique-oriented prisons the warfare is already simmering down. Combattants are getting tired of attacking others and facing attack. Many of the most belligerent are being killed, growing old, or finally being crushed by too much isolation in adjustment centers. New potential gladiators with foreknowledge of the past wars are less willing to enter the battles and more willing to negotiate. New accommodations and alliances are forming among the violent cliques.

While the tension and violence abate inside, relevant changes are occurring outside. The crest of the crime wave has passed. The segment in society that has always committed most of the street crime — armed robberies, burglaries, assaults, rapes, and murders — grew during the late 1950s and early 1960s to an unprecedented size. This segment is composed of poor, inner-city young men, and its percentage in the population increased by 50 percent.[18] The migration that produced this bulge was mostly nonwhite, and to the usual problems of poverty faced by the new urban poor was added extreme racism. In addition, expectations were raised higher in the 1960s than in former periods. The result was a large increase in street crime, the types of crime to which these persons are restricted. But, like the violent activities in the prison, street crime has peaked. The heavy influx of new urban poor has slacked off. The young male urban poor of the 1960s and 1970s are aging, tiring, withering, or dying (few are prospering).

[18] Although he fails to consider other forms of crime than street crime and then goes on to draw insidious conclusions, James O. Wilson does an excellent job of analyzing the street crime wave of the 1960s (*Thinking About Crime* [New York: Vantage Books, 1975], chap. 1).

The public will eventually calm down about street crime. Inflation, corruption, and waste will draw its attention. Conservative politicians, who have been so successful in using the public's fear of crime for their own political advancement, will have to find other issues. Television news reporting, which has capitalized on street crime, will have to turn to other events to excite their viewers. The pressures of escalated prison populations, the higher costs of incarceration, and the resurgence of humanitarian sentiments may again prepare the way for another push toward rational and humane changes in prison policies. If this occurs, what should we do?

STEPS TOWARD A HUMANE AND RATIONAL PUNISHMENT SYSTEM

When we return to the search for a more humane and rational response to crime, we must keep in mind that the prison is tied to other social and political arrangements that limit what changes are possible. The criminal justice system in general is at least partially involved, directly and indirectly, advertently and inadvertently, in repressing groups and classes of people and in maintaining unfair social, political, and economic relationships. Fundamental changes in its operation are impossible unless some higher degree of social justice has been achieved and the criminal justice system is relieved of these tasks. But, for the purpose of considering what is possible in penology *if* this progress is being made, we shall assume that we are moving toward social justice and are now considering our response to crime as part of our general program of change.

Should We Have Prisons   The first issue to settle is this: Should we have prisons? This question has been confused with euphemisms. Let us begin with an agreement that any place in which people are held against their will for a felony is a prison. At present some prisons, such as Jackson in Michigan and San Quentin in California, are huge, decaying fortresses. Others, such as Eagle River in Alaska, Butner in North Carolina, and Pleasanton in California, are new, small, attractive facilities. Most prisons fall in between these extremes. Moreover, halfway houses or other community locations to which convicted felons are sent as alternatives to prison are possible only if

230

there is a more secure place, a prison, to which the felons can be sent if they repeatedly wander off and do not come back. The issues of what type of prison we promote or tolerate or which felons we send to prison are different from that of accepting imprisonment as a form of punishment.

Most persons who argue for abolition of prisons actually argue for diversion of *most* persons to probation, halfway houses, and other forms of punishment, but for imprisonment of a few, variously labeled violent, dangerous, or serious offenders, in some place that has a new label. For instance, one of the early and more famous abolitionists, George Bernard Shaw, seems to argue for complete abolition when he states: "If any person is addressing himself to the perusal of this dreadful subject in the spirit of a philanthropist bent on reforming a necessary and beneficient public institution, I beg him to put it down and go about some other business." Later in his discussion, however, he recommends euthanasia for "incorrigibly dangerous persons" and "detention and restraint" for "persons defective in the self-control needed for a free life in modern society." [19] Most of the contemporary abolitionists are guilty of the same inconsistencies and hypocrisies.

There are some sincere abolitionists. They, however, do not offer an alternative form of punishment, but point us to the day when society will not need to punish. They recommend, as Gordon Hawkins puts it, "other changes in social organization, changes so universal in scope and radical in nature that by comparison the abolition of prisons seems a relatively minor adjustment." [20] These radical abolitionists usually argue that any reform of prisons or present punishment systems merely delays the eventual radical changes that we must make.

I reject the radical abolitionists' argument, because I have no confidence in their prediction of a crime-free society. Further, I am convinced that most citizens (including myself and the radical abolitionists) will demand that something be done about the crime that they believe to be serious and will agree that small steps toward humanity do not delay but, in fact,

[19] *Crime, Punishment and Cure,* as quoted in Gordon Hawkins, *The Prison* (Chicago: University of Chicago Press, 1976), pp. 6–7.
[20] Hawkins, *The Prison,* p. 5.

must lead to higher levels of humanity. However, I find the argument of those abolitionists who recommend the detention of some small group of residual offenders in some place not called a prison to be more insidious. By pretending that there will be no prisons, suggesting that most people will be sent to nonpunitive alternatives, and claiming that only a few who must be detained will be detained, these soft abolitionists brush aside the most difficult problem: selecting who is detained (imprisoned). This group may or may not be a smaller number than are sent to prisons today. (So far, the use of alternatives to incarceration has not reduced the number sent to the old style of prison and has greatly increased the number of people in some type of detention situation.) The problem is that the residuals of whom these abolitionists speak do not stand out as a distinct, identifiable group of persons who are obviously "defective in the self-control needed for a free life in modern society." Locating such a group of persons rests on the task of predicting future serious or dangerous criminal acts. How this is done (and how it will always be done) is through the use of a set of indicators of future criminal activity. The indicators are any piece of information about an individual that, when measured in a group of people who are followed through time, shows a relationship to future criminal activity. Examples of commonly used indicators that have consistently shown a relationship to future criminal acts are being arrested the first time very early in life and being arrested the first time for auto theft. The relationship between these and future criminality are relatively strong, but always on the order of 0.2 or 0.3, in the language of correlations. To predict future criminality, a set of indicators are combined into an index or score, and persons are grouped into categories according to their scores. The rates of recidivism (return to criminality as indicated by rearrest) are measured for those with different scores by following successive "cohorts," or persons passing through some process together. When several indicators are present, the recidivism rate is sometimes as high as 60 or 70 percent.

I must emphasize that these indicators are not the causes of criminality nor measurements of criminal personality. We do not know exactly what they represent. They may reflect being immersed in criminal belief systems, having reduced life options, being well-known and, therefore, more closely watched by police agencies, as well as possessing aggressive or criminal tendencies. An important fact in considering their validity is that indicators identified in one period, such as the 1930s when this type of research began, do not work in future periods. They are constantly gaining or losing in predictive strength. We do not know exactly why.

I must also emphasize that knowing a group rate of recidivism does not give us an individual's chances of relapsing. In other words, if we add up an individual's score on indicators and place him in a group that in the past had a recidivism rate of 65 percent, this does not tell us that he has a 65 percent chance of returning to crime. We cannot know his chances, for probability theory is about group rates only.

Let me use a comparison that clarifies the theory. Suppose that we are dealing with driving patterns, and our concern is predicting the likelihood of an eighteen-year-old male's being involved in an accident. Actuarial data indicate that males between the ages of sixteen and twenty-one have a relatively high accident rate. Sex and age are not the causes of accidents, but we may theorize that young males are more likely to drive carelessly, show off in front of friends, and occasionally drive while in that youthful drunken state that results in recklessness. Keep in mind, however, that these are the habits of some young males and not all of them. Knowing that a person is male and twenty does not tell us whether he is one of the persons who drives recklessly, shows off, and so on. Even knowing that he was involved in an accident before and that this places him in a subclass with a higher rate does not tell us this. Many accidents are situational or truly unavoidable and do not reflect bad driving habits by one or all drivers involved. And even knowing that in the past this young man drove recklessly does not tell us that he will continue to drive recklessly in the future. Human beings are not bundles of unchangeable habits. They reflect on their past, mend their ways, and act differently in the future. So knowing that this young male falls into a class of people who in the past had an accident rate of, say, 30 percent does not mean that *he* has a 30 percent chance

233

of having an accident. Many complex personal characteristics (most of which we have not measured, cannot measure, or do not know about), unpredictable future situational factors, and his own choices over which he has some control will determine his chances. The 30 percent rate tells us only that if we continue to follow many persons with the indicators (here, age and sex) and if other relevant conditions do not change (for example, radical changes in speed limits, gasoline shortages, a depression, or a war, all of which may alter the overall driving picture), then in the future the *group* will have something very close to a 30 percent accident rate.

Even if these difficulties did not exist, that is, if the predictors did not shift and they truly measured criminal characteristics in the individual, then we would still have the problem of making decisions on class rates and knowing that we include in our class many "false positives," persons about whom the prediction is made, but who do not fulfill the prediction.[21] The percentage of false positives is always significant; in the category containing the highest risks, it is 30 or 35 percent. This confronts us with an insoluble dilemma. If our intention is to incapacitate persons who will commit serious or violent acts in the future, we shall always include and thereby falsely punish a significant percentage who would not commit these acts in the future. The percentage is at least 30 when we are merely talking about recidivism. It is much higher if the recidivism is for a violent act.[22]

The injustice inherent in this process is compounded when we consider that we gain little in the reduction of future criminal acts by incapacitation, because most violent and serious crime in the future will be committed by persons other than those defined as dangerous by these methods. The scale tips further when we consider that unless we hold those defined as

[21] For a more thorough discussion of this problem of prediction, see Andrew von Hirsch, *Doing Justice* (New York: Hill and Wang, 1976), chap. 3.

[22] Ernest Wenk, James Robison, and Gernal Smith followed a sample of released youthful offenders, 25% of whom had been involved in violent crimes. After fifteen months only 2.5% had recidivated for a violent crime ("Can Violence Be Predicted," *Crime and Delinquency*, v. 19, 1972), p. 5.

dangerous for life or at least for very long periods (twenty years or more), until such time as they mature out of crime, there is virtually no reduction in crime at all, just a minor delay.

This dilemma and attendant injustice exist even if our predictive techniques locate true criminal tendencies in the individual. This injustice grows when we recognize that most or at least some of the indicators reflect reduced life options and tendencies of the system to identify, watch, and incarcerate certain classes of people. To some degree, a tendency to recividism grows out of being incarcerated too young and too many times. What we identify as tendencies for which we incarcerate persons may be tendencies implanted through incarcerating them too much in the past.

There is no way out of these dilemmas. Although I have focused on predictions based on actuarial or probability theory, the same problems exist in all means of predicting future danger. Psychiatrists or other clinicians who attempt to predict future criminal acts are merely applying a set of indicators that they have adopted through their experience with offenders. Their indicators, which usually remain implicit, vague, and inconsistent, are no better than those discovered through actuarial research and are subject to the same shortcomings.

Norval Morris, in his discussion of the future of imprisonment, argues that there is a special type of prediction, labeled "anamnestic prediction," that is different.

> A prototypical example of an anamnestic prediction of criminal behavior might be based on your observation of that redheaded young man who works in the steel mills stepping through the tavern door one hot payday evening. Over the past year or two, he has been involved in a series of tavern fights when alcoholically well lubricated. You make an anamnestic prediction that your friend may have need for lawyer-like or doctor-like services that evening.[23]

I disagree with Morris and suggest that anamnestic prediction is also an example of unsystematic and implicit application of

[23] Norval Morris, *The Future of Imprisonment* (Chicago: University of Chicago Press, 1974), p. 31.

correlates of outcomes and in no way avoids the difficulties of the more systematic predictive techniques.[24]

This discussion of the problems in prediction has been very long, but it was necessary to make the essential point that those who advocate the abolishment of prisons for everyone except a few serious or dangerous criminals are leading us into a trap. Pursuing this policy would result (or is already resulting) in many persons' being held for very long periods of time, even though their crimes do not warrant severe punishment. This includes false positives and persons who are recidivists because of reduced life options. Most of the punishment delivered because of predictions of future dangerousness will fall on young, male, nonwhites who have been arrested early and have several arrests because they fall into the highest risk category. This system will also have the result that many persons who commit very reprehensible crimes will not be imprisoned at all because they fall into very low risk categories. By and large, these persons will be white and middle-class or above. Thus, while not reducing crime more than a very insignificant degree, a policy of only imprisoning "the few" defined as dangerous or serious offenders aggravates the most serious problem in the criminal justice system, that of discriminatory selection for severe punishment.

What Should Prisons Do?   We still have not answered our initial question. Should we have prisons? Before attempting to answer this, we must settle the issue of purpose. We have just rejected incapacitation as a reason for prisons. In earlier

[24] We certainly can make highly accurate predictions about some behavior when we know other people well. For instance, it is no feat to predict that a friend who goes to work every workday will go to work tomorrow if it is a workday. The difficulty is predicting when people will or will not repeat behavior that has dire consequences for them, consequences such as imprisonment. We must assume that they have some desire to avoid imprisonment and will try to avoid it. The indicators of recidivism relate to forces that override this desire—other strong desires, reduced options, a secret (or unconscious) desire to be in prison—and cause them to go against it. But we cannot predict when they will decide not to take chances and stick to their decision. This holds true for Morris's redhead above. If his periodic fighting resulted in more than some bruises (numbed by alcohol) and minor legal difficulties (compensated for by enhanced reputation), then we could not make the prediction of another fight with the same confidence.

chapters, the near impossibility and the abuses of imprisonment for rehabilitation were discussed. In summary, rehabilitation places a responsibility on the prison that it cannot accomplish and leads to increased punishment and arbitrariness. However, rejecting rehabilitation as a purpose of imprisonment does not preclude offering help to felons. Norval Morris, in arguing for rehabilitation, defines it in such a way that its benefits are present and its abuses avoided:

> Rehabilitation, whatever it means and whatever the programs that allegedly give it meaning, must cease to be a purpose of prison sanction. This does *not* mean that the various developed treatment programs within prisons need to be abandoned; quite the contrary, they need expansion. But it does mean that they must not be seen as *purposive* in the sense that criminals are to be sent to prison *for* treatment.[25]

Morris refers to treatment programs that are voluntary and not related to the length of sentences. Actually, this guts the historical meaning of rehabilitation. Although I may be quibbling over terms, in *Struggle for Justice* we felt safer calling the services *help* instead of *rehabilitation*. We also made the important point (as Morris does) that any help offered convicted felons must be available to all free persons:

> In recommending the separation of helping and coercive functions of the criminal law, we may have conveyed the impression that we support abandoning the goal of helping the defendant or prisoner. This is far from the truth. We envision a vast expansion of the range of educational, medical, psychiatric, and other services available not only to prisoners but to all people. Quality services now enjoyed by an elite group should be made free and accessible to all. High priority should be given to using this country's resources to allow each member of our society to develop his or her potentialities to the fullest.[26]

If rehabilitation and incapacitation are not the purposes of prisons, what are? Punishment and general deterrence, the other two possible purposes, are left. We are not and probably

[25] *The Future of Imprisonment,* p. 14–15.
[26] Pp. 152–153.

never will be sure about how much deterrence results from punishing those convicted of crimes. Zimring and Hawkins, in the most thorough examination of deterrence to date, include in their preface a cautionary statement, which reveals the difficulty in answering the question: "Does punishment deter crime? This question, though not entirely meaningless, is unanswerable in categorical terms for we confront a complex of issues about human behavior in a great variety of situations; and there are significant differences in situations which condition the existence, extent and nature of deterrence."[27] The manner in which each of us plans our own action should convince us that the threat of punishment does have some force in regulating behavior. (Our driving habits are the most instructive here.) While the evidence on what types of threats increase deterrence is inconclusive, there is some data that suggest that certainty rather than severity increases it more.[28] This does not directly support imprisonment as a form of punishment, but it does suggest uniformity and is not inconsistent with imprisonment. We must assume that to some extent the threat of imprisonment does deter, and a legitimate purpose of prisons is deterrence.

The main purpose of imprisonment, however, should be punishment. We are dishonest and foolish if we do not admit that punishment is basic in our response to crime. This is not a brutish retributive atavism in human beings; it is an essential part of the bargain that we make to live by rules. When they are breached, particularly in a manner producing extreme harm to others, we want something done. When nothing is done, the rules lose their meaning and persons lose their social commitment.

Historically, societies have used a variety of forms of punishment, many of which (such as whipping, mutilation, and perhaps execution) are presently unacceptable to us and others

[27] Franklin E. Zimring and Gordon J. Hawkins, *Deterrence* (Chicago: University of Chicago Press, 1973), pp. 6–7.
[28] After examining some of the literature on deterrence, Richard Salem and William Bowers conclude that certainty is "the primary deterrence factor" ("Severity of Formal Sanctions as a Deterrent to Deviant Behavior," *Law and Society Review,* August, 1970, p. 21).

(such as banishment) are impossible. In the last hundred years, many new and apparently more humane forms (such as probation, fines, and mandatory work in public institutions) increasingly have been used. Each has some minor problems, such as the tendency of organizations to misuse free labor and the differential capacity to pay fines. All share one inherent flaw: they are not sufficiently punitive for serious crimes. We must keep in mind that the public will continue to want persons guilty of crimes like murder, violent rape, and mayhem to receive more than probation, fines, or work in public service.

The only humane option that is seen as sufficiently punitive is imprisonment, a modern form of banishment. If our intention is to find the least inhumane form of punishment that society will accept for serious crime, we shall do better by drawing the line at imprisonment. Then we can insist that imprisonment is sufficient, and we can work to remove all punishment beyond that which is necessary to maintain a system of incarceration. If we want to reduce the number of people who receive imprisonment, our most extreme form of punishment, then we must alter the social arrangements that promote serious crime and remove some crimes from the category of serious offenses. It is neither fair nor effective to reduce the number of persons who receive imprisonment by selecting a few out of the pool of persons convicted of serious crime. If we want to reduce prison populations, short sentences can be added to the two changes just recommended. But we are stuck with prisons, so let us be fair in sending people to them and remove from them any unnecessary, added punishment.

I defend prisons because they are the only feasible punishment for serious crime. Perhaps the purpose of general deterrence is served, but the main purpose is punishment. Rehabilitation and incapacitation are impossible, unjust, and inhumane. Therefore, I accept prisons *because* they are punitive. However, once this hurdle is crossed, the path is open to consider other positive functions of imprisonment. One potential positive function, atonement, was envisioned by the Quakers when they planned prisons, but they considered it only as part of a total religious conversion. Many persons who complete their prison terms, although they experience no contrition for their preprison activities and are not "born again," do feel atoned. They express this in frequently repeated statements, such as "I did my time!" They are out of debt, stronger in knowing that they took their punishment, and securer in knowing that they have a response to any blame aimed at them after imprisonment.

Another potential benefit is imprisonment as a "respite." This runs against the dominant, humanitarian opinion on incarceration: imprisonment is necessarily damaging to the prisoners and their social lives because it extricates and segregates them from their outside communities, families, and work. I would argue that many, if not most, convicted felons were not nestled in the types of communities, families, or work situations that persons who believed the above had in mind or even in which, given a real choice, felons would like to remain. More likely, they were caught in somewhat destructive social webs or were being swept along out of control, careening and ricocheting through the days. Imprisonment affords these persons a respite from their involvements, during which they can extricate themselves from destructive dynamics, sort through their values and beliefs, pull themselves together, and make new plans and preparations for a new effort at life. The longer the respite lasts, the more likely it becomes that prisoners drift into special prison-nurtured belief systems and lose subtle skills required to function in the outside world. Short periods of confinement, perhaps one year or less, particularly if they are accompanied with resources that prisoners may use at their own discretion to equip themselves, can allow many benefits of a respite and avoid the deterioration of long imprisonment.

By and large, these benefits are realized only when convicts serve their time in a setting that is safe and not excessively mean, deprived, and arbitrary and has resources, meaningful options, and freedom to choose and plan so that they may pull themselves together and improve themselves. Privacy, some educational and vocational training resources, and voluntary systems of change (for example, individual therapy, group therapy, TM, yoga, or whatever prisoners believe to be effective) should be available. The benefits are reduced or disappear if convicts are constantly confronted with murderous violence and whimsical, arbitrary, and malicious control practices.

A first order of business is reducing the violence in the violent prisons. This is no easy task. But methods being pursued by administrators, classification and segregation, are ineffective and escalate the other negative conditions, the whimsical, arbitrary, and malicious control practices. The new hope is small prisons, but fiscal conservatism may thwart this solution. It would not necessarily work, anyway. If small prisons are filled, administered, and controlled in an arbitrary manner, then they will be as punitive and unconducive to the benefits mentioned above as the old fortresses.

We need a new system of control over prisoners that is not based on arbitrary decision making or on the old informal convict social system and its single prisoner code. There is only one possibility, a formal system of decision making in which all diverse parties (prisoners and guards included) have some input and in which the conditions of work and confinement, the rules of the institution, and the special problems and grievances of different parties (individuals and groups) are negotiated. Since a prison will always have special problems of social control, the administration will need the preponderance of power. But there could be systematic and open negotiation of policy and rules, a swift procedure for the inferiors (prisoners, guards, and other employees) to bring grievances to the administration, and an appeal mechanism involving outside authorities, preferably an independent body with a mixture of private and governmental representatives. The administration would not lose control of the prison under these arrangements, but would only be pressured to act openly, reasonably, and fairly. This is the direction taken when differences and hostilities divide people, groups, states, colonies, and nations. But in the prison realm, where authoritarianism has prevailed and prospered in the past and where one of the most significant groups is prisoners, who have been considered less than human or not entitled to any rights, the idea is repulsive. The big barrier is allowing prisoners to have organizations that formally represent prisoners in decision making. It was considered seriously in California, and the plan and its history are instructive. We described both in an issue of the *Outlaw*:

> For over eight months, the Prisoners' Union has been meeting with top administrators of the California Department of Corrections. The meetings have proceeded on two tracks. One has dealt with general problems of access to prisons — media, visitation, correspondence, etc. The other has been an effort to see if we could arrive at a plan for allowing prisoners to participate in organizations.
>
> *The Basic Idea*
>
> Most everyone who knows about prisons regards them as a terrible failure; full of misery, despair and violence. We believe a root cause of these problems is the isolation and powerlessness of people who are locked up. Our goals of abolishing the Indeterminate Sentence, ending economic exploitation and restoring civil and human rights (including the right to organize) all seek in one way or another to empower prisoners.
>
> The empowerment of prisoners is important for everyone. No one point of view can encompass all the complexities of a vast system of prisons. Participation by everyone concerned is necessary for any part of our political system to work and this includes prisoners. At present, there is no way for the prisoners' point of view to be effectively presented, either on behalf of an individual or for the class. This results in many stupid, uninformed, or accidental decisions that have very destructive effects on people inside and ultimately on us all.
>
> *Progress*
>
> After five years of opposition, we were initially dubious. The attitude and intense questioning by those with whom we met convinced us they were sincerely interested. Whether we would ever be able to agree on any form of institutionalized power for prisoners was another matter.
>
> In early January, we arrived at a tentative proposal permitting prisoner organizations. Call them Unions or whatever, these organizations would have the right to hold meetings inside attended by outside members; elect officials to represent its members at appeals, transfers or disciplinary hearings; and to meet and confer with administrators to examine prison policies. Prison officials did not let loose any of their control prerogatives or any of their decision-making author-

ity. They were entitled to immediately suspend any such organization and to kick it out for any reason, provided they held a public hearing. This proposal was a very weak version of what we think should be happening inside prisons but we went for it because it was a real beginning — it recognized the right to representation (Abraham Lincoln once said, "Any lawyer who represents himself has a fool for a client.") and it made possible an organizational structure inside, something that is essential if solid, well-supported positions on prison issues are to be developed. The entire document is printed following this article.

The proposal was a very broad one, more concerned with setting limits than with specifying who does what when. Our hopes were to continue refining in discussions with people who would actually be involved, beginning with a pilot project in one large prison. We wanted to hold a series of workshops with our members and prison staff to get across the limits and the possibilities of an organization and to work out the innumerable specific details of functioning. Only after months of such workshops and a secret ballot election would we be ready to operate. Knowing that the fate of the first such program would have national reverberations, we wanted it to happen right, at a slow and steady pace.

Our concerns were with the lack of a broad base of support in the community (many potentially sympathetic people were unaware of what was happening) and the reservoir of opposition to any change within the CDC. We decided that we could best develop the former and deal with the latter when and if we had something concrete to talk about.

The next step, after reaching broad accord, was to begin an ever-widening circle of discussion. We were going to begin this process by circulating the tentative proposal to the wardens, superintendents and parole district supervisors and appearing at their regular meeting to answer their questions. We never got any further.

Stall

On January 19, 1976, the day before our scheduled meeting with prison administrators, leaders of the California Correctional Officers' Association (CCOA) released the proposal to the press and announced their bitter opposition.

They threatened to strike if it or anything like it were adopted. They demanded that Director Jiro Enomoto and

Secretary Mario Obledo of Health & Welfare be fired for even entertaining such an "idiotic" and "insane" idea. The only substantive comments made about the proposal betrayed a total misunderstanding of what it was about. Their hysteria was infectious.

The next day, in a highly unfavorable climate created by their intense reaction and threats, the wardens and superintendents came out strongly against the plan. Concern was also expressed by those above the CDC over the banner headlines of contradictory content that were popping up like mushrooms everywhere. In this pressurized atmosphere, the plan was placed on the back burner, on very low heat.

Opposition

What kinds of opposition does the idea of organized prisoners face? One kind is the calculated hysteria of the first press comments of the CCOA leaders. This is essentially a political threat that has nothing to do with the idea. Another kind are specific concerns we have heard from guards, such as a feeling that a grievance procedure might be utilized to harass or fire one individual or that they be included in the planning of any major change. Such concerns are quite legitimate and can be talked over and worked out.

A more formidable obstacle, however, is an insidious, mistaken notion which we feel strongly is at the root of the prison administrator's unwillingness to accept the proposed plan. This is the belief that prisoners are fundamentally inferior. They are either dangerous animals or mostly weak people subject to domination by the few dangerous animals. They are, according to this view, incapable of participating in sustained, responsible action and becoming dignified, honorable human beings.

Of course, prison officials have many examples of failure to document their position. But many, perhaps most, of these are the fulfillment of a long operation of this viewpoint. Prisoners, as any group which has been persistently viewed as inferiors, moral degenerates or incapable persons, because of no opportunity to act otherwise or because of rage at having been constantly viewed and treated this way, will act accordingly.

Many prison administrators believe that any such organization of prisoners would rapidly be "taken over" by one of the other "gang of thugs and hoodlums." Our arguments that although such an organization would not likely be spotless, it had such a marked benefit for all who are locked up and so little in the way of material benefits that it was not likely to be "taken over," were regarded as the words of naive idealists. Our arguments that the various groups in prison would unite for the limited purpose of working for change in those areas that affect *everyone* inside were also generally regarded as naive.

Prison administrators were being "realistic" when they predicted that the expansion of the rights of jailhouse lawyers and law libraries would create chaos in the prison; that the extension of constitutional protection to the Nation of Islam would result in death and destruction. None of this has materialized. Warden Jake Gunn of Folsom Prison said during the meeting of January 20th, that 80% of the convicts inside Folsom wouldn't want a Union anyway. We will wager the existence of the Prisoners' Union against Warden Gunn's pension that a secret, anonymous referendum held inside Folsom over whether or not a Union was desired would show a majority in favor. We think the point of view we represent is no less realistic and a lot more fruitful.[29]

The Prisoners' Union's primary purpose with this plan was to increase prisoners' rights and power and to reduce abuses in prisons. However, we did consider the plan's impact on the informal world of the prison and offered it partly as a solution to the murderous clique activity inside California prisons. We did not predict immediate or complete cessation of violence, but we sincerely believed that if a formal structure with some real power in the decisions that influence the prisoners' situation and with access to effective grievance mechanisms were to develop, then the prisoner organization would gain respect and be able to negotiate and reduce disputes among prisoners. More importantly, it would offer many prisoners, who are potentially capable leaders and who at present have gone into hiding to avoid becoming involved in the rapacious violence, a means to display leadership, earn respect, and establish a new, dignified identity in the prison world. This type of

[29] *Outlaw,* January–February 1976, pp. 1–2. See Appendix B for "The Tentative Plan" agreed on by us and the top administrators of the California Department of Corrections.

organization and leadership would steadily chip away at the power and support of the cliques.

The 1973 events at Walpole Prison in Massachusetts support these predictions. After conflicting with a prisoner organization for several weeks and not being allowed by the state's top correctional administrator to suppress the organization forcefully, the guards walked out of the prison and guarded only the prison's perimeter. The prisoners, who had been divided on racial lines, selected a racially balanced committee to govern them and with relative lack of violence and other difficulties managed the prison for eleven weeks. This meant carrying on all the activities that prisoners, staff, and guards normally perform. This does not prove that prisoners can autonomously run a trouble-free prison. It was a short period, and evidently, at the end of the eleven weeks, troubles among prisoners were escalating. But it does demonstrate that prisoners, even when bitterly fractionalized, can come together when they have some real stake in managing their conditions. Imagine what would be possible if there existed preestablished, orderly mechanisms for selecting representatives, a sharing of power with other parties, a body of established rules and policy, and mechanisms for changing these in an orderly and rational fashion and for remedying aggrieving violations.

Since the events in 1975 and in January 1976, the California Department of Corrections has moved far away from its position of serious consideration of the above plan. (The conservative swing has carried them along.) In fact, across the country the concept of prisoners' having the right to organize and participate in decision making now seems ludicrous to most prison administrators and the public. In the meantime, I have become more convinced that formal prisoner organizations with input in decision making and access to independent grievance processes will be necessary to reestablish a safe prison and to establish for the first time a prison free from excessive punishment and arbitrary and malicious practices. Without this formal structure, many prisoners will remain divided into hostile factions, and the majority will withdraw in fear. Administrations will continue in or lapse into self-serving and arbitrary practices.

246

In advocating this solution, I am not optimistic about its possibilities in the near future. It appeared to have a chance in the early 1970s in California and perhaps Minnesota, where there were significant prisoner union organizations and somewhat receptive prison administrations. However, the public has reacted, the prison administrators have backed away from the idea, and the prisoners' unions have lost most of their momentum and support. Even in Sweden and Norway, countries much less punitively oriented toward prisoners, serious drives to introduce prisoner democracy failed, despite backing by influential outside organizations.[30] However, this does not mean that the plan is not fair or will not work. We do not have to search far to locate social arrangements that now are accepted as correct and appropriate even though they were resisted by the majority in the past. What the resistance means is that more time will have to pass before it can be accomplished.

One of the important obstacles that must be removed is the public conception of the prisoner. Presently, this conception is formed from the rare, but celebrated and horrendous crimes, such as the mass murders by the Manson cult, Juan Corona, or the "Hillside Strangler." Whereas prisoners like George Jackson, viewed as a heroic revolutionary fighting back from years of excessive punishment for a minor crime (an eighty-dollar robbery), shaped the conception of the prisoner in the early 1970s, persons like "Son of Sam" do so today.[31] These extraordinary cases distort the reality. Most prisoners are still in prison for relatively petty crimes, and even those convicted of the more serious must be understood in the context of society in the United States. What we need is a new

[30] See Thomas Mathiesen, *The Politics of Abolition* (Oslo, Norway: M. Robertson, 1974), and David A. Ward, "Sweden: The Middle Way to Prison Reform?" in Marvin E. Wolfgang, ed., *Prisons: Present and Possible* (Lexington Mass.: Lexington Books, 1979).

[31] A few days after writing this sentence, I was reading an article by Eve Pell. One of the prison movement activists during the late 1960s and early 1970s, she had written the following statement: "But fashions change; the public grows bored, and today the image of the man behind bars is no longer that of a social protester such as George Jackson, but rather of a mass murderer such as Son of Sam" ("Revisiting the Prison Movement," "California Living" section, *San Francisco Sunday Examiner and Chronicle,* March 25, 1979, p. 6).

theory of crime and penology, one that is quite simple. It is based on the assumption that prisoners are human beings and not a different species from free citizens. Prisoners are special only because they have been convicted of a serious crime. But they did so in a society that produces a lot of crime, a society, in fact, in which a high percentage of the population commits serious crime. Those convicted of serious crimes must be punished and imprisoned, because it is the only option that satisfies the retributive need and is sufficiently humane. Knowing that imprisonment itself is very punitive, we need not punish above and beyond imprisonment. This means that we need not and must not degrade, provoke, nor excessively deprive the human beings whom we have placed in prison. It also means that we must not operate discriminatory systems that select which individuals should be sent to prison and, once incarcerated, who should be given different levels of punishment.

Since we assume that convicts are humans like us and are capable of myriad courses of action, honorable and dishonorable, we also assume that they will act honorably, given a real choice. This means that we provide them with the resources to achieve self-determination, dignity, and self-respect.

This theory continues to be rejected not because it is invalid, but because it challenges beliefs and values to which large segments of the population comfortably cling. These beliefs serve the selfish interests of many bureaucrats, prison employees, politicians, and private entrepreneurs who bloat their sense of importance, protect their jobs, win reelection, and divert attention from their own corrupt, unscrupulous, and criminal acts. They do so by identifying groups of people in society as subhumans and then treating them inhumanely. In pushing this theory, I admit that many prisoners, like many free citizens, act like monsters. But they are not monsters and often choose to act like monsters when their only other real option is to be totally disrespected or completely ignored, while being deprived, degraded, abused, or harassed.

Appendix A

FOLSOM

Folsom Prison Demands

Brothers and Sisters,

This list of demands comes from our brothers at Folsom Prison—Black, Brown, Red, Yellow, and White. They believe that now is the time to determine the direction of their own lives, and to stop letting themselves be the Pawns of the Adult Authority and the California Department of Corrections. Their struggle is your struggle. The walls that wall our brothers in wall us out. Consider how these demands affect all of our lives. To continue their effort and to make these demands STATE-WIDE, they need our utmost support. . . .

November 3, 1970—Continuing

ALL POWER TO THE PEOPLE! ! !

Manifesto of Demands, 11/3/70

1. *We demand* the constitutional rights of legal representation at the time of all Adult Authority hearings, and the protection from the procedures of the Adult Authority whereby they permit no procedural safeguards such as an attorney for cross-examination of witnesses, witnesses in behalf of the parolee, at parole revocation hearings.
2. *We demand* a change in medical staff and medical policy and procedure. The Folsom Prison Hospital is totally inadequate, understaffed, prejudicial in the treatment of inmates. There are numerous "mistakes" made many times, improper and erroneous medication is given by untrained personnel. The emergency procedures for serious injury

249

are totally absent in that they have no emergency room whatsoever; no recovery room following surgery which is performed by practitioners rather than board member surgeons. They are assisted by inmate help neither qualified, licensed, nor certified to function in operating rooms. Several instances have occurred where multiple injuries have happened to a number of inmates at the same time. A random decision made by the M.D. in charge as to which patient was the most serious and needed the one surgical room available. Results were fatal to one of the men waiting to be operated upon. This is virtually a death sentence to such a man who might have lived otherwise.

3. *We demand* adequate visiting conditions and facilities for the inmates and families of Folsom prisoners. The visiting facilities at this prison are such as to preclude adequate visiting for the inmates and their families. As a result, the inmates are permitted two hours, two times per month to visit with families and friends, which, of course, has to be divided between these people. We ask for additional officers to man the visiting room five days per week, so that everyone may have at least four hours visiting per month. The administration has refused to provide or consider this request in prior appeals using the grounds of denial that they cannot afford the cost of the (extra) officers needed for such change. However, they have been able to provide twelve new correctional officers to walk the gun rails of this prison, armed with rifles and shotguns during the daytime hours when most of the prison population is at work or attending other assignments. This is a waste of the taxpayers money, and a totally unnecessary security precaution.

4. *We demand* that each man presently held in the Adjustment Center be given a written notice with the Warden of Custody signature on it explaining the exact reason for his placement in the severely restrictive confines of the Adjustment Center.

5. *We demand* an immediate end to indeterminate adjustment center terms to be replaced by fixed terms with the length of time served being terminated by good conduct and ac-

cording to the nature of the charges, for which men are presently being warehoused indefinitely without explanation.

6. *We demand* an end to the segregation of prisoners from the mainline population because of their political beliefs. Some of the men in the Adjustment Center are confined there solely for political reasons and their segregation from other inmates is indefinite.

7. *We demand* an end to political persecution, racial persecution, and the denial of prisoners to subscribe to political papers, books, or any other educational and current media chronicles that are forwarded through the United States mail.

8. *We demand* an end to the persecution and punishment of prisoners who practice the constitutional right of peaceful dissent. Prisoners at Folsom and San Quentin Prisons according to the California State Penal Code, cannot be compelled to work as these two prisons were built for the purpose of housing prisoners and there is no mention as to the prisoners being required to work on prison jobs in order to remain on the mainline and/or be considered for release. Many prisoners believe their labor power is being exploited in order for the State to increase its economic power and continue to expand its correctional industries which are million dollar complexes, yet do not develop working skills acceptable for employment in the outside society, and which do not pay the prisoner more than the maximum sixteen cents per hour wage. Most prisoners never make more than six or eight cents per hour. Prisoners who refuse to work for the two to sixteen cent pay rate, or who strike, are punished and segregated without the access to the privileges shared by those who work, this is class legislation; class division, and creates class hostilities with the prison.

9. *We demand* an end to the tear-gassing of prisoners who are locked in their cells, such action led to the death of Willie Powell in Soledad Prison in 1968 and of Fred Billingslea on February 25, 1970 at San Quentin Prison. It is cruel and unnecessary.

10. *We demand* the passing of a minimum and maximum term

251

bill which calls for an end to indeterminate sentences whereby a man can be warehoused indefinitely, rehabilitated or not. That all prisoners have the right to be paroled after serving their minimum term instead of the cruel and unusual punishment of being confined beyond his minimum eligibility for parole, and never knowing the reason for the extension of time, nor when his time is completed. The maximum term bill eliminates indefinite lifetime imprisonment where it is unnecessary and cruel. Life sentences should not confine a man for longer than ten years, as seven years is the statute for a considered lifetime out of circulation and if a man cannot be rehabilitated after a maximum of ten years of constructive programs, etc., then he belongs in a mental hygiene center, not a prison. Rescind Adult Authority Resolution 171, arbitrary fixing of prison terms.

11. *We demand* that industries be allowed to enter the institutions and employ inmates to work eight hours a day and fit into the category of workers for scale wages. The working conditions in prisons do not develop working incentives parallel to the money jobs in the outside society, and a paroled prisoner faces many contradictions on the job that adds to his difficulty to adjust. Those industries outside who desire to enter prisons should be allowed to enter for the purpose of employment placement.

12. *We demand* that inmates be allowed to form or join Labor Unions.

13. *We demand* that inmates be granted the right to support their own families, at present thousands of welfare recipients have to divide their checks to support their imprisoned relatives who without the outside support could not even buy toilet articles or food. Men working on scale wages could support themselves and families while in prison.

14. *We demand* that correctional officers be prosecuted as a matter of law for shooting inmates, around inmates, or any act of cruel and unusual punishment where it is not a matter of life or death.

15. *We demand* that all institutions who use inmate labor be

made to conform with the state and federal minimum wage laws.

16. *We demand* an end to trials being held on the premises of San Quentin Prison, or any other prison without the jury as stated in the U.S. Constitution as being picked from the country of the trial proceedings and of the peers of the accused; that being in this case, other prisoners as the selected jurors.

17. *We demand* an end to the escalating practice of physical brutality being perpetrated upon the inmates of California State Prisons at San Quentin, Folsom, and Soledad Prison in particular.

18. *We demand* appointment of three lawyers from the California Bar Association for full-time positions to provide legal assistance for inmates seeking post-conviction relief, and to act as liaison between the Administration and inmates for bringing inmate complaints to the attention of the administration.

19. *We demand* update of industry working conditions to standards as provided for under California law.

20. *We demand* establishment of inmate workers insurance plan to provide compensation for work related accidents.

21. *We demand* establishment of unionized vocational training program comparable to that of the Federal Prison System which provides for union instructors, union pay scale, and union membership upon completion of the vocational training course.

22. *We demand* annual accounting of Inmate Welfare Fund and formulation of inmate committee to give inmates a voice as to how such funds are used.

23. *We demand* that the Adult Authority Board appointed by the Governor, be eradicated and replaced by a parole board elected by popular vote of the people. In a world where many crimes are punished by indeterminate sentences; where authority acts within secrecy and within vast discretion, and gives heavy weight to accusations by prison employees against inmates, inmates feel trapped unless they are willing to abandon their desire to be independent men.

24. *We strongly demand* that the State and Prison Authorities conform to recommendation #1 of the "Soledad Caucus Report," to wit, "That the State Legislature create a full-time salaried board of overseers for the State prisons. The board would be responsible for evaluating allegations made by inmates, their families, friends, and lawyers against employees charged with acting inhumanely, illegally, or unreasonably. The board should include people nominated by a psychological or psychiatric association, by the State Bar Association, or by the Public Defenders Association, and by groups of concerned, involved, laymen."

25. *We demand* that prison authorities conform to the conditional requirements and needs as described in the recent released Manifesto from the Folsom Adjustment Center.

26. *We demand* an immediate end to the agitation of race relations by the prison administrations of this state.

27. *We demand* that the California Prison System furnish Folsom Prison with the services of Ethnic Counselors for the needed special services of Brown and Black population of this prison.

28. *We demand* an end to the discrimination in the judgment and quota of parole for Black and Brown people.

29. *We demand* that all prisoners be present at the time that their cells and property are being searched by the correctional officers of state prisons.

ATTICA

Attica Prison Demands

DEMANDS SUBMITTED TO NEW YORK PRISON AUTHORITIES AND OTHER GOVERNMENT FUNCTIONARIES ON "MAN'S RIGHT TO KNOWLEDGE AND THE FREE USE THEREOF"

We, the inmates of Attica Prison, have grown to recognize beyond the shadow of a doubt that, because of our posture as prisoners and branded characters as alleged criminals, the administration and prison employees no longer consider or respect us as human beings, but rather as domesticated animals selected to do their bidding in slave labor and furnished as a personal whipping dog for their sadistic, psychopathic hate.

We, the inmates of Attica Prison, say to you, the sincere people of society, the prison system of which your courts have rendered unto, is without question the authoritative fangs of a coward in power.

Respectfully submitted to the people as a protest to the vile and vicious slavemasters:

THE GOVERNOR OF NEW YORK STATE
THE N.Y.S. DEPARTMENT OF CORRECTIONS
THE N.Y.S. LEGISLATURE
THE N.Y.S. COURTS
THE UNITED STATES COURTS
THE N.Y.S. PAROLE BOARD

And those who support this system of injustice.

Manifesto of Demands

1. WE DEMAND the constitutional rights of legal representation at the time of all parole board hearings; and the protection from the procedures of the Parole Authorities whereby they permit no procedural safeguards such as an attorney for cross-examination of witnesses, witnesses in behalf of the parolee, at parole revocation hearings.

2. WE DEMAND a change in medical staff and medical policy and procedure. The Attica Prison hospital is totally inadequate, understaffed, prejudiced in treatment of inmates. There are numerous "mistakes" made many times, improper and erroneous medication is given by untrained personnel. We also *demand* periodical check-ups on *all* prisoners and sufficient licensed practitioners 24 hours a day instead of inmate help that is used now.

3. WE DEMAND adequate visiting conditions and facilities for the inmates and families of Attica prisoners. The visiting facilities at this prison are such as to preclude adequate visiting for the inmates and their families.

4. WE DEMAND an end to the segregation of prisoners from the mainline population because of their political beliefs. Some of the men in Segregation Units are confined there solely for political reasons and their segregation from other inmates is indefinite.

5. WE DEMAND an end to the persecution and punishment of

prisoners who practice the Constitutional right of peaceful dissent. Prisoners at Attica and other N.Y.S. prisons cannot be compelled to work, as those prisons were built for the purpose of housing prisoners and there is no mention as to the prisoners being required to work on prison jobs in order to remain in the mainline population and/or be considered for release. Many prisoners believe their labor power is being exploited in order for the state to increase its economic power and to continue to expand its correctional industries (which are million dollar complexes), yet do not develop working skills acceptable for employment in the outside society, and which do not pay the prisoner more than an average of forty cents a day. Most prisoners never make more than fifty cents a day. Prisoners who refuse to work for the outrageous scale, or who strike, are punished and segregated without the access to the privileges shared by those who work; this is class legislation, class division, and creates hostilities within the prison.

6. WE DEMAND an end to political persecution, racial persecution, and the denial of prisoners' rights to subscribe to political papers, books, or any other educational and current media chronicles that are forwarded through the United States mail.

7. WE DEMAND that industries be allowed to enter the institutions and employ inmates to work eight hours a day and fit into the category of workers for scale wages. The working conditions in prisons do not develop working incentives parallel to the many jobs in the outside society, and a paroled prisoner faces many contradictions of the job that adds to his difficulty in adjusting. These industries outside who desire to enter prisons should be allowed to enter for the purpose of employment placement.

8. WE DEMAND that inmates be granted the right to join or form a labor union.

9. WE DEMAND that inmates be granted the right to support their own families; at present, thousands of welfare recipients have to divide their checks to support their imprisoned relatives who, without the outside support, cannot even

buy toilet articles or food. Men working on scale wages could support themselves and families while in prison.

10. WE DEMAND that correctional officers be prosecuted as a matter of law for any act of cruel and unusual punishment where it is not a matter of life or death.

11. WE DEMAND that all institutions using inmate labor be made to conform with the state and federal minimum wage laws.

12. WE DEMAND an end to the escalating practice of physical brutality being perpetrated upon the inmates of N.Y.S. prisons.

13. WE DEMAND the appointment of three lawyers from the N.Y.S. Bar Association to full-time positions for the provision of legal assistance to inmates seeking post-conviction relief, and to act as a liaison between the Administration and inmates for bringing inmate complaints to the attention of the Administration.

14. WE DEMAND the updating of industry working conditions to the standards provided for under N.Y.S. law.

15. WE DEMAND the establishment of inmate workers insurance plan to provide compensation for work-related accidents.

16. WE DEMAND the establishment of unionized vocational training programs comparable to that of the Federal Prison System which provides for union instructions, union pay scales, and union membership upon completion of the vocational training courses.

17. WE DEMAND annual accounting of the Inmates' Recreation Fund and formulation of an inmate committee to give inmates a voice as to how such funds are used.

18. WE DEMAND that the present Parole Board appointed by the Governor be eradicated and replaced by a parole board elected by popular vote of the people. In a world where many crimes are punished by indeterminate sentences and where authority acts within secrecy and within vast discretion and gives heavy weight to accusations by prison employees against inmates, inmates feel trapped unless they are willing to abandon their desire to be independent men.

19. WE DEMAND that the State Legislature create a full-time, salaried board of overseers for the State prisons. The Board

would be responsible for evaluating allegations made by inmates, their families, friends, and lawyers against employees charged with acting inhumanely, illegally, or unreasonably. The Board should include people nominated by a psychological or psychiatric association, by the State Bar Association, or by the Civil Liberties Union, and by groups of concerned, involved laymen.

20. WE DEMAND an immediate end to the agitation of race relations by the prison administration of this state.

21. WE DEMAND the Department of Corrections furnish all prisoners with the services of ethnic counselors for the needed special services of the Brown and Black population of this prison.

22. WE DEMAND an end to the discrimination in the judgment and quota of parole for Black and Brown people.

23. WE DEMAND that all prisoners be present at the time their cells and property are being searched by the correctional officers of state prisons.

24. WE DEMAND an end to the discrimination against prisoners when they appear before the Parole Board. Most prisoners are denied parole solely because of their prior records. Life sentences should not confine a man longer than ten years as seven years is the considered statute for a lifetime out of circulation, and, if a man cannot be rehabilitated after a maximum of ten years of constructive programs, etc., then he belongs in a mental hygiene center, not a prison.

25. WE DEMAND an end to the unsanitary conditions that exist in the mess hall, i.e.: dirty trays, dirty utensils, stained drinking cups, and an end to the practice of putting food on the tables hours before eating time without any protective covering put over it.

26. WE DEMAND that better food be served to the inmates. The food is a gastronomical disaster. We also demand that drinking water be put on each table and that each inmate be allowed to take as much food as he wants and as much bread as he wants, instead of the severely limited portions and limited (4) slices of bread. Inmates wishing a pork free diet should have one since 85% of our diet is pork meat or pork-saturated food.

27. WE DEMAND that there be one set of rules governing all prisons in this state instead of the present system where each warden makes the rules for his institution as he sees fit.

IN CONCLUSION

We are firm in our resolve and we demand, as human beings, the dignity and justice that is due to us by right of our birth. We do not know how the present system of brutality and dehumanization and injustice has been allowed to be perpetrated in this day of enlightenment, but we are the living proof of its existence and we cannot allow it to continue.

The taxpayers, who just happen to be our mothers, fathers, sisters, brothers, daughters, and sons, should be made aware of how their tax dollars are being spent to deny their sons, brothers, fathers, and uncles of justice, equality, and dignity.

ATTICA LIBERATION FACTION

Practical Proposals

1. Apply the New York State minimum wage law to all State institutions. STOP SLAVE LABOR.
2. Allow all New York State prisoners to be politically active, without intimidation or reprisals.
3. Give us true religious freedom.
4. End all censorship of newspapers, magazines, letters, and other publications coming from the publisher.
5. Allow all inmates, at their own expense, to communicate with anyone they please.
6. When an inmate reaches conditional release, give him a full release without parole.
7. Cease administrative resentencing of inmates returned for parole violation.
8. Institute realistically rehabilitation programs for all inmates according to their offense and personal needs.
9. Educate all correctional officers to the needs of the inmates, i.e., understanding rather than punishment.
10. Give us a healthy diet, stop feeding us so much pork, and give us some fresh fruit daily.

11. Modernize the inmate educational system.
12. Give us a doctor that will examine and treat all inmates that request treatment.
13. Have an institutional delegation comprised of one inmate from each company authorized to speak to the institution administration concerning grievances (quarterly).
14. Give us less cell time and more recreation with better recreational equipment and facilities.
15. Remove inside walls, making one open yard and no more segregation or punishment.

Proposals Acceptable to Commissioner Oswald at This Time (September 11, 1971)

1. Provide adequate food, water, and shelter for all inmates.
2. Inmates shall be permitted to return to their cells or to other suitable accommodations or shelter under their own power. The Observer Committee shall monitor the implementation of this operation.
3. Grant complete administrative amnesty to all persons associated with this matter. By administrative amnesty, the State agrees:
   a. not to take any adverse parole actions, administrative proceedings, physical punishment, or other type of harassment such as holding inmates incommunicado, segregating any inmates, or keeping them in isolation or in twenty-four hour lock-up;
   b. The State will grant legal amnesty in regard to all civil actions which could arise from this matter.
   c. It is agreed that the State of New York and all its departments, divisions, and subdivisions, including the State Department of Corrections and the Attica Correctional Facility, and its employees and agents shall not file or initiate any criminal complaint or act as complainant in any criminal action of any kind of nature relating to property, property damage, or property-related crimes arising out of the incidents at the Attica Correctional Facility during September 9, 10, 11, 1971.
   d. The District Attorney of Wyoming County, New York, has issued and signed the attached letter as of this date.

4. Recommend the application of the New York State minimum wage law standards to all work done by inmates. Every effort will be made to make the records of payment available to inmates.
5. Establish by October 1, 1971, a permanent ombudsman service for the facility staffed by appropriate persons from the neighboring communities.
6. Allow all New York State prisoners to be politically active, without intimidation or reprisal.
7. Allow true religious freedom.
8. End all censorship of newspapers, magazines, and other publications from publishers, unless there is determined by qualified authority which includes the ombudsman that the literature in question presents a clear and present danger to the safety and security of the institution. Institution spot censoring only of letters.
9. Allow all inmates, at their own expense, to communicate with anyone they please.
10. Institute realistic, effective rehabilitation programs for all inmates, according to their offense and personal needs.
11. Modernize the inmate education system, including the establishment of a Latin library.
12. Provide an effective narcotics treatment program for all prisoners requesting such treatment.
13. Provide or allow adequate legal assistance to all inmates requesting it or permit them to use inmate legal assistance of their choice in any proceeding whatsoever. In all such proceedings, inmates shall be entitled to appropriate due process of law.
14. Reduce cell time, increase recreation time, and provide better recreation facilities and equipment, hopefully by November 1, 1971.
15. Provide a healthy diet; reduce the number of pork dishes; increase fresh fruit daily.
16. Provide adequate medical treatment for every inmate; engage either a Spanish speaking doctor or inmate interpreters who will accompany Spanish speaking inmates to medical interviews.
17. Institute a program for the recruitment and employment

of a significant number of black and Spanish speaking officers.

18. Establish an inmate grievance commission comprised of one elected inmate from each company which is authorized to speak to the Administration concerning grievances, and develop other procedures for inmate participation in the operation and decision-making processes of the institution.

19. Investigate the alleged expropriation of inmate funds and the use of profits from the metal and other shops.

20. The State Commissioner of Corrections' Services will recommend that the penal law be changed to cease administrative resentencing of inmates returned for parole violation.

21. Recommend that Menenchino hearings be held promptly and fairly.

22. Recommend necessary legislation and more adequate funds to expand work release program.

23. End approved lists for correspondence and visitors.

24. Institute a thirty-day maximum for segregation arising out of any one offense. Every effort should be geared toward restoring the individual to regular housing as soon as possible, consistent with safety regulations.

25. Remove visitation screens as soon as possible.

26. Paroled inmates shall not be charged with parole violations for moving traffic violations or driving without a license, unconnected with any other crime.

27. Permit access to outside dentists and doctors at the inmate's own expense within the institution, where possible, and consistent with scheduling problems, medical diagnosis, and health needs.

28. It is expressly understood that members of the Observer Committee will be permitted into the institution on a reasonable basis to determine whether all of the above provisions are being effectively carried out. If questions of adequacy are raised, the matter will be brought to the attention of the Commissioner of Correctional Services for clearance.

Appendix B

The "Tentative Plan" negotiated between the Prisoners' Union and the top administrators of the California Department of Corrections during 1974 and 1975 (as reported in *Outlaw,* Jan.–Feb., 1976).

Certification of Inmate Representing Organizations

Each Inmate Representing Organization deciding to represent its members in their relations with the California Department of Corrections shall file annually with the Director of the Department of Corrections, a statement containing the following information:

1. Name and address of the organization.
2. Names and mailing addresses of the organization's principal officers and representatives.
3. A statement that the organization:
   a. Has 1,000 or more inmates in the Department of Corrections, as certified by the organization and subject to independent audit by an outside person who may not disclose the names of individual members to the department.
   b. Is prepared to represent its members in matters relating to the condition of their confinement and departmental-inmate relations.
   c. Recognizes that the provisions of Section 923 of the Labor Code are not applicable to inmates, residents, or parolees of the Department of Corrections.
   d. Affirmatively supports the constitutional form of government in the United States and of the State of California.
   e. Permits membership without regard to race, color, creed, national origin, age, or sex.
   f. Recognizes the Director may suspend relationships with

263

any Inmate Representing Organization, without notice, e.g., in times of emergency or serious disruption within the institution.

Statement of Department-Inmate Organization Relations

The following statement of policy and principles governs the relationships between the California Department of Corrections and Inmate Representing Organizations. It is the purpose of this statement:

a. To assure a uniform and equitable basis for department-inmate organization relations within Corrections in California.

b. To maintain open channels of communication that permit the exchange of ideas in a cooperative and informal manner.

c. To bring together the points of view of the Department of Corrections and the inmates, residents and parolees under its jurisdiction in order to insure humane and safe conditions and to improve the well-being of both inmates and staff.

d. To enhance the general effectiveness of the Inmate Appeal Procedure as a means of identifying and resolving inmate grievances.

Right to Organize

Inmates, residents, and parolees of this department have the right to organize or join Inmate Representing Organizations of their own choice for the purpose of representation on all matters of department-inmate organization. Inmates, residents, and parolees also have the right to refuse to join in such activities or to withdraw from such organizations and have the right to represent themselves individually in all matters covered by this statement.

Inmates, residents, and parolees may belong to more than one organization and may, therefore, be represented on different matters by different organizations. Inmates, residents, and parolees will not be discriminated against or granted preferential treatment or have equitable treatment withheld because of either membership or non-membership in Inmate Representing Organizations.

Scope

The scope of representation will include all matters relating to the Rules of the Director of Corrections, departmental policies, and conditions of confinement, including classification, program assignment, transfer, and discipline.

Right to Meet and Confer

The department will meet and confer with representatives of Inmate Representing Organizations upon request and will consider such presentations as are made by the inmate organization on behalf of its members prior to arriving at a determination of rule, policy, or course of action.

If, as a result of meeting and conferring in good faith, the departmental and organizational representatives achieve a mutual understanding, a written memorandum will be prepared, signed by both, and made available to interested parties.

If no mutual understanding is achieved, a written memorandum will be prepared describing the areas and extent of difference between the respective positions. Such memoranda will be signed by both parties and made available to interested groups and individuals.

Grievances

The departmental Inmate Appeal System exists to insure opportunities to deal with complaints. Grievances will be resolved at the lowest feasible level in the department and in the most expeditious manner possible. Inmates, residents, and parolees have the right to representation by an official of an Inmate Representing Organization in the preparation and presentation of his or her grievance at all levels of the process. The right to freedom from reprisal for using the grievance procedure is assured.

Access

Reasonable access to the facilities of the department will be granted to Inmate Representing Organization officers and representatives on matters relating to the performance of their function. This does not include visits for purpose of solicitation of membership. Access will be permitted for the purpose of routine organizational meetings and any necessary attendant workshops. Where specific problems exist which necessitate the organization representative seeing the specific area to understand the situation, access will also be granted. Such representatives will notify and obtain the approval of the appropriate official before entering the facility as follows:

1. Any institution—Warden or Superintendent.
2. Any parole facility—Deputy Director, Parole, and Community Service Division.

Representatives are subject to all laws, rules, and regulations governing entrance to and behavior within a correctional institution.

Each institution Warden or Superintendent will prepare a list of those locations to which access for the purpose of contact with an inmate shall be barred because of security reasons. Such a list should be kept to an absolute minimum consistent with institution security; it is anticipated that representatives will be permitted access to most areas of the institution.

Contact with an inmate will be done in such a way as to minimize the possibility of incidents or breaches in the institution security.

Use of State Facilities and Time

Uniform standards of treatment will be applied to all inmate representing organizations concerning the use of state facilities, equipment, and work time. Organizations may be granted the use of state facilities for organization meetings provided space is available. Assigned working hours will not be used for conducting or participating in organization meetings and membership campaigns.

All services provided inmates through any organization which involve the utilization of institution facilities, grounds, equipment, or staff must be approved in writing by the Warden or Superintendent.

Subject to the approval of the Warden or Superintendent,

266

organizations may be assigned office space and the use of an inmate clerk if such space and assistance are available.

Distribution and Posting of Organization Literature

This department will provide a reasonable amount of space for posting organization bulletins or will provide space for organization bulletin boards. Organization representatives may post or distribute material in accordance with local procedures provided such activities do not disrupt normal institution activities. Material that calls for disruption of institutional routines, work stoppages, or other organized demonstrations and material containing personal attacks directed toward employees of the departmental staff or inmates in the Department of Corrections are specifically prohibited. Prior approval of the content of the material for posting or circulation will be obtained from the appropriate administrator as listed above authorizing access to work locations. Approval to post or circulate material will not in any way constitute endorsement by the department of any of the statements contained in the material.

Statewide Operations

Inmate Representing Organizations will not be allowed to begin full operations at any institution until it has held a series of meetings with inmates and staff during an introductory period of not less than two months. An Inmate Representing Organization will not be allowed to expand full operations to more than one institution until it has completed six months of successful operations at one location.

Suspensions of Relationships

If the Director suspends relationships with any Inmate Representing Organization without notice, within 10 days of such suspension the department will provide such inmate organization with written reasons for any modification or cancellation of its relationship with the prisoners. The department will meet and confer with such inmate organization within 20 days of such suspension. If the inmate organization is dissatisfied with the decision of the Director, following such meeting, it may within 10 days request in writing an administrative hearing on the matter, which the department will schedule within 30 days of such request. Such hearing will be open to the public. Within 20 days of such hearing, the Director will issue a written decision on the matter, giving reasons for any modification or cancellation of such organization's relationship with the prisoners and the department.

Index

271

276